SUSTAINABLE INFRASTRUCTURE INVESTMENT

This book provides examples and suggestions for readers to understand how public investment decisions for sustainable infrastructure are made. Through detailed analysis of public investment in infrastructure over the last few decades in the United States, the United Kingdom, and Finland, the author explores how the decision-making processes for major public works spending, many of them requiring quite rigorous and detailed computational methodologies, can result in plans that underserve large portions of the population, are inequitable, and fail to efficiently preserve public property. Beginning with some of the commonly offered explanations for the slow pace of investment and repair in a supposedly prosperous society facing serious environmental challenges, the book then explores media's role in shaping the public-at-large's understanding of the situation and the unimaginative solutions put forward by politicians. It continues with some case studies of infrastructure investment, or lack thereof, including an exploration of competing uses for government funds. It concludes with some suggestions. It is aimed at a large readership of professionals, students, and policy makers in political science, urban planning, and civil engineering.

Eric Christian Bruun has been Visiting Professor at the School of Civil and Environmental Engineering at Aalto University in Espoo, Finland, and adjunct faculty at the University of Pennsylvania School of Engineering and Applied Sciences. He has taught short courses at several universities around the world. He has managed or participated in numerous national and international consulting projects. He is the author of *Better Public Transit Systems: Analyzing Investments and Performance* (2nd edition, 2013), and co-author of *An Introduction to Sustainable Transportation: Policy, Planning and Implementation* (2010), both from Routledge/Earthscan. Eric has Bachelor and Master of Science in Mechanical Engineering degrees from the University of Washington and a PhD in Systems Engineering from the University of Pennsylvania.

"This is a very important book. It analyses a wide breadth of problems – concerning transportation,education,health care and others – across the whole policy spectrum. It does so in three different countries (the US,the UK and Finland) with three very different systems of political economy and governance. 'Systems' is a key word here because the systematic inter-relations of cause and effect with regard to policies,is necessary to understand why,what often seem on the surface to be wise practices,so frequently fail. The answer as to why such occurs is both simple and complex. The simple answer is that purported policy solutions to problems when considered in isolation usually produce unintended consequences. Of course,there is a more complex answer as well, and Dr. Bruun provides it...in case after case. His cogent arguments and sound logic are matched by a wealth of empirical fact...as said before,embracing problems and issues across three very different political-economic systems. This is a very important book!"

Garry Potter, *Professor of Sociology,*
Wilfred Laurier University Waterloo, Ontario, Canada.

"It suggests hope for a better future,and in fact I see the book as being well sprinkled with constructive ideas on how we can do better in the future."

Glen Weisbrod

SUSTAINABLE INFRASTRUCTURE INVESTMENT

Toward a More Equitable Future

Eric Christian Bruun

Routledge
Taylor & Francis Group
NEW YORK AND LONDON

Cover image: © Getty Images

First published 2022
by Routledge
605 Third Avenue, New York, NY 10158

and by Routledge
4 Park Square, Milton Park, Abingdon, Oxon, OX14 4RN

Routledge is an imprint of the Taylor & Francis Group, an informa business

Library of Congress Cataloging-in-Publication Data
A catalog record for this title has been requested

ISBN: 978-1-032-15798-6 (hbk)
ISBN: 978-1-032-15797-9 (pbk)
ISBN: 978-1-003-24570-4 (ebk)

DOI: 10.4324/9781003245704

Typeset in Bembo
by codeMantra

CONTENTS

ACKNOWLEDGMENTS

I am grateful to several people with very different knowledge bases than my own. Professor Garry Potter read the manuscript carefully from the perspective of a social theorist and was invaluable to me in making sure that I was not speaking in jargon but in a clear and logical manner. My sister Rita Bruun used her background in the history of political ideology and US constitutional law to make sure my thinking was clear and my level of detail was sufficient. Otso Kivekäs Is member of the Green Party of Finland and took the time to provide me with details about investment policy I could not access myself with my limited skills in reading Finnish. Thanks also to my friends who made field trips or rummaged through archives to obtain photos for me. Their names are given in the photo credits. I also must say that I found my inspiration to write this book from the many comments I received from the anonymous reviewers of my research proposals on the topic of multidisciplinary infrastructure analysis and planning.

1
INTRODUCTION

> "….the construction of a new city is not the answer to these problems. Nor can it be a substitute for better urban planning. Instead of new cities/urban settlements, we need to invest heavily in improving the deteriorating infrastructure — water supply, drainage, education, health, environment etc — in the existing ones. Also, the government needs to bring these public services to smaller towns in order to control unchecked growth in labour migration from less developed areas to major urban centres for jobs and better services."

This book was written at the tail end of the Trump Administration and the beginning of the Biden Administration. The hot topics of the proposed Green New Deal plus racial and economic justice are very much intertwined with what choices the US government makes with regard to its public investment strategy. From my perch as a person who has lived mostly in the USA but also outside of it in a couple of other prosperous countries, when combined with my systems analysis background, gives me a unique view of infrastructure and the public services it supports. What investments are languishing, what are the economic-related justifications and excuses, and what role has the historical evolution of the USA, in particular, played? It is a complex story that this book tries to summarize with the assistance of some selected case studies. If there seems to be a bias by picking some of them to illicit outrage, then I am guilty as charged. In my defense, I also try to offer productive suggestions.

Given the reality of Brexit, the UK is already looking toward the USA for ideas and business relationships regarding public services. For this reason, as well as the Lockean philosophical ties that still bind the English-speaking countries, I have also paid special attention to comparisons that might be of interest to readers in the UK. More than any other prosperous country, the UK has followed the USA in privatization of what are elsewhere understood to be public services – from education to transportation. Transportation was the first to be lopped off and I focus most heavily on that. For many years after it deregulated transit in the 1980s during the Thatcher revolution, the UK Central Government would simply refuse to help any city build rail transit, arguing that it would be unfair competition to unsubsidized buses. Whether or not a city democratically decided it wanted a publicly planned, integrated transit system based on a hierarchy of modes, like its peers over on The Continent, was immaterial.

I have been working in topics related to urban transportation for over 30 years. Now, I am increasingly bothered by hearing the same old debates in the USA that go on without

DOI: 10.4324/9781003245704-1

resolution, not just about transportation but all infrastructure. Not that we do not hear about it, as messengers like the American Society of Civil Engineers point out the need to do something every year (ASCE 2020, 2021). The problems these debates address are the same and even intensifying. I feel especially qualified to weigh in on this debate as my areas of special expertise, transit system analysis and urban form changes and supply chain changes to support sustainable development, sit at the intersection of engineering and the social sciences. Furthermore, I have made several unsuccessful attempts to find funding for the study of the interactions between various types of infrastructure, making the argument that decisions about land use and the transportation choices that support it link the cost and efficiency of all urban infrastructure.

It is not as though these unresolved problems have taken us by surprise. The inability for those without their own cars to get to work is nothing new. Heavy traffic and saturated traffic at signals had been forecast years ago. The ability of municipalities to finance maintenance of their sewers, wastewater treatment plants, their school and library buildings, their public housing, their roads, and their parks has been an ongoing struggle. So much so that visions of improvements are no longer even offered by our leaders or pondered by the citizens. I came to this last realization after living in Helsinki the last ten years where the city continually reveals new proposals and improves already very good transit systems and biking facilities, and where roads are closed temporarily to install central heating pipes that reduce the fuel burn at the power stations.

Flint, Michigan and Jackson, Mississippi are extreme cases where even safe drinking water is no longer taken for granted. And there are periodic stories of dams that fail, water mains that burst, and sinkholes that open. That used to be a large part of what I knew about the state of infrastructure outside my own silos. But I had come to recognize that many of the issues were analogous across public works and widened out my interests. I found that concerned citizens and officials involved in their various silos were often being played off against each other. Here is an example: if City Council wants to fill the potholes and repave some streets that means the water treatment plant replacement will have to be deferred. They both would have to come out of the same budget, typically with little or no help at all to be expected from the state government. But perhaps some matching funds can be expected from the Feds if one is willing to wait in a long line. So, if the public is even consulted at all, the question they are asked is: which do you want?

What I also noticed was that sometimes money does appear even after the local and state governments have been pleading poverty for many years. Why was there money for a new arena for the Detroit Red Wings at the same time the City of Detroit was in bankruptcy? Why did lower-income people have their water shut off if there was money for entertainment venues for higher income people? Why did the largest free-standing concrete dome in the world, Seattle's King Dome, get imploded when it still had 15 years of bond payments left and get replaced by separate baseball and football stadiums? How did a $500M people mover connecting the BART trains to Oakland Airport go to the head of queue when a proposed $125M Bus Rapid Transit line that would benefit the lower-income parts of Oakland languished on the official to-do list of the Metropolitan Planning Organization for many years? The residents had to be without this badly needed improvement but not before its cost had risen to $232 million by the time it finally opened in the summer of 2020 (Wanek-Libman 2020).

I could go on. There are convention center expansions, new prisons, even casinos have received public support. The City of Detroit has a new automation feature in its downtown parking garage that will pack in cars tighter when much of the city has gone back to nature (Phelan and Wall Howard 2020). It will also eliminate the need for valets while the city suffers from high unemployment. One could understand how the public might choose to neglect sewer repairs since they are out of sight and out of mind. But does the citizenry really favor venues for private entertainment over repairing leaking roofs in their school buildings or filling the

FIGURE 1.1 Detroit – these railroads were used to support the automobile factories.
Source: Shutterstock (94909557)

FIGURE 1.2 Detroit – demolishing Joe Louis Arena as if there were not already enough destruction.
Source: Shutterstock (1609733881).

potholes? I could guess the answer, but the truth is that we usually don't really know the public's preferences. Elected officials can game the system. They won't let the public vote on things they know would be unpopular, and they force a vote on things that are popular, but by attaching odious terms like an increase in property and sales taxes that hit hard those with fixed incomes.

And higher levels of government have distorted the decision process. The US Interstate Highway system was built with 90 percent Federal Funds, that is, "free money." But the Feds offered nothing at all if you would rather expand or build a rapid transit line. Only in the 1980s did a few cities like Portland, Oregon first manage to get highway funds transferred to transit. Modal favoritism still goes on, with many state departments of transportation refusing to help transit. The State of Indiana's legislature actually made it illegal for the citizens of Indianapolis to choose light rail transit, ostensibly to protect the taxpayer. Even today, there is a maximum 80-20 split for highway projects but typically only 50-50 for transit for Federal matching funds. Beginning in 2001, the State of Maryland started a widening project for I-95 parallel to their MARC commuter rail system thereby undermining its purpose. An upgrade to MARC was finished as recently as 1992 in this same corridor. No doubt, some free money played a role.

The misnamed Interstate Highways are currently undergoing a new round of widening. In the Virginia suburbs of Washington, D.C., I-66 is becoming a DMZ or Berlin Wall severing the north and south sides of Fairfax County. The Zoo interchange on the freeway encircling the City of Milwaukee was recently (not quite) finished using a combination of State and Federal funds at a total cost of over $1.7 Billion, a portion of that from rural residents of Wisconsin (Midwest Environmental Advocates 2020). As for the State's contribution to transit "...over the last 12 years the Milwaukee County Transit System has eliminated 21 regular bus routes, 4 freeway flyer routes and numerous route segments, and reduced the frequency and span of many bus routes (Silver 2018)." No plans at all were made to serve the new FoxConn factory, located far outside the city, when the State of Wisconsin offered this company an extremely generous subsidy. This would put pressure to divert money from other transit services when existing "JobLines" routes to other suburbs were already in jeopardy (Williams 2018). Similarly, Austin, Texas is in a fast-growing region with substandard transit, but the state's idea of help is to widen Interstate 35 by 4 lanes right through the heart of the city (Lee 2021). The city will have to go it alone with a transit plan that required a public vote, additional local taxes, and perhaps federal matching funds, but only if they are willing to delay for five or ten years due to intense competition with other cities also drowning in a sea of cars (Egan 2020).

I don't want to exaggerate. Some cities have done better than others in maintenance and repairs. And some have even modernized their public works and expanded them. But a closer look reveals that the improvements tend to be concentrated in more prosperous areas. If they weren't prosperous before, they become so. Control of property along corridors where infrastructure is coming is the stuff of much of urban folklore and history.

The number of cities that are at the point where one can live without a car due to decent transit remains limited. These locations are where, to use Richard Florida's term "the creative class" now flock. These include large cities with legacy transit systems, but also some smaller and newer cities. But the pace of construction has been slow, so transit is not ubiquitous and not all parts of town are well served. The irony is that the transit dependent are being displaced, and those displacing them may never even use transit. Furthermore, many of the jobs that the transit dependent would like to take are being displaced to sites where land is cheap: on the perimeter where infrastructure is limited and transit systems cannot afford to reach. Yes, some of the lower paid jobs are accessible because they are in the city center, but it involves long commutes, often with quite high fares which offset lower rents. A person in the Bay Area might be facing $12 in separate fares each way, involving three different transit agencies. Around London, people are facing £400+ monthly passes. Again, all of this was totally predictable by academic theories like bid-rent curves that show that higher transportation costs offset lower housing costs.

Why are predictable pathologies allowed to happen? Juergen Habermas, the world-renowned political philosopher, argued that no force except 'the force of the better argument' should decide public policy. This has clearly not happened, unless one defines the public more narrowly than the public-at-large. In fact, life is good for a large minority of the population. This book explores how the decision-making processes for major public works spending, many of them requiring quite rigorous and detailed computational methodologies, can still manage to justify plans that underserve large portions of the population and fail to efficiently preserve existing public property.

The second chapter of the book discusses some of the commonly offered explanations for the slow pace of investment and repair. The third chapter continues with some discussion about the media's role in the public-at-large's understanding of the situation. The fourth chapter moves on to some lamentations about the lack of visions put forward by politicians at all levels of government despite a supposedly prosperous society facing serious economic and environmental challenges. Then Thomas Frank's viewpoints are summarized in the fifth chapter, hopefully accurately, about why it is so hard to fix things in the face of a political system that mostly responds to a minority of roughly 20 percent of the population or less, depending upon the specific issue. This is much larger than the oft-repeated 1 percent of the population.

There is strong empirical evidence for Thomas Frank's framing of the US political economy in the persistence and intensification of the phenomenon recognized as the "dual economy" over recent decades, even with an increasingly educated population and increasing awareness of economic injustice and the environmental imperative to address climate change. The origin of the dual economy in the USA has its beginnings as a slave economy, making the concept even more engrained that most of its peer countries:

> When we think about the Industrial Revolution, when we think about public investment in rail lines and shipping industry, we often don't think about it in conjunction with the institution of slavery. But it was the institution of slavery and cotton that was the impetus for it all.
>
> Moving on to the modern economy, and cotton in the 19th century and how it transforms the U.S. economy really is the engine behind the U.S. economic ascent in the 19th century, making the U.S. an economic powerhouse in the world.
>
> *(Christy Clarke Pujara 2021)*

That Frank's viewpoint offers a missing element to the common explanations is then supported in the sixth chapter by looking at case studies of several different types of vital services heavily dependent upon public works. The seventh chapter then describes some other public services that compete for the same funds, like schools, police departments, healthcare, housing, childcare, and institutions that do not contribute to the tax base, like universities. The money in a government budget is fungible and must be viewed in its totality. Especially so since some types of capital investments and operating budgets are traditionally funded by users of the currency, state and local governments, and others are funded by the issuer of the currency, the US government.

The eighth and last chapter provides some suggestions on how to make public investment decisions responsive to a larger share of the population and more considerate of the minorities that have been in the lower tier of this dual economy the longest. Even more imperative, these decisions must become more long-sighted, scientific, and careful about global warming because of greenhouse gas generation and about resource conservation, especially water, arable land shortages, and raw material shortages, demand it. Fortunately, the two sets of goals of enhancing democratic participation to widen the benefits and sustainable development need not conflict but can be mutually reinforcing.

By the way, the opening quote refers to Lahore, Pakistan, not a city in the USA (Editorial 2020).

References

American Society of Civil Engineers (ASCE). 2020. Failure to Act: Current Investment Trends in our Surface Transportation Infrastructure: Preliminary Findings. Available at: https://www.infrastructure-reportcard.org/wp-content/uploads/2020/09/FTA_SurfaceTransport_Study%E2%80%94FINAL.pdf

ASCE. 2021. Executive Summary. A Comprehensive Assessment of America's Infrastructure. 2021 Report Card for America's Infrastructure. Available at: https://infrastructurereportcard.org/wp-content/uploads/2020/12/2021-IRC-Executive-Summary-1.pdf

Editorial. 2020. Ravi City Project. *Dawn*. August 10. Available at: https://www.dawn.com/news/1573575/ravi-city-project

Egan, John. 2020. Austin's $10 Billion Transit Package with 3 New Light-Rail Lines Drives Forward. *Culture Map Austin*. June 15. Available at: https://austin.culturemap.com/news/city-life/06-15-20-three-new-light-rail-lines-drive-10-billion-transit-plan-for-austin/

Lee, Jonathan. 2021. City Council Critiques TxDOT's I-35 Plans. *Austin Monitor*. March 29. Available at: https://www.austinmonitor.com/stories/2021/03/city-council-critiques-txdots-i-35-plans/

Midwest Environmental Advocates. 2020. *Milwaukee Zoo Interchange: Case Summary*. Madison, WI. Available at: https://midwestadvocates.org/issues-actions/actions/milwaukee-zoo-interchange Accessed November 24, 2020.

Phelan, Mark and Phoebe Wall Howard. 2020. Detroit Parking Garage Will Feature Automated Parking System by Ford, Bosch in Self-Driving Car Demonstration. *Detroit Free Press*. August 28. Available at: https://eu.usatoday.com/story/money/cars/2020/08/28/self-driving-cars-ford-bosch-automated-valet-parking-detroit/5642487002/

Pujara, Christy Clark. 2021. Teaching Hard History: Episode 3, Season 1 Slavery & the Northern Economy. *Learning for Justice Podcast*. Available at: https://www.learningforjustice.org/podcasts/teaching-hard-history/american-slavery/slavery-and-the-northern-economy

Silver, Maayan. 2018. As Funding Wanes, Bus Routes Connecting Milwaukeeans With Suburban Jobs May Disappear. *Radio UWM Milwaukee's NPR*. April 17. Available at: https://www.wuwm.com/post/funding-wanes-bus-routes-connecting-milwaukeeans-suburban-jobs-may-disappear

Wanek-Libman, Mischa. 2020. AC Transit Begins Service on East Bay's First BRT Line. August 10. Available at: https://www.masstransitmag.com/bus/article/21149531/ac-transit-begins-service-on-east-bays-first-brt-line?utm_source=MASS+NewsViews+Newsletter&utm_medium=email&utm_campaign=CPS200810031&o_eid=7000E952418911B&rdx.ident%5Bpull%5D=omeda%-7C7000E952418911B

Williams, Nick. 2018. Faster Connections to Jobs, Health Care Fuels MCTS' Push for Redesign of Bus Routes. *Milwaukee Business Journal*. November 19. Available at: https://www.bizjournals.com/milwaukee/news/2018/11/19/faster-connections-to-jobs-health-care-fuels-mcts.html

2

COMMON EXPLANATIONS FOR SLOW INVESTMENT AND REPAIR

There has been no shortage of discussion about the issue of stagnation or outright decay of many cities, even in regions where suburbs might be growing at a steady pace. This includes anti-poverty advocacy groups, environmental-oriented groups, and academia, including sociologists, political scientists, urban planners, and historians. Detroit has gotten the most publicity. It has large sections that have gone back to nature and gardening as a skill-learning opportunity,

FIGURE 2.1 Intercity bus waiting area adjacent to Philadelphia 30th Street Station, 9 October 2013.
Source: Eric Bruun.

DOI: 10.4324/9781003245704-2

and business has grown dramatically. The Kensington section of North Philadelphia is known as a major open-air drug market for the east coast. But while these are dramatic examples, many cities and especially small towns have main streets with boarded up storefronts and hundreds of empty lots. Methamphetamine and opioid addiction have come in three waves since the 1990s (CDC 2020), and it generally is believed that city decay and lack of job opportunity is one of the main contributors.

Lots of suspects for this decay have been investigated. What follows is a brief discussion of many of them. The thesis of this book is that most of the explanations commonly offered do not fully explain the phenomenon of urban decay in the face of an ever-growing economy, even though many have been going on for a long time. It is not as if there is no investment. Later chapters will show where this money goes, which should provide some insight into additional reasons.

FIGURE 2.2 Suburban Virginia residential street.
Source: Rita Bruun.

Inevitability

This is in some sense the default argument. It means there is not a major issue for the public purse, as this is what one must expect to happen as technology changes and the world economy evolves. Besides, there are offsets. The rest of the nation is getting more prosperous so that people in the descending regions can find opportunities elsewhere in the ascending regions. In this view, the dislocations of families and communities, while unfortunate for those involved, are not a valid government concern to slow down, let alone reverse. The waste involved in abandoning existing infrastructure and replacing it with new elsewhere when larger cities have to absorb this steady trickle of internal refugees is not addressed.

Yes, of course, technology marches on, and there will be pressures due to changes where particular resources can be found and what they will cost that are beyond the control of any individual government. If this were adequate as an explanation, there would be no need for books such as the one you are now reading.

In reality, there are many ways in which public policy has contributed to the situation a nation finds itself. There are also many ways in which public policy could change directions and prospects for cities, metropolitan regions, and the rural hinterlands. People realize this and will not accept this line of reasoning. They see it in their personal lives. Some prominent politicians have met with great success in tapping into these concerns. The real question is what policies should be enacted going forward.

Corporate masters

One of the reasons, if not the most common reason offered, is that we are subject to corporations that have captured control of our political institutions. In times past, companies were more rooted in their communities. Even large companies selling nationwide had an interest in the public being able to afford to purchase their products, like the Model T. After the New Deal strengthened the safety net and gave labor stronger negotiating power, there was a period of what John Kenneth Galbraith described as "countervailing power" where productivity gains were shared with labor and an activist government worked with both (Galbraith 1952). By the late 1970s, labor's share of output reached record highs. Much higher energy costs and global competition started to erode this relationship. Since then, labor's negotiating strength decreased through corporate threats to move overseas to lower cost locations, intensifying after the passage of NAFTA in 1994 and then the admission of China to the WTO (World 101 Course 2017). Without this countervailing power, the loyalty of large corporations to their cities where their factories and offices used to be lessened, and ability to manipulate government policies through lobbying became increasingly effective. They managed to achieve a steady reduction in their tax rates as well, so cities suffered from reductions in both worker income and corporate tax revenues.

Many books have been written about the influence of the oil industry lobby. It would be foolish to deny that. Indeed, it is always one of the biggest spenders at the Federal level. The oil industry has been very effective in maintaining subsidies such as the oil depletion allowance and in avoiding full clean-up costs of their operations. They have also been opponents of increases in the federal gasoline and diesel fuel taxes. The reason is simple: supply and demand dictate that people will buy less if the price is higher. Moreover, as fuel prices get higher people change travel habits and buy smaller cars, thereby setting in motion further reductions in consumption. The lobby has been extremely successful. The federal fuel tax is unchanged since 1993, and it is not even indexed as a percentage of sales price but merely 18.4 for gasoline and 22.4 cents per gallon for diesel, so it is in fact decreasing in real terms. Many states have also been very slow to increase their taxes (Davis 2020). More recently, the industry has played a role in keeping a carbon tax off the table. But credit does not go to them alone. Other industries using petroleum as an input like petrochemicals, plastics, coal, natural gas, and other companies involved with hydrocarbons had a common interest.

The auto industry has been portrayed as a group that has been active through conspiracies to bring about the downfall of transit systems, especially after World War II. Many cities had very worn out electric-powered transit systems that were operating 24/7 with minimal maintenance and no need for precious rationed gas or diesel fuel. Los Angeles rail lines supported military airplane factories, Philadelphia streetcars supported naval shipyards, and so on. After the war, some cities had their systems purchased and then converted to buses rather than receiving an overhaul. While it is true that General Motors conspired with Firestone tires through National City Lines (NCL) to make such bus conversions and was convicted, it is also true that cities they did not succeed in converting also chose to shut down much of their transit systems. Large cities like New York and Chicago, which NCL never controlled, largely stopped expanding their subways. (The Orange Line in Chicago in 1983 was its last. New York is discussed in a later chapter.) So there had to be a multiplicity of interests that helped to phase out existing transit lines. The population density was also decreasing in some districts as more people could escape crowded tenements and perhaps dropping overall due to outmigration to expanding suburbs which would require service cuts in a for-profit operation.

The auto industry's biggest lobbying accomplishment has been to avoid the imposition of a larger-than-normal sales tax on new cars as is common in European countries, especially those without auto industries. It has also benefited, of course, from low fuel taxes that enable them to use technological efficiency improvements to make larger cars for the same fuel consumption and to withstand pressure from financially strapped auto-dependent consumers to make smaller cars. Similar to the military hardware industry, the auto industry has dispersed its operations into far more states over a much larger geographic area than the old days where it had large factories around several major cities. Thus, it is seen to be a vitally important local employer by many elected officials who might see reduction of auto dependence and promotion of transit as threats to the industry. In fact, they often compete to attract automotive parts manufacturers through incentives. In particular, European and Japanese manufacturers were enticed to open large assembly plants on terms they could never get in their home countries. There is the Nissan plant in Canton, Mississippi, the BMW plant in Spartanburg, South Carolina, the Mercedes plant in Vance, Alabama, and the Volkswagen plant in Chattanooga, Tennessee. In addition to benefiting from playing states off against one another, all are non-union and get support from elected officials who all oppose unions and attempts at unionization (in the last case the German head office abstained during a vote). All of them are located in host states where the state governments offer little to no financial support for transit services and are almost totally auto dependent. While Japan has a reputation for company unions, the German companies have real unions back home that have a say on their Boards of Directors, negotiate work sharing instead of layoffs, and whose workers have five-week vacations and health benefits in common with other citizens instead of a company-mandated benefit.

Many property developers clearly have an interest in maintaining the current methods of urban expansion. There are parts of the urban area that receive steady investment even while other parts might not even receive basic maintenance, let alone upgrades. Does this belong in a discussion about the corporate role in urban investment? Yes, because so much development is from national companies that bring the same chains of stores and similar suburban neighborhood designs to numerous locations. They, in turn, are financed by Wall Street investment banks that demand that certain chain stores be in the malls and that the housing stock be aimed at certain demographics. Unlike manufacturing industries that only occasionally use new locations, property developers must get local permits as a matter of course and pass modest environmental assessments (depending upon the state), meaning regular opportunities for local citizens and elected officials to try to intervene to block them. These interventions have been largely ineffective and sprawl continues unabated. Distant corporations continually winning without recurring significant and powerful local support seems unlikely. More about this in the discussion of urban planning in a later chapter.

Ribbon cutting

Another reason offered for neglect of routine maintenance in favor of new construction is that one is visible, the other is not. New construction entails an opportunity for "ribbon cutting" for which politicians and senior governmental officials can take credit with the voters. While there certainly are lots of photos when a major phase of a large project is completed and no doubt that people like to be in the shot, PR value is not overly convincing as a motivation, at least for public works projects. These take more years to plan, to get through the Environmental Impact Statement approval, and to get money appropriated than the length of almost all election cycles, even the US Senate, which is every six years. Unless someone is in a safe district, or has built oneself into a self-appointed mega-manager, like the legendary Robert Moses did in New York City and New York State, one cannot be guaranteed of getting any credit near election time. And in a safe district, why would one need the public credit in the first place?

A more convincing explanation is that elected officials and senior governmental department managers can build a reputation with various interests: under their administration, suburban infrastructure financing schemes will not be interrupted. New construction projects signal that the elected officials are amenable to approving and perhaps even helping to fund public works that construction companies and trade unions want but the public probably does not, like expanded jails, expanded convention centers, highway widenings, or sports stadiums. Not only does this get them steady campaign financing, it can score points with voters in the favored area. This is not the same as appealing to the public at large for votes. Even if one loses an election, the skids are greased for a revolving door job as an executive at a consultancy, a government agency, or as a lawyer or accountant at a real estate development firm.

Excessive regulations

This reason is closely related to corporate lobbying. Most attempts to pass new statutory requirements that mean more regulations for corporations, and attempts to issue new regulations re-interpreting existing statutes, will trigger lobbying to prevent them if they threaten the bottom line. New housing on virgin land, new arterials to access this land, and freeway widenings to add long-distance commuting capacity as traffic volumes build are continuing despite the adverse effect on local air pollution, on auto dependency, on global warming, and global demand for oil production and all that this entails for the environment. There has been virtually no improvement at all in overall private vehicle fuel efficiency in the USA for ten years (BTS 2020). Traffic safety gains have been reversed as larger vehicles and increased driving offset better crash resistance features for those cocooned inside. Attempts at land conservation for farming and forestry and habitat preservation have also met with limited success as anyone who has been driving out of the same city over the decades can observe. Every year, the number of stoplights and strip malls increases making the proverbial weekend trip to the countryside an ever more tedious affair. My personal experience was a regular motorcycle ride between central Philadelphia and the Virginia suburbs of Washington, D.C. through Baltimore. I have watched the gap close to about 30 miles of sprawl leaving Philly and about 30 miles of sprawl approaching Baltimore with only about 30 miles of farmland remaining in between.

The evidence for new regulations completely stopping the approval of public works, in general, is weak. If anything, there has been some opposite effect as regulations have slowed down the more environmentally friendly investments in favor of more of the status quo designs. Sprawl is incorporated into many city and regional master plans and thus the supporting infrastructure is also "grandfathered" in. The burden of proof that something more harmful than usual will happen to the ecosystem or there will be some kind of serious environmental injustice will fall on citizen activists and environmental/conservation organizations to prove that such plans applied to particular locations are harmful. They will need strong ammunition such as an endangered species habitat to invoke Federal laws and a major Environmental Impact Statement (EIS).

An alternative that *prima facie* is likely to reduce the environmental footprint like a rail line with apartments around stations instead of typical auto dependent subdivisions almost certainly requires an expensive EIS for which significant funds must be raised and might take two years or more to complete. Strategies like densification of urban districts by removing parking requirements or allowing of garage apartments in alleyways usually require zoning changes that can be quite hard to get officially considered, let alone pass. In such cases, existing regulation indeed has played a role in defending the status quo. Thus, excessive existing regulation might have some merit as a reason for slowing down more environmentally friendly infrastructure plans but is incomplete because changes can involve large injections of money that have to come from somewhere outside the local decision-makers.

Allegations of fraud, waste, and abuse: no need to raise taxes

Another explanation on the list is that government agencies cannot be trusted to accomplish projects in an efficient manner as there is too much "fraud, waste and abuse." Raising taxes on users needed for maintenance would only encourage more waste. Taking this logic a step further, elected officials blocking public works projects are seen to be responsible stewards of the public purse. As an example, in 2014 the Indiana state legislature banned a modern and popular type of urban investment known as light rail transit, anywhere in the state in order "to protect the taxpayer." Indianapolis, a long-time laggard in transit investment among its peer cities, finally did a more modest upgrade based on buses instead. Whether any waste and fraud allegations are true or not is irrelevant, because the effect is the same: it can simply serve as a pretext for not supporting projects that might be popular with the public at large. The same politician may very well support other projects that would use many of the same construction companies and face many of the same issues of risk of cost overruns associated with most large construction projects, especially those involving tunnelling (Flyvbjerg 2007). Or change their minds, like the Indiana legislature, when they tried to attract Amazon, conveniently forgetting their stated concern about protecting the taxpayers (Associated Press 2018).

There are indeed measurements besides monetary costs for determining waste. For transportation infrastructure, one is the time savings generated for users. Many projects have been justified by a faster commute for auto users, shorter travel times for trucks, and so on, when they are finished. But the disruption and delays during construction can be huge, and these are not always factored in. A very good example is the Springfield Interchange in suburban Virginia, commonly known as the "mixing bowl," where the western and eastern halves of the Washington, D.C. Beltway meet. This project involved massive new flyovers and an expansion to 24 lanes on one stretch. It cost $676 million in then-current dollars starting in 1999 and took eight years to complete (Kozel 2017). There were incessant traffic delays every day. One analysis estimated the total delay would average 1,750 hours per commuter over the course of the project (McCann et al. 1999). This time could never be made up later. If time waste were a concern amongst decision-makers, this would probably never have been funded after a preliminary analysis.

The accusation of waste can also be quite vague. The perception of what is waste is in the eye of the beholder. Critics may not mean that excessive monetary costs were involved, they might mean that the whole concept or goal is a waste. Mary Peters was the Secretary of Transportation under President George W. Bush from 2006 to when he left office in early 2009. In an interview on a national TV news show she said that about 20 percent of the budget was wasted but did not explain in detail. She clearly did not think that bicycle paths and trails are part of the national infrastructure (Maus 2007), but this is only about 1 percent of the total from the Highway Trust Fund. Transit, however, receives 20 percent, so it seems she was implying that spending Federal tax dollars on transit is a waste. If one asked the opinions of some bicycle or transit advocates, they would say that highway projects she favored are a waste as well.

Fraud claims are exaggerated. There is no particular history of falsified billing in the public works related industries that stand out from other public spending. There have been huge spikes in construction materials costs like steel that can exceed budgets, but this is because it is on a worldwide market and demand might have been skyrocketing in places like China. In the USA, two sectors involving public spending that stand out for fraud are medical billing and military procurement. Medicaid and Medicare have documented cases including large fines and legal settlements (Sherman 2014). The Pentagon is notorious for being lax against overbilling and leakage of funds (Serbu 2020). Recall the speech by Secretary of Defense Donald Rumsfeld on September 10, 2001 that $2.1 Trillion dollars is missing. Ten years into the Afghanistan war, the US Inspector General found that $70 Billion in cash delivered to Afghanistan could not be traced (Baron 2011). And a recent attempt to audit the Pentagon failed (Buble 2020). If fraud were really the concern, focus should turn to the largest targets. Why it does not is a subject for later chapters. The sewers still need to be repaired and bridges rebuilt. It is a poor excuse to neglect public property to say that our state and local governments are institutionally incapable of doing what governments in other industrialized nations can do.

Abuse is a throwaway line and not really deserving of too much of an analysis. It makes for a good phrase to include it behind fraud and waste. A vague accusation, it is probably intended to imply that governments exceed their mandate by imposing projects that are harmful or unwanted. In 2014, the Tennessee state legislature banned "constructing, maintaining or operating any bus rapid transit system" expressing concern that bus stops might be unsafe and the project might require taking land from private interests (Barry 2014). Cost was not the primary stated concern. Let us give them the benefit of the doubt that they were sincere and not just responding to an anti-transit lobby. Perhaps they believed they were protecting taxpayers from abuse by cities (in this case, Nashville) that want to build transit that will make their citizens less safe and unfairly confiscate private property. As with waste, what is abuse can be in the eye of the beholder. I am quite sure that people who had their entire neighborhood confiscated and uprooted for a freeway (Dewey 2020) or had an incinerator placed inside it would have liked someone to protect them from abuse too.

Voter suppression, gerrymandering, and other voting distortions

The voting systems in use in most of the USA are certainly one reason why investments play out the way they do. A significant opportunity to increase the use of various techniques to alter voting patterns came with the Shelby County versus Holder decision by the Supreme Court in 2013. It removed the "preclearance" requirement under the Voting Rights Act of 1965

(Newkirk 2018). It allowed some governments and elected officials to go back to their old ways and think up some new techniques as well.

One of the most important techniques is gerrymandering. An example is the horseshoe shape of Dan Crenshaw's suburban Houston district. It reduces proportional representation. In turn, this leads to disproportionate allocation of benefits and costs to various constituencies. One can look at swing states like North Carolina or Ohio or until recently, Pennsylvania, as examples where Republicans hold legislative and Congressional seats far out of proportion to their share of votes. A state legislature that is overrepresented by rural interests can be expected to downplay urban investment needs. Similarly, minority communities can be expected to be underserved if they are broken into small units in several districts known as "cracking" or concentrated in a few districts known as "packing". Cities can also be unrepresented in the Congress by pizza-slicing its population into several districts, with Austin, Texas being a very good example. Fairness dictates pointing out that gerrymandering is a bipartisan tradition, as the shape of the late Elijah Cummings' district drawn by Democrats in Maryland makes clear.

Voting is also reduced due to voter suppression. Much has been written about how this is done, and it would be disingenuous for anyone to deny it. Some people still do, claiming that there is a problem with voter fraud that necessitates strict ID requirements. Thus, hapless citizens who have voted at the same location for many years may have to obtain a birth certificate costing hundreds of dollars. They must burden their friends and relatives with trips to often remote Department of Motor Vehicle locations. The cost in both time and money of obtaining an acceptable ID will tend to filter out lower income people, and in rural areas, people without cars. It will also filter out retired people who can either no longer drive or have no further desire to drive and have stopped renewing their licenses. This already generates a voting bias against support for transit and non-motorized modes since non-auto owners will be underrepresented. Even simpler is closing voting booths in urban districts (Milwaukee, Georgia) made possible when Justice Roberts and the Supreme Court gutted the 1965 Voting Rights Act in its Shelby County decision in 2013 (Dirr and Spicuzza 2020; Fowler 2020). Then there is a long list of tactics that have been tried, many of which make the wait long if one gets over the hurdles involved in getting to the polls (Berman 2015; Berman and Vicens 2020; DeVega 2020).

All true that the election system is distorted. But it can only be a partial explanation for denial of investment funds. Rural areas are not necessarily receiving a bounty of investment in public works just because a rural-tilted legislature or Congressional delegation deprives cities. Austerity has been the order of the day for a majority of citizens, rural and urban alike, long before the latest opportunity for a state legislature to gerrymander after the 2010 Census by a political party to suppress voting. One needs to have a look at specific demographic groups and business interests, not just geography, to more fully understand where investment is likely to be offered.

Retirement scares and other obstacles to funding

How major public works projects are funded varies from state to state also depending on the particular type of infrastructure involved. In some states, initiatives are allowed and give an avenue for members of the public to try to originate or terminate something. In others, referenda enable elected officials to punt sensitive or controversial proposals to the voters. In yet others, people are entirely dependent on their elected officials except for the public input phase mandated by the National Environmental Policy Act or state laws. Some projects are simply funded with little fanfare through existing revenue sources, but if a project is going to be expensive enough to be transformative in some sense, it will need additional funding. It is the selection or requirement to use a particular funding source that can strongly influence whether a project moves forward.

According to the user pays principle of neoclassical economics, the best solution is to charge the capital cost to the people who will use this new resource over its entire life through amortization. The typical instrument would be a municipal or service district bond, or perhaps some kind of investment fund with a large principal. Sometimes a Tax Increment Financing (TIF) scheme is authorized where increased property value created by infrastructure is partially captured but how this works is a subject for a later chapter. Without such possibilities there needs to be support from higher levels of government. It is this absence of ability to bond sufficiently or to receive regular and reliable support that will cause infrastructure managers to take loans at higher interest rates than a bond would cost to be able to address extremely urgent repairs. In general, they will have to defer routine maintenance never mind the upgrading of public property.

According to this same principle, current operating costs would be charged through monthly fees based on usage. This might make sense for a bridge, but it clearly makes no sense for something like a school or daycare center if the "user" is defined as the child. The users are the parents and everyone who ever sends their kids to school. But it gets more complicated. An extreme version of this principle asserts that if I never use something, I should be exempt. This argument was in fact made in a legal challenge against the Affordable Care Act mandates (Lovelace and Higgins 2019). If this view were to legally prevail for public programs in general, one who never has children or never goes to higher education would not have to contribute at all to public schools or public universities. The more common (and sensible) viewpoint is that everyone in society benefits and everyone should pay at least part of the cost. Thus, there are really two funding issues, the type(s) of revenue generator(s) and the degree to which various subgroups should help to pay. The design of a popular voting scheme to finance public works must take into account the likely response based on the particular mix of viewpoints that the voting population might have.

One explanation for the difficulty in keeping up with maintenance, let alone expansions of public works, is that the voters themselves are largely to blame. They get opportunities to step up to take better care of public property, or to improve the liveability of their city but turn it down. This need not be voting down a particular project with a specific funding proposal, but by consistently voting for politicians whose agenda is to limit public spending at current levels or even to cut taxes. There is merit to this argument, but it begs the question of why individuals vote the way they do. They may not be so selfish or anti-social, but have some legitimate concerns, which brings us to another reason.

State governments will allocate money from their general fund for some infrastructure projects, especially highways. When a state-level government declines to participate in a major proposed project, a local/regional tax or fee will have to be used that is allowable under the state laws. That is, if your local government(s) are lucky. In some states, the legislature will neither help nor allow a local/regional vote. In many states, it is illegal to use the gasoline tax for anything other than roads, and some groups have advocated for changing state constitutions. But this is really a moot point as the tax provides no surplus in any case due to chronic under taxation. There will be no money left over for flood control or bicycle trails or parks. So, the funding sources might well have to be not directly related to users. Some of these options could be quite unpopular.

The electorate have diverse current financial positions and future outlooks. This future is of concern when a tax or fee might stay in place for decades. An increase in the property tax could be significant for some people who are on fixed incomes. People with pensions are increasingly on defined contribution instead of defined benefit plans, which means they may not even know how much money they will have. Social security retirement age has gone up to 66 (even though average life expectancy is going down). Other more prosperous citizens may have a 401K plan that will give them an affluent retirement and the increase is not a concern. A property tax has some rough correspondence to benefit from infrastructure as people with more expensive property are likely to drive more, use more electricity, generate more wastewater, etc. On the other hand, many of them will be quite old and will get less years of benefits, sometimes not at all.

Sales and excise taxes are the other common solution for local governments. They may be allowed to raise the sales tax rate by one fourth or one half or even 1 percent. This hits the lowest income people the hardest, as they spend all of their money every pay period. It also has no link whatsoever to use of public resources. The excise tax is a periodic tax targeted at a specific product and a little bit closer linked. There can also be car rental, hotel and other such taxes targeted at visitors, which could be substantial depending upon location.

Would it be any wonder that some voters say no? Property and sales tax are increasingly unviable for funding infrastructure, especially in states with no income tax. In 2002, Miami-Dade County voters thought they would be getting a bigger rail system. The money has been spent on other things. The traffic congestion and liveability problems have only worsened. It is no surprise that the State of Florida did not want to help with so many other unmet needs, not just in the Miami area, but across the state. Politicians and public agency managers are struggling to find a solution. Part of it will be user fees but this cannot be the full solution as much of the population is too poor to charge high enough prices to reduce or eliminate operating subsidies let alone recoup the capital investment. Part of the solution has been private investment, such as the recent *Brightline* train service from Miami to West Palm Beach and soon to Orlando. But even this involved some financing backstops from the Federal government. Despite the lack of action by any level of government, this private effort to fill a major service gap was met with stiff resistance through federal lawsuits (TaxWatch Staff 2018).

Florida was selected as an example for a reason. In addition to all its other infrastructure deficiencies, the sea level is rising. During storms, flooding occurs and there is danger of saltwater entering the fresh water supply. Other low-lying cities have similar problems, as Super Storm Sandy showed about the New Jersey/New York metropolis. Other places have to deal with more frequent flood control, with drought, with longer forest fire seasons, and so on. Add to this list, the request for charging infrastructure for electric buses and private cars and more solar collectors on public buildings. It all points toward increasing demands from the public purse. It is totally unrealistic to think that adequate funds will be provided through local/regional sources. Most national governments recognize this as a national issue requiring a national contribution. The US response has been either stagnant or even declining financial commitment to help local/regional efforts. So this lack of commitment in the face of needs further examination and one of the main motivations for this book.

Is there some kind of plan?

The idea that something needs to be done has received attention at the national level for a long time. Every year, the American Society of Civil Engineers releases its infrastructure report card. Every year the grades are very low for almost every type of infrastructure. The 2020 average was a C- while transit, my specialty, earned a D- (ASCE 2021). The stimulus plan in 2009 allocated money toward "shovel ready" projects that could create employment quickly. This included a high-speed rail vision complete with money to start on projects in several locations, which was quickly deflated because ironically it proved to capture the public imagination. The Republicans did not want to give President Obama a winning issue. This did not bode well for future efforts. It revealed that instead of a sense of urgency to catch up with our peers, upgrades were seen through a political benefit lens.

Since the one-time stimulus after the 2008 crash, there has been periodic talk of a new national infrastructure spending initiative. The latest one under President Trump came to nothing when his program would give a temporary increase at the federal level, but actually decrease by 2023. This shifts the burden state and local level, which really changes almost nothing (Leibenluft 2017). It gained very little support at the state and local level, not surprisingly. There is also increased concern for infrastructure resiliency, meaning making further investments to help resist storms and other increased stresses from climate change without significant damage (Voisin 2020). This is all on top of the already huge backlog of repairs.

The double standard on public spending

The list of reasons above certainly explains some of the chronic underfunding and inability to come up with either local/regional or national plans. Something is still missing. The tax cut from 2017 is estimated to cost 1.9 trillion dollars in lost federal tax revenue over the next ten years (House Committee on the Budget 2019). Such huge funds being readily available for upward transfers makes a mockery of the unaffordability argument. This difference is not only because of independent actions of the Federal Reserve Bank, but because many of these types of expenditures get heavy support from the US Congress.

Governance structures are supposed to evolve to cope with evolving situations. But they do not. Not even in the face of needs that are only intensifying. Huge sums of money become available for bailing out companies on short notice during a crisis. The Federal Government gave just shy of one billion dollars to a single company to develop a Covid-19 vaccine and this company even gets to keep the patent (Levey 2020). But no similar generosity happened for the ongoing infrastructure crisis that was further exacerbated by the Covid-19 lockdown tax revenue collapse. As this book goes into final editing, an infrastructure bill finally passed that largely continues the traditional funding distribution formula. The "reconciliation" bill that would put new environmental and equity constraint on public works projects and extend the definition of public works to childcare facilities languishes in the US Congress. There must be some interests who like the system as it is.

Comparison to Finland: funding through user taxes instead of unrelated taxes

Voting on a particular project with a specific targeted new or increased tax is not the normal way of deciding its fate. First, there is no need as the existing sources are usually adequate instead of chronically underfunded as is the pattern in the USA. Some projects are closing out while others are in the initial stages so that investment can be smoothed out and continuous. In the ten years I have lived in Helsinki, there has been a long extension of the Metro line to the west, a loop line connecting two regional rail lines via the airport, extensions and fleet expansions to the ten-line streetcar system, new trunk bus routes, upgrading of one trunk bus route to rail is underway, and a conversion of a former freight rail spur to a bicycle highway and park. In the 20 years prior that I lived in the Philadelphia metro area, three times the size, nothing at all has been built. Indeed, two more streetcar lines were closed down.

If the cash flow from current years or existing bonding schemes would be inadequate, then there might have to be a discussion between city councils, regional planning authorities and the national government. Each level of government will typically have to contribute something considering equity and ability to pay. There may be some funds available from the European Union as well to promote rural development or to develop an EU-wide high capacity, high performance transport network of air, sea, and land modes. It is designed to better knit together the various regions culturally and economically, known as the Trans European Transport Network, or TEN-T (European Commission: Mobility and Transport 2020). The USA had such a thing with the build-out of the US Interstate Highways and a first-rate Air Traffic Control system, but nothing of the kind for a national passenger bus or rail network. Freight rail and trucking are privately conceptualized with occasional concern shown by state governments, but with no overall national vision.

Finland, like some other members of the EU, has an extra-high sales tax on new automobiles. There is some dispute among academics and public agencies whether this is counterproductive. Having paid so much money is all the more reason to drive everywhere. With higher monthly car payments, there is also less disposable income with which to buy a monthly transit pass. Paying a tax on a per kilometers driven basis and scaled to the size and weight of the car would better match the tax to the costs the owner imposes on the environment, community, and wear to physical infrastructure. But it is a hard sell politically, and a non-starter if the extra-high sales tax is not removed.

Comparison to the UK: very high level of central versus regional government control

The UK is an interesting contrast to the USA in that it does not undercharge auto users through a gasoline and diesel tax that is too low to cover direct costs. The tax is sufficient to have money left over for complementary transit and non-motorized improvements and problems caused by impervious pavements. In theory, this is fair, as auto use generates social and environmental costs which can be mitigated by trying to alter the balance of modes. Nevertheless, the UK is the laggard of Europe in alternatives to the auto, outside of Greater London. Any annual surplus is used to allow tax cuts instead of public investment.

Indeed, the UK has been quite extreme in the level of privatization of public works, including the water supply. The national railway is broken up into multiple operators some of which are subsidiaries of national railroads on the Continent that make a profit on their operating contracts. The Central Government has been trying hard to minimize its responsibility for public works in general. It has provided pressure on the regions to find private solutions as well by sharply limiting assistance and by statutory requirements, some of which would be considered absurd in countries that didn't have an ideological foundation laid by limited government theorist John Locke. An example involving transit in the UK will be in a later chapter.

The further integration into the aforementioned TEN-T network is unclear after Brexit. The EU funds will not be available and there will be customs delays crossing between the UK and France and some of the trading patterns will change. These together will almost certainly cause some overseas shipping to change ports to avoid ferries and the Channel Tunnel. It is also unclear what will happen with privatized utilities. A majority of the public would like to bring back British Rail.

An irony of not being subject to the European Commission's (EC's) procurement rules is that it may actually be easier to unprivatize in the UK, at least from a legal standpoint. The EC might well have challenged attempts to give what it sees as "state aid" in the form of buyouts of private companies. Other capital injections and operating assistance would almost surely be needed to bring back a group of private holdings into the public sector and to align it with changes in the mission of the railway. It would probably be done in a manner similar to what happened with failing private transit companies in the USA decades ago. The EC might well even challenge the very legitimacy of government investing and attempts to change the mission to one where the railway is treated as a vital public service (Commission of the European Community 2000). In 2000, there was a serious struggle between city governments and the

EC when it proposed that transit should not be subsidized. The EC did not want to accept the idea that the subsidies are justified and not just free handouts to transit operators, even when neoclassical economic theory also provides a justification of public benefit, which is that public transport has decreasing marginal cost whereas autos have increasing marginal cost such that the total cost to the community is decreased if people switch from autos to transit (Vuchic 2017). Manchester very recently declared that it is taking back control of public planning and fare structures of transit based on authority it has asserted because of a devolution of responsibilities (and costs) by the Central Government in 2017 (Topham 2021). Without Brexit, the possibility of a repeat struggle with the EC would have been real.

References

American Society of Civil Engineers (ASCE). 2021. 2021 Report Card for America's Infrastructure. Available at: https://infrastructurereportcard.org/wp-content/uploads/2020/12/National_IRC_2021-report.pdf

Associated Press. 2018. Lawmakers Reconsider Indianapolis Light Rail Ban for Amazon. *WFYI Radio Indianapolis*. January 29. Available at: https://www.wfyi.org/news/articles/lawmakers-reconsider-indianapolis-light-rail-ban-for-amazon

Baron, Kevin. 2011. U.S. Has Lost Sight of Cash from $70 Billion Sent to Afghanistan: *Inspector General. Stars and Stripes*, July 20. Available at: https://www.stripes.com/blogs/stripes-central/stripes-central-1.8040/u-s-has-lost-sight-of-cash-from-70-billion-sent-to-afghanistan-inspector-general-1.149731

Barry, Keith. 2014. UPDATED: Deal Would Allow Tennessee Bus Rapid Transit Project to Proceed. *Wired*, April 15. Available at: http://www.wired.com/2014/04/tennessee-bans-bus-rapid-transit/

Berman, Ari. 2015. *Give Us the Ballot: The Modern Struggle for Voting Rights in America*. Picador.

Berman, Ari and AJ Vicens. 2020. 29 Ways Trump and the GOP Are Making It Harder to Vote. *Mother Jones*, October 5. Available at: https://www.motherjones.com/politics/2020/10/29-ways-trump-and-the-gop-are-making-it-harder-to-vote/?fbclid=IwAR2iSRtyTbEHyOw0Od6X3rv82Iud0EQtYM-fHoQgWsA1LYwDwaqwu4itWiCM

Buble, Courtney. 2020. Pentagon Audit Shows Progress, But Also Deep Challenges in Financial Management. *Government Executive*, March 10. Available at: https://www.govexec.com/defense/2020/03/pentagon-audit-shows-progress-also-deep-challenges-financial-management/163654/

Bureau of Transportation Statistics (BTS). 2020. Average Fuel Efficiency of U.S. Passenger Cars and Light Trucks. *US Dept. of Transportation*. Available at: https://www.bts.gov/content/average-fuel-efficiency-us-passenger-cars-and-light-trucks (Accessed November 24, 2020).

Centers for Disease Control and Prevention (CDC). 2020. Opioid Overdose: Three waves of Opioid overdose *Deaths*. Available at: https://www.cdc.gov/drugoverdose/epidemic/index.html (Accessed 25 November 2020).

Commission of the European Community. 2000. Proposal...On Action by Member States Concerning Public Service Requirements and Award of Public Service Contracts in Public Transport by Bus, Rail and Inland Waterway. *Proposal 2000/0212 (COD)*. Available at: http://europa.eu.int/eur–lex/en/com/pdf/2000/en_500PC0007.pdf

Davis, Carl. 2020. How Long Has It Been Since Your State Raised Its Gas Tax? Institute on Taxation and Economic Policy. February 26. Available at: https://itep.sfo2.digitaloceanspaces.com/022520-Gas-Tax-Policy-Brief.pdf

DeVega, Chauncey. 2020. Investigative Journalist Greg Palast: Here's How Trump Will Steal the 2020 Election. *Salon*, June 15. Available at: https://www.salon.com/2020/06/15/investigative-journalist-greg-palast-heres-how-trump-will-steal-the-2020-election/

Dewey, Caitlin. 2020. Advocates Rally to Tear Down Highways That Bulldozed Black Neighborhoods. *Stateline*, July 28. Available at: https://www.pewtrusts.org/en/research-and-analysis/blogs/stateline/2020/07/28/advocates-rally-to-tear-down-highways-that-bulldozed-black-neighborhoods

Dirr, Alison and Mary Spicuzza. 2020. What We Know So Far about Why Milwaukee Only had 5 Voting Sites for Tuesday's Election While Madison Had 66. *Milwaukee Journal Sentinel*, November 4. Available at: https://www.jsonline.com/story/news/politics/elections/2020/04/09/wisconsin-election-milwaukee-had-5-voting-sites-while-madison-had-66/2970587001/

European Commission: Mobility and Transport. 2020. Trans-European Transport Network (TEN-T). Available at: https://ec.europa.eu/transport/themes/infrastructure/ten-t_en (Accessed November 26, 2020).

Flyvbjerg, Bent. 2007. Policy and planning for large-infrastructure projects: problems, causes, cures. *Environment and Planning B: Urban Analytics and City Science* 34(4): 578–597. https://doi.org/10.1068/b32111

Fowler, Stephen. 2020. 'It Was Very Chaotic': Long Lines, Voting Machine Issues Plague Georgia Primary. *National Public Radio*, June 9. Available at: https://www.npr.org/2020/06/09/873054620/long-lines-voting-machine-issues-plague-georgia-primary

Galbraith, John Kenneth. 1952. *American Capitalism: The Concept of Countervailing Power*, 1st Edition. Reissued 1993 by Routledge.

House Committee on the Budget. 2019. CBO Confirms GOP Tax Law Contributes to Darkening Fiscal Future. *US House of Representatives*, February 5. Available at: https://budget.house.gov/publications/report/cbo-confirms-gop-tax-law-contributes-darkening-fiscal-future

Kozel, Scot. 2017. Springfield Interchange Project. Roads to the Future. September 17. Available at: http://roadstothefuture.com/Springfield_Interchange_Project.html

Leibenluft, Jacob. 2017. Trump's Bait and Switch on Infrastructure. *Center on Budget and Policy Priorities*, June 7. Available at: https://www.cbpp.org/blog/trumps-bait-and-switch-on-infrastructure

Levey, Noam N. 2020. Vaccine Maker Got $1 Billion from Taxpayers. Now It's Boosting Drug Prices. *The Los Angeles Times*, September 14. Available at: https://www.latimes.com/politics/story/2020-09-14/drug-maker-got-1-billion-from-taxpayers-boosting-prices

Lovelace Jr, Berkeley and Tucker Higgins. 2019. US Appeals Court Rules Obamacare Individual Mandate Unconstitutional, Leaves Law Intact. *CNBC*, December 18. Updated December 19. Available at: https://www.cnbc.com/2019/12/18/appeals-court-rules-obamacare-individual-mandate-unconstitutional-but-leaves-law-intact-for-now.html

Maus, Jonathan. 2007. DOT Secretary Says Bike Paths Are Not Transportation Infrastructure. *Bike Portland*. August 16. Available at: https://bikeportland.org/2007/08/16/dot-secretary-says-bike-paths-are-not-transportation-infrastructure-4832

McCann, Barbara and Bianca DeLille, Hank Dittmar, and Michelle Garland. 1999. Road Work Ahead: Is Construction Worth the Wait? *Surface Transportation Policy Project*. Available at: http://www.transact.org/wp-content/uploads/2014/04/Road_Work_Ahead.pdf

Newkirk II, Vann R. 2018. How Shelby County v. Holder Broke America. *The Atlantic*, July 10. Available at: https://www.theatlantic.com/politics/archive/2018/07/how-shelby-county-broke-america/564707/

Serbu, Jared. 2020. Pentagon's Longstanding Audit Failures Also Pose a Recruiting Challenge. *Federal News Network*, July 27. Available at: https://federalnewsnetwork.com/defense-main/2020/07/pentagons-longstanding-audit-failures-also-pose-a-recruiting-challenge/

Sherman, Amy. 2014. Rick Scott 'Oversaw the Largest Medicare Fraud' in U.S. History, Florida Democratic Party Says. *Politifact*, March 3. Available at: https://www.politifact.com/factchecks/2014/mar/03/florida-democratic-party/rick-scott-rick-scott-oversaw-largest-medicare-fra/

TaxWatch Staff. 2018. Drop the Lawsuits and let Brightline Roll. *Florida TaxWatch*, February 5. Available at: https://floridataxwatch.org/Press-Room/ArtMID/35144/ArticleID/18420/Drop-the-lawsuits-and-let-Brightline-roll

Topham, Gwyn. 2021. Greater Manchester Bus Services to be Brought Under Public Control. *The Guardian*, March 25. Available at: https://www.theguardian.com/uk-news/2021/mar/25/greater-manchester-bus-services-to-be-brought-under-public-control-mayor-andy-burnham

Voisin, Sara L. 2020. Why Climate Change Is About to Make Your Bad Commute Much Worse. *The Washington Post*, August 8. Available at: https://www.washingtonpost.com/local/trafficandcommuting/why-climate-change-is-about-to-make-your-bad-commute-worse/2020/08/08/7ad97ba8-d5b6-11ea-aff6-220dd3a14741_story.html?hpid=hp_hp-more-top-stories_climateinfrastructure-815pm%3Ahomepage%2Fstory-ans

Vuchic, Vukan R. 2017. *Transportation for Livable Cities. Chapter 2: The City-Transportation Relationship*. eBook 31 October. Routledge (First Published 1999). https://doi.org/10.4324/9781351318167

World 101 Course. 2017. Module 7: What Happened When China Joined WT0? *Council on Foreign Relations*. https://world101.cfr.org/global-era-issues/trade/what-happened-when-china-joined-wto

3
REPORTING QUALITY

New items from Associated Press (AP) – "At least 1,600 dams across the US pose potential risk."

We are all used to seeing pronouncements like this, especially after some disaster that might have been avoided with proper maintenance occurs, in this case the Spencer Dam in Nebraska (Lieb et al. 2019). There will also be some spectacular footage of the damage occurring, perhaps from a helicopter. There is a flurry of discussion on the talks shows. Then there is the annual American Society of Civil Engineers annual report card where the different types of infrastructure all score low "grades" like Cs and Ds which again initiates a few news stories expressing embarrassment over how the USA got so bad. Maybe there will be a hilarious skit about infrastructure on one of the satirical news shows (John Oliver 2015). This lack of progress has been going on for decades now. In the end not too much really changes in the coverage except that there are more types of media than newspapers, weeklies, and TV and radio news shows in the internet era.

Failure to connect the dots

Media coverage has played a role in the continued lack of investment. Coverage is, of course, episodic in nature in the traditional media such as TV and radio as it really about holding your attention between commercials. "If it bleeds, it leads" is the unofficial motto of television news programming. Even seemingly natural disasters where infrastructure fails often have a human-caused dimension. The Hurricane Katrina disaster would not have occurred if a dike (one of those numerous dams posing a potential risk) at the north end of the city had been reinforced as was the Army Corp of Engineers' plan until the money was transferred. Also, National Guard trucks that could have driven in deep water to rescue people had been transferred to Iraq. President Bush turned down an offer from the regular US Army to supply their trucks. There was a failure to connect the dots quickly enough so that the event would have been interpreted as more a scandal and less a natural catastrophe.

A failure to connect the dots is a good way to describe much of the reporting where public services or lack thereof should be an integral part of understanding issues. For example, transit or lack thereof plays a role in unemployment. The idea that there are plenty of jobs available is because of the so-called U3 percentage released by the US Bureau of Labor Statistics which is

DOI: 10.4324/9781003245704-3

defined by the International Labor Organization as "U3: the official unemployment rate that occurs when people are without jobs and they have actively looked for work within the past four weeks" (Kozlovich 2015). This has been cited by lazy or rushed reporters for so long that U3 qualifier is not even used any longer. But it excludes people who might actually like to work but cannot because public services and public works are lacking. When assessing a job opening a candidate takes into account pay as well as location. If a job pays too little to be able to afford childcare it simply does not make sense. Applicable to a far larger portion of the population than just people with small children is the location. In sprawled areas, the majority of urban/suburban USA, few jobs are in walking or bicycling distance. If the pay is low, it might not make sense to buy a car as too much of the after-tax income would be consumed in monthly payments, insurance, and fuel. And this is assuming that one is even able to drive. In most metro regions, transit is very likely to be too poor to be realistic, taking far too long via a connection somewhere. Even if this connection is well timed, there might still be with lots of unproductive waiting time before work starts and after work ends because buses operate on 30- or even 60-minute headways.

FIGURE 3.1 The dilemma so many people face.
Source: www.andysinger.com

Occasionally there are some more thorough investigations. Indeed, they bring to light what life is like for many workers. Longa et al. (2020) reviewed the records of the Albuquerque Police Department, dividing a person's record into a primary reason for a traffic stop and then secondary violations. These secondary violations were typically for lapsed registrations and especially liability insurance. Violators were supposed to pay the registration and insurance plus a fine. When they did not pay then they also got a bench warrant which added another $100. Some defendants told the authors they did not come because children were not allowed in the courtroom and no childcare was available elsewhere. Others did not come because they were afraid of being put in jail because they simply did not have the money. They had to drive because transit was too poor, so they were, in effect, pressured into breaking the law. Some lost their jobs because of this bench warrant, which I guess solves the commuting problem if not the payment problem. Some went on to lose their driving licenses as well when they could not pay, which seems illogical if the point is to get them to pay up.

There is even more to the story as it also highlights that the Albuquerque Police Department is either overcommitted or underfunded, given the amount of money allocated by state and local governments. Either by intent or neglect, fines are now a significant part of the police budget, making it hard to change a system that depends upon kicking people when they are down. Reform would require either a trimming back of police duties or a replacement for revenue from fines or both. Anger over the number of fines and the frequency of being stopped by residents was the kindling waiting to be lit by the police shooting of Michael Brown in Ferguson, Missouri in 2014. There are occasionally stories about how changes have been slow in coming in our examples of Albuquerque (James et al. 2020) and Ferguson (CBS News 2020). Dependence upon fines for significant operating revenues by city governments persists and when combined with outsourcing of enforcement on a commission basis can hit the lower income communities hardest (Bradley and Sherman 2021).

As these stories show, many aspects of public services are in fact financially intertwined with each other and with social issues that at first glance are not associated with one another. These services provided by municipal governments, in turn, require support from higher levels of government, especially when the tax base is limited due to modest income levels of its residents. Moreover, at times it will be necessary for higher levels to contribute far larger sums for a few years for major projects like a transit upgrade or wastewater treatment plant replacement. It is the isolation and self-dependence of local governments, even in the case of states with prosperous regions that is the real context for many news stories currently treated as a short video clip and a few statistics about who was injured, what property was damaged and who went to jail.

Projects formulated with media coverage in mind

Because of the money involved, large projects are going to be debated in the media. Even more so if there is a request for a tax increase. Politicians, public service planners and interest groups who are in favor will hope for positive coverage. The explanations can be quite involved but this does not match the sound bite nature of most radio and TV coverage. The written media is more likely to handle a complicated story well. It is also clear that those opposed will also be looking to contribute to the story that reporters write. And, they often have the resources to buy advertisements. They are not necessarily interested in the public investment money involved, but rather the impacts on their businesses. The role of social media is less clear. It provides avenues for self-education on public works around the world and perhaps on local projects. But like radio and TV, perhaps even more so, people can confine themselves to sources that have viewpoints to which they already agree.

Proponents face a dilemma. Go small or go big? How this will be covered in the press is a serious consideration. Small makes the investment money requested less but it also will serve fewer people. Big makes the price tag larger but spreads the benefit around. Small means that one must go back to ask again later. Big allows continuity. Opponents can work with either approach to criticize the project. If it is small, then the argument is that everyone pays but only a few people benefit. If it is large, then the argument is it costs too much and takes too long for everyone to benefit. The proponents are put in a position of having to say either way that this is the best we can do given the funding that we can realistically expect.

The Nashville transit proposal put to the voters in 2018 is a case in point. The city of Nashville has a population of about 680,000 and adjacent Davidson County has about 700,000 people. This proposal did not even include Williamson County, which actually has equal commuter travel in both directions with Nashville (West 2018). In common with most of the other southern states, the legislators of the state of Tennessee do not see fit to give a lot of support to transit, leaving this to local governments. But they cannot cope without some assistance if there is to be anything other than a rudimentary bus system running in mixed traffic with low frequencies. Like other cities in a similar situation, Nashville turns to the Federal Government for additional funds. There are some formula funds that help to buy replacement buses with bonuses for the extra cost of being able to run on alternative fuels, for Intelligent Transportation Systems (ITS) technologies to help manage the fleet and provide the public with information on their phones and websites, mobile ticketing, and other modern conveniences the public has come to expect. There are competitive grants with program names such as Small Starts for smaller operations wanting to install the beginnings of a dedicated rights-of way network, and then major grants up to 50 percent of the total capital cost of a major project. Highway projects still get up to 80 percent from Uncle Sam, transit projects very rarely do even though it would be legal. This double standard also had to be taken into account as highway proponents have the advantage of more "free money" that could be brought into the region if highways are extended and widened instead.

The non-formula-based programs to which the Nashville transit agency (known as the MTA) could apply are always oversubscribed. Various locations across the entire country compete with one another based on the ratings they receive from the US Federal Transit Administration (FTA). Even with a very high rating, it can take years before the first award, thereby slowing down development plans. If a place is in a hurry, and given the traffic and the complaints from the electorate this is quite common, they may need to start with local funds if their state happens to be one of those that is parsimonious toward transit. This puts pressure on cities or counties or regional transit districts, depending upon local organization, to try raise a local tax as soon as possible to get the project started. In the absence of a state-level match, they will need this anyway to get a high rating from the FTA. Then, as the matching funds arrive later the project can keep expanding.

The MTA and planning authorities opted to go big with an oft-repeated price tag of $5.2 Billion in infrastructure construction and about $9 Billion in total if one includes ongoing long-term operating and maintenance expenses. They had the support of the Chamber of Commerce who were concerned about the future ability of the region to attract younger workers and to remain competitive in the race for the "creative class" (Florida 2003). The MTA and the regional planning authority provided a vision of a comprehensive network that eventually would cover the whole region including the suburbs. But it would take many years to complete with some segments of the five corridors not receiving the separated-lane higher performance rail transit, the most appealing part of such projects, for a couple of decades. These might get improved frequency and better area coverage with buses in the meantime but not necessarily immediately. It ended up losing by a margin of two to one despite outspending the anti-side by a larger margin (Capps 2018; Garrison 2018; Stockton 2018).

There was drama along the way, including the resignation of a quite popular mayor who was a major proponent of the plan over a misspending scandal (Kennedy 2018). There were a couple of major efforts from the anti-side, one, in particular, *NoTax4Trax,* included visible opponents as well as darker but still legal Section 501(c)(4) money. They spent $1.2 Million on television ads. One group who called themselves *Plan B* prepared a website where potential voters could learn additional (dis?)information. The Plan B website had multiple arguments which to a layperson seem logical, and indeed there are some contexts where their arguments have merit. For instance, they promote the idea of shared ride mass transit which can indeed fill in the gaps of traditional transit services (Maddox and Porisch 2018). But the Plan B website gives the impression this could be an alternative to an entire traditional fixed route system, which is a stretch to say the least for a metro area the size of Nashville and Davidson County. There was also a suggestion of improved highway interchanges as a way to reduce highway congestion. This is also woefully inadequate if the regional population is projected to expand by another one million people over the next 20 years. (More on interchanges shortly.) Where the transit future of Nashville and Davidson County stands as of this writing is that the current Mayor has prepared to go small, this time with a new proposal having a more modest price tag of about $1.5 Billion (Sichko 2020).

This type of pro- and anti-back and forth calls out for skilled reportage including interviewing of persons without a local connection that might indicate prejudice and by comparison with other regions that might be a peer in some sense. A good recent example of the latter is David Gutman's (2017) story in the *Seattle Times* explaining why Seattle now has higher spending than other comparable cities in the USA. There is a legacy of quite detailed coverage of each of several transit proposals over the decades. How highway projects are typically covered in the press is the subject of the next section.

Highway coverage versus transit coverage

Most short news stories about major infrastructure proposals begin with the price tag and everything else is included as time or space allows. This can create quite misleading impressions, as one cannot cost public works project out the way one prices a vacation package. When a vacation is over it is over, and one can simply sum up the expenses. Public works will be around for a long time, and there are many uncertainties both before construction and afterwards. One of the most important is that the demand for its services must be estimated. So, if numbers are being thrown around, there should be some discussion about the assumptions that were involved. There are also individuals and organizations who might have hidden motivations for their positions for or against. Furthermore, the costs and benefits of major public works projects are not evenly distributed so subtracting the total cost from the total benefits to get a net benefit, the method used by private companies, would be misleading as well. Not only misleading, some consequences can be so severe that many protests might occur beforehand and many lawsuits afterwards.

Such a topic cannot be explored without in-depth stories. Most certainly it is not about minimizing costs, a position which the primary media focus on total project costs might invite. My dissertation supervisor and transit guru Professor Vukan Vuchic was quick-witted on more than one occasion to make this point during public testimony. In one case he replied to a hostile questioner by responding "if we always did what was cheapest, we would all be riding around on mopeds." In reference to a complaint about "the gold-plated metro" in Washington, D.C., he pointed out that "It is the nation's capital after all. If we always did what was cheapest, the Capitol Building would have had a flat roof."

Some daily newspapers and especially weeklies (*The Stranger, Philadelphia City Paper, The Village Voice*, etc.) have done an admirable job in trying to contribute information which concerned citizens might consider. Alas, they have been disappearing, and with them beat reporters who build up expertise and contact networks. A few e-magazines like *The Verge* have been picking up the slack to some extent but cannot hope to cover the details of every city in the nation. *Wired* is an interesting example as it has expanded out from its original "tech" sector boosterism roots to wider coverage of technology across society from an agnostic standpoint. Some business news services like the regional manifestations of the *Business Insider* provide insight as well, albeit often behind paywalls. Nevertheless, there are some flaws in the coverage that persist. It would be surprising if there were not. This is a complicated topic for which people go to the university in a variety of disciplines and then spend years as consultants, government employees, and academics to gain more nuanced understanding over time.

One of these persistent flaws is the lack of a proper comparison between public spending on roads versus transit in the same region. The price tag of a transit project will include right-of-way acquisition (which can be very substantial indeed in built up areas), the construction cost of tracks or separated roadways, power supply and distribution networks if electrified, stations or stops, major terminals, and depots. Projects may be broken into several phases, which may or may not be properly quoted with discounting for the reduced value of money in the future. Then comes the operating subsidy which is the difference between what is covered by user fares and the total operating cost, with the added complexity that the future amount that can be collected from users also depends on factors typically outside the planners' control. Examples include any housing and commercial densification that may occur along the transit corridors and, especially in the USA, huge fluctuations in the price of gasoline due to the low proportion of price that is taxes by world standards. Perhaps hard to imagine at the moment, but if global warming starts being taken seriously there might be a public policy of carbon taxes that increase fuel costs dramatically combined with spending more money to dramatically increase the frequency of transit.

Meanwhile, on the highway side, in press reports there might be some mention that car drivers are subsidized too, but not in nearly enough detail. A proposed new highway project will also have substantial investment costs. Many freeways are now 50 years old, and the reinforcement bars are starting to show through the worn and cracking concrete. One project, the Zoo Interchange outside of Milwaukee – actually, a complex or highways and access roads – took six years and over $1.7 Billion to reconstruct. While they were at it, designers added some features to make "an aesthetically-pleasing, mobility gem" in order to help get through the mandatory public participation process when Federal funds are involved, while also sneaking in a few more lanes here and there in the spaghetti of overpasses, underpasses, and access roads. Ostensibly these are to remove congestion just like the Plan B website advocated for Nashville (Jacobs Engineering 2020).

It turns out that the price quoted for the Zoo Interchange was for the "core" system which was completed in June 2018. There is still a north leg which the Wisconsin DoT estimated to cost another $238 million. In 2019, the State appropriated a total of $465 Million with $320 Million for other highways, the balance toward completing Zoo (Kirchen 2019). I saw no breakdown or estimate of how much non-drivers or rural non-users of these suburban freeways will be paying. It is understandable because pooled revenues from multiple taxation and grant sources can be hard to trace and then disaggregate over a multiyear project, in this case six years. But it would still make for more balanced reporting if there could at least be a mention that no money at all was allocated toward transit by the State of Wisconsin legislature. The very latest proposal passed through the Wisconsin state legislature's budget committee recommends $223.5 million of borrowing for roads and infrastructure over the next two years rather than using the current account where it would compete with other priorities or by raising the fuel taxes. The Governor wanted to borrow more than twice as much (Schmidt 2021).

In the interest of fairness, reports could maybe also mention that this capacity increase is not for "interstate" travel but for intra-suburban travel and all Wisconsin taxpayers are contributing, just as if the State had seen fit to support transit. This is a very important omission, as politicians regularly argue that transit is a local responsibility. Indeed, the Republican 2016 Platform says exactly this

> More than a quarter of the [Trust] Fund's spending is diverted from its original purpose. One fifth of its funds are spent on mass transit, an inherently local affair that serves only a small portion of the population, concentrated in six big cities.
>
> *(Republican Party 2016, page 5)*

There was no 2020 platform.

Some portion of the "reconstruction" not covered by the Federal Government has to be paid by the taxpayers of Wisconsin. But this is not all, just as with transit, there will be ongoing maintenance costs, which must be born totally at the state and/or local levels. Since the gasoline tax covers 40 to 50 percent of the direct cost of construction and maintenance of roads, the portion covered by non-users should be discussed. This contribution that will also go on for decades does not require a vote for a new local tax, it is simply appropriated by the state legislature without the drama of a public vote. This would explain why reporters do not connect these dots too often.

FIGURE 3.2 Guide to drivers during reconstruction of the Zoo Interchange outside Milwaukee.
Source: Wisconsin DoT.

Another of these persistent flaws is the non-discussion of the enormous and long-lasting fiscal impacts on the governments involved due to the consumption of land. It can be enormous on highway interchange projects, necessitated by the large radii required to allow speeds to stay high. This is at best low value land for life-expired vehicle or construction equipment storage or something similar. It certainly is not usable as park space, as anyone who stands near these know. The huge shadows, the roar of vehicles moving at high speed and need for circuitous navigation by the non-motorized, all preclude that. It really is just land removed from the tax rolls. This is not insignificant. One report compared the size of an interchange in Houston with the center of Siena, Italy, where 30,000 people live (BBBC 2020). Professor Norman Garrick and his students investigated Bridgeport, Connecticut in detail with photos taken over a century to the present day where much of the central business district has disappeared from mixed uses to government buildings, highways, and parking lots, all off the tax rolls (Schmitt 2017; Garrick 2021). Other cities have received similar photo analyses, this is not an extreme case (Hampton 2014). Entire modestly sized cities based on 19th-century horse-era designs and entire Central Business Districts of many modern cities could easily fit within the same footprint.

It is true that urban critics and architects regularly criticize the ugliness of multilane elevated highways, but this is perhaps not as helpful in a discussion about proposed new projects as when compared to the footprints of the alternatives because of the relative fiscal impacts from so much untaxed land. It would be more financially realistic to place transit alternatives in a tunnel if judged to be too noisy and unpleasing in appearance (which is what happened with the Seattle Light Rapid Transit project instead of a modest new low bridge over the Ship Canal). In an era when visualization tools are so plentiful, the local and regional media need not rely on officially sanctioned studies in their reporting. They can provide independent contributions and not merely "he said, she said" coverage. Have a look at the Interstate 5 bridge across the Lake Washington Ship Canal in Seattle as seen in Figures 3.3 or 3.4, or on an internet search for other examples like the Buffalo Skyway. To borrow an insight from a friend, he suggested that anthropologists a few thousand years from now in the post-apocalypse will see the giant remnant columns and think our civilization had built monuments to our gods just like the ancient Egyptians. By comparison, rail bridges of similar throughput would have been much narrower and not need two levels. And many formerly elevated sections, like the 3rd Avenue Elevated in NYC, were eventually placed underground, unthinkable for the I-5 monstrosity.

There is one use for land around interchanges and large bridges that does indeed get some media attention. This is as shelter for the homeless. Figure 3.5 shows that Anatole France's observation that the law forbids the rich as well as the poor from sleeping under the bridges is obsolete: bridge undersides are now typically fenced off. Shelter might be a temporary use reflecting the current political economy, but surely the embankments in such places will never be a cherished part of the city fabric. Fair coverage would demand that some proposed transit facilities would also be visualized. Bus storage depots and railyards can also be large, becoming long-term non-contributors to the tax base and sources of blight, although there is more latitude about where they are placed as buses and trains need not be stored near their users, but cars do. The point is that comparisons should be independently available and not only ones provided by official project sources released to newspapers (Seattle Times staff 2012). Prominent architects and planners as well as advocacy groups could be invited to submit their visions of the city 30 years in the future if each of the various alternatives were to be selected. Project alternatives might have to be revised or even eliminated with more comprehensive and stimulating coverage.

FIGURE 3.3 Interstate 5 over the Ship Canal in Seattle – huge and noisy structures attract industrial uses.
Source: Ralph Jenne.

FIGURE 3.4 Looking south under Interstate 5 toward the Ship Canal in Seattle.
Source: Ralph Jenne.

FIGURE 3.5 Under the north side of the University Bridge in Seattle.
Source: Ralph Jenne.

FIGURE 3.6 Homeless living in a Seattle park.
Source: Ralph Jenne.

Conflict of interest

There are multimedia companies with vast resources as a result of the deregulations of the 1990s that allowed content providers to merge with communications infrastructure providers. (A type of infrastructure not discussed so far as it is mostly in private hands in the USA.) Already mentioned and certainly not news to well-informed people, TV and radio shows want ratings and websites want clicks, so they lean toward short stories, short reads, and sensational aspects of proposed projects. Understandable behavior since detailed coverage costs more money. But it goes deeper. Why would a company that can make money off a heated pro versus anti-battle want to intercede? If they do a thorough job, then the voters can make informed decisions. Advertisements are far less likely to be effective.

There have been multiple attempts at campaign reform, including free airtime, but it clearly has been a failure, by and large. Remember the McCain Feingold Act of 2002? Payments for ad buys are still one of the largest costs of any campaign, even for what can be very technical subjects requiring professional staffs to justify or refute a candidate project. My personal experience was that people on my side were asked to volunteer their time and even couch surf if travel was required, while on the other side, paid help would stay in hotels. Such cost saving would be one way to compensate for having less money for advertising. In fairness it must be noted that having more money does not always mean a side will win. The pro forces lost dramatically in Nashville even with far more money. Thus, in the USA, major decisions about the future of a city or region are often more like a series of sensational jury trials than an exercise in democratic participation.

Being a reporter in the modern multimedia environment is not easy. It is very competitive to hold a full-time position and apparently the pace can be hectic. Never mind investigative journalism which used to mean weeks or months on one story. Perhaps this makes requests like mine for in-depth storytelling a fantasy. Yet, these stories are incredibly important to the future of a city. What its urban form will be like and hence how much walking and bicycling there will be, what types of foods will be readily available and at what price, how much exercise and human contact people will get and taxpayer bills all depend on decisions made decades ago. Residents might have a certain lifestyle because of the results from an off-season election with low turnout or because of maneuvers by crafty politicians seeking to avoid public input. When newspapers are losing money or radio talk shows have lost advertising to social media, it becomes hard even for well-intentioned organizations to stay on the beat. There are people like Bill Weir, the chief climate reporter at CNN, who feel that "Eventually, we're all going to be climate reporters, whether we call it that or not. Because it's going to touch everything in more obvious ways every year" (Hertsgaard 2020).

Comparison with Finland

As a rule, support or opposition to a major infrastructure project is something that helps define a candidate in an election for both City Council and the Parliament. The candidates are trusted to make decisions in line with the ideologies of their parties, of which there are at least seven. They are not able to avoid taking responsibility for enabling legislation or a major decision on a project, which is one way to interpret the invoking of a requirement for local votes. The City of Philadelphia has a population of about 1.5 million and 17 City Council members. The City of Los Angeles has about 4 million and 15 members. Contrast this with the City of Helsinki that has about 700,000 residents but 85 members.

As a practical matter, it is possible to avoid new fundraising efforts that require a special vote because the gasoline tax is high enough to support a package of infrastructure rather than make roads

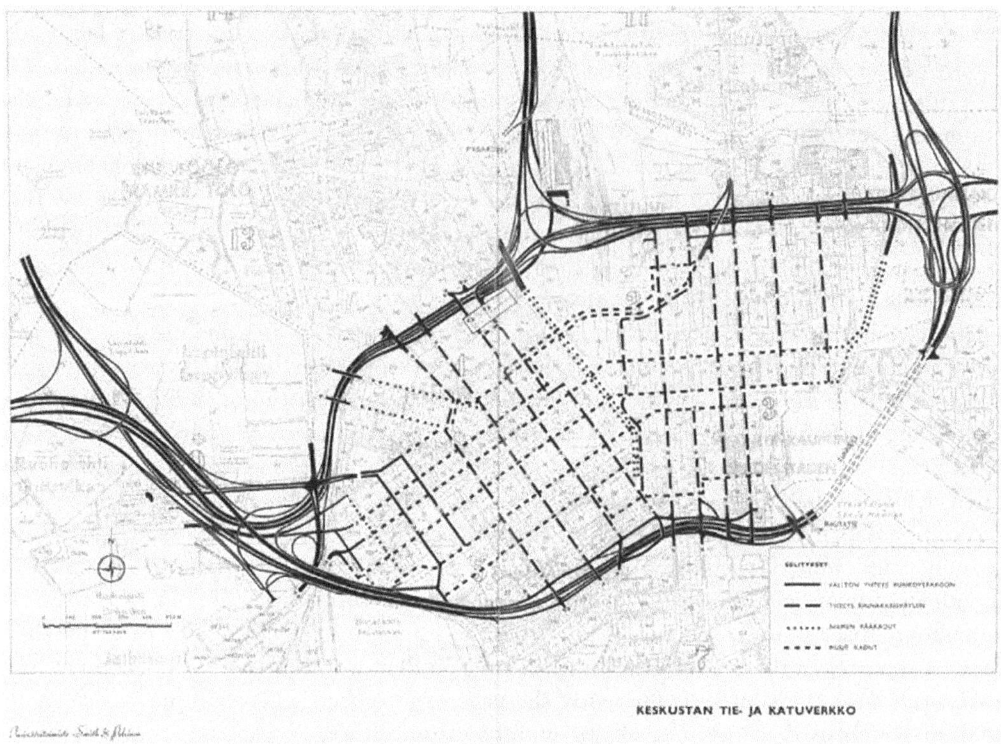

FIGURE 3.7 Central Business District of Helsinki if Smith Polvinen plan of 1968 had been executed. *Source*: Wilbur Smith & Associates and engineering consultant Pentti Polvinen: Helsinki transport study, 1968 © The Museum of Finnish Architecture
https://guides.hamhelsinki.fi/work/smith-polvisen-liikennesuunnitelma-1968/

and highways compete with all other infrastructure, which is one of the main causes of multiple funding crises across the USA. The national tax structure is in the domain of the Parliament.

It is an interesting observation that a Finnish company, *Pentti Polvinen*, teamed with *Wilbur Smith* in 1968, a prominent US highway engineering firm, to propose a series of elevated highways and rail lines across Helsinki including a highway interchange next to the central train station. It was soundly defeated because of the public outcry. In the USA at about this same time, such a project would probably have succeeded despite public opposition especially if the alignment went through a minority community as evidenced by how many freeways actually did get built during that era. *Polvinen* went out of business not too long afterwards.

References

Bradley, Ryan and Alex Sherman. 2021. Mutant Meter Maids. *The Baffler*, April 28. Available at: https://thebaffler.com/latest/mutant-meter-maids-bradley-sherman?utm_source=Baffler+Readers&utm_campaign=7c34f79f07-weekly_04282021&utm_medium=email&utm_term=0_3541d01f8a-7c34f79f07-46816556

Building Better, Building Beautiful Commission (BBBC). 2020. *Living with Beauty: Promoting Health, Well-Being and Sustainable Growth*. UK Government. Available at: https://assets.publishing.service.gov.uk/government/uploads/system/uploads/attachment_data/file/861832/Living_with_beauty_BBBBC_report.pdf

Capps, Kriston. 2018. Nashville's Transit Plan Just Got Trounced. *Bloomberg City Lab*, May 2. Available at: *https://www.bloomberg.com/news/articles/2018-05-02/nashville-voters-reject-5-2-billion-transit-plan*

CBS News. 2020. 6 years after Michael Brown's Death, Activists Continue to Mobilize for Change in Ferguson. *Yahoo News*, August 29. Available at: *https://news.yahoo.com/6-years-michael-brown-death-000000477.html?guccounter=1&guce_referrer=aHR0cHM6Ly9kdWNrZHVja2dvLmNvbS8_dD1mZm50JnE9ZmVyZ-3Vzb24rbW8rcG9saWNlK3Byb3Rlc3QmaWE9d2ViJmlhaT1odHRwcyUzQSUyRiUyRm5ld3MueW-Fob28uY29tJTJGNi15ZWFycy1taWNoYWVsLWJyb3duLWRlYXRoLTAwMDAwMDQ3Ny5odG1s-JnBuPTE&guce_referrer_sig=AQAAAI0tZgzWFuIG4An0lIfhGrded-EvBrl0YTXMkX7u4fVnQAlh1i-uHPo5dP0xHb-wfN0Ab2_URLxdQsw0foUYWKlofzH59j_TsJD8oei8aLlRbqM48s0S6rIY1Yc7w7Zpe-2WAw2Vs_qk5Xr1lc87UN2KtemCXDh-9z-7W-BRJcsllF*

Florida, Richard. 2003. *The Rise of the Creative Class*. Turtleback.

Garrick, Norman. 2021. *Just and Sustainable: Transportation and Land Use Planning*. The Sustainable Cities Group: University of Connecticut.

Garrison, Joey. 2018. Nashville Voters Overwhelmingly Reject Transit Referendum. *The Tennessean*, May 1. Available at: *https://eu.tennessean.com/story/news/politics/2018/05/01/nashville-transit-vote-davidson-county-mass-transit/564991002/*

Gutman, David. 2017. Seattle Area Spends Most Per Capita to Build Transit and Here's Why. *Seattle Times*, March 19. Available at: https://www.seattletimes.com/seattle-news/transportation/seattle-area-spends-most-per-capita-to-build-transit-heres-why/

Hampton, Shane. 2014. 60 Years of Urban Change: Midwest. *Institute for Quality Communities, University of Oklahoma*, December 12. Available at: http://iqc.ou.edu/2014/12/12/60yrsmidwest/

Hertsgaard, Mark. 2020. Will Climate Break Through in Big Media's Elections Coverage? *The Nation*, August 5. Available at: *https://www.thenation.com/article/environment/election-paris-accord-climate/*

Jacobs Engineering. 2020. Zoo Interchange Reconstruction. Available at: *https://www.jacobs.com/projects/wisconsin-department-of-transportation-zoo-interchange* (Accessed November 29, 2020)

James, Keegan, Sarmiento Kloer and David Correia.2020. Mayor Keller's Killer Cops: An Assessment of Court-Ordered Police Reform in Albuquerque. *Counterpunch*, August 19. Available at: https://www.counterpunch.org/2020/08/19/mayor-kellers-killer-cops-an-assessment-of-court-ordered-police-reform-in-albuquerque/

John Oliver Last Week Tonight. 2015. Infrastructure. *Home Box Office*, March 2. Available at: *https://www.youtube.com/watch?v=Wpzvaqypav8*

Kennedy, Merrit. 2018. Nashville Mayor Resigns, Pleads Guilty To Felony Theft. *National Public Radio*, March 6. Available at: *https://www.npr.org/sections/thetwo-way/2018/03/06/591146030/nashville-mayor-resigns-pleads-guilty-to-felony-theft*

Kirchen, Rich. 2019. Evers Budget Includes Tax Cut and Funding for Zoo Interchange, Medical College. *Milwaukee Business Journal*, July 3. Available at: *https://www.bizjournals.com/milwaukee/news/2019/07/03/evers-budget-includes-tax-cut-and-funding-for-zoo.html*

Kozlovich, Rich. 2015. Classifications of Unemployment U1 through U6. *Paradigms and Demographics*, February 8. Available at: https://paradigmsanddemographics.blogspot.com/2015/02/classifications-of-unemployment-u1.html.

Lieb, David A., Michael Casey and Michelle Minkoff. 2019. AP: At least 1,680 dams across the US pose potential risk. *New York Post*, November 11. Available at: http://www.livingrivers.org/pdfs/Press/AtLeast1680DamsPosePotentialRiskUSA.pdf

Longa, Ernesto, David Correia, and Matias Fontenla 2020. What Good are Police on Patrol? An Analysis of Traffic Enforcement in Albuquerque by Counterpunch. *Counterpunch*, August 27. Available at: https://www.counterpunch.org/2020/08/27/what-good-are-police-on-patrol-an-analysis-of-traffic-enforcement-in-albuquerque/

Maddox III, John Hayes and Johann Porisch. 2018. We Aren't Against Mass Transit. Just This Plan. *Nashville Plan B* website. Available at: *http://nashvilleplanb.com/* (Accessed August 15, 2020).

Republican Party. 2016. Republican Party Platform. August 1. Available at: *https://prod-cdn-static.gop.com/media/documents/DRAFT_12_FINAL[1]-ben_1468872234.pdf*

Schmidt, Mitchell. 2021. Budget Committee Reduces Borrowing for Road Projects, Cuts Transit Aid to Madison, Milwaukee. *The Wisconsin State Journal*, June 10. Available at: https://madison.com/wsj/news/local/govt-and-politics/budget-committee-reduces-borrowing-for-road-projects-cuts-transit-aid-to-madison-milwaukee/article_b0fb5ed5-54f0-5bb2-b2e2-e73620f6d3ac.html

Schmitt, Angie. 2017. How Highways Squeezed Taxable Land Out of Cities. *StreetsBlog USA*, October 27. Available at: *https://usa.streetsblog.org/2017/10/27/how-highways-squeezed-taxable-land-out-of-cities/*

Seattle Times staff. 2012. Renderings of the New SR 520 Floating Bridge. *The Seattle Times*, March 28. Available at: *https://www.seattletimes.com/news/renderings-of-the-new-sr-520-floating-bridge/*

Sichko, Adam. 2020. Nashville Mayor John Cooper crafting $1.5 Billion Mass-Transit Expansion. *Nashville Business Journal*, August 17. Available at: *https://www.bizjournals.com/nashville/news/2020/08/17/nashville-mayor-cooper-new-mass-transit-plan.html*

Stockton, Nick. 2018. Why Traffic-Choked Nashville Said 'No Thanks' to Public Transit. *Wired*. May 9. Available at: *https://www.wired.com/story/nashville-transit-referendum-vote-plan/*

West, Emily R. 2018. What Nashville's Transit Vote Means for Franklin and Brentwood. *The Tennessean*, May 1. Available at: https://eu.tennessean.com/story/news/local/williamson/2018/05/01/nashville-transit-referendum-vote-williamson-suburbs/529416002/

Wilbur Smith & Associates and Engineering Consultant Pentti Polvinen: Helsinki Transport Study, 1968 © *The Museum of Finnish Architecture*. Available at: https://guides.hamhelsinki.fi/work/smith-polvisen-liikennesuunnitelma-1968/

4

POLITICIANS ARE SUPPOSED TO HAVE A VISION

Infrastructure comes into discussions about the future. Being a politician is closely tied to what kind of city one envisions for the future, even if one feels that technology is destiny. There were exceptions, of course, when someone suggests that little public investment will be needed but the burden would then be on them to explain how this might be possible. Or so it seemed, until the fight in the US Congress after Biden was elected over the proposed infrastructure and reconciliation bills where almost half of them opposed both. It shows that a do-nothing attitude is becoming increasingly widespread. This despite the mounting evidence of a backlog of maintenance needs and a population growing by about 3 million per year.

An argument used to typically include a statement that at least some of the existing infrastructure must be maintained, while the same politician might declare other parts were obsolete or were entirely the purview of state and local governments, with the debate then turning to questions like "will automation eliminate truck drivers?" or "will new technologies make ICE engines obsolete?" and "If so, how long from now?" Further questions are "what kinds of funds will be available to perhaps help the private sector?" and "what will the voting public accept or reject?" In short, there are visions, whether spoken or not, based on what politicians believe and what they think they can deliver. It is this author's distinct impression that most people running for office have not been pressured too much about their longer-term vision, with most of the questions revolving around current events and the next term. The point of this chapter is to explore whether I am exaggerating. And if I am not, who is filling the visioning vacuum?

Different levels of governments often conflict

It is said that clever politicians try not to get too pinned down, as they could lose voters when people have a clearer idea of what they will do. Furthermore, if they make promises, these can be reviewed by reporters, by opponents, and during election time, in attack ads. This is overly cynical, as some politicians do have genuine convictions. Indeed, for those who have very little money compared to their opponents, getting coverage for their distinct ideas might their best strategy. Consider how detailed the national Green Party platform is compared to the national Democratic Party platform in 2020. One sets deadlines for some major investments and drastic

DOI: 10.4324/9781003245704-4

changes, the other could not commit to basic precepts of a Green New Deal. As mentioned in the previous chapter, the Republicans simply re-used their 2016 platform in 2020 despite the huge changes to the nation and the world since then, demonstrating that they don't even seem to think that a vision is necessary, only some platitudes and general principles.

This lack of a strong plan on the Federal level leaves the state level and local/regional level candidates with largely a blank canvas. They can be quite free to develop campaigns unencumbered by promises made by the national party apparatus. This does not mean they are totally free to say whatever they want, as support can be withheld, or primary opponents boosted if some unspoken lines are crossed. They can still feel pressured into local commitments that bring them into conflict with national-level candidates. This is very much in evidence in military spending reduction proposals that risk cuts to their own districts. But it is also in evidence about public works with potentially large environmental impacts, such as pipelines to deliver oil and fracking gas or freeway widenings.

Candidates must also be concerned with media coverage, especially about the situation discussed in the previous chapter where the total, multi-year cost is mentioned in sound bites but not the corresponding benefits or necessity for the project. Thus, politicians in many urban regions speak in an atmosphere where their breathing space can be quite constricted or even toxic, both literally and figuratively.

Ideology against picking winners and losers actually picks winners

One of the most common explanations for not highlighting a position on public investment is the belief that a politician should not be picking winners, meaning winners in the narrow sense that profits can be made. But there are different consequences from the way that companies earn money they are ignoring. Some lines of business have far more externalities than others. Would it be the same if a city attracted an electroplating plant, many of which used to be in Silicon Valley, or the back-office operations of a bank? Some winners are going to impose costs on public service agencies or degradation to the environment, or both. These must be considered beforehand and not as afterthoughts. Did we really still have to make this point in the year 2020? It seems we do and not just because of egregious Executive Orders like the ones negating the Endangered Species Act. Expect ongoing attempts at deregulation bills, regardless of history of violations or environmental mitigation justifications, in the US Congress. For example, to bring back electroplating and even steel mills that are without modern pollution controls on the excuse that this is the only way that the USA can compete. This laxity at the Federal level enables city and state level politicians to pay little attention to externalities if they so choose.

Is it that politicians are dense? Some might be. There are some who have ideologies that do not take environmental impacts, or even the need for planning, seriously. There can be other reasoning as well. With finely grained political subdivisions, it is quite possible that one jurisdiction can capture a lot of the benefit and another a lot of the cost from the same project. As a common example, this fact can be and is used as a threat by big box stores. If one town does not give a permit for a megastore because of the concern for traffic generation and/or because its town center will lose some of its customer base, the store can simply say we are going to build on the edge of town. Thus, the town gets the dreaded effects in any case but no tax revenues. As a project grows in size, the impacted area also grows until it is a regional concern.

Such was the case with the FoxConn factory deal signed by the Governor of Wisconsin, apparently commonly referred to as the "Fox Con" deal to residents of Wisconsin. An area to the south of Milwaukee might get huge tax revenues if the plant comes to fruition because of thousands of jobs (which now seems very unlikely). The company and the town of Mount Pleasant both avoid the brownfield clean-up costs associated with more logical placement in Milwaukee proper where the utilities are already in place and there may even be usable buildings. These costs can be substantial and typically fall to public agencies as the Milwaukee City Transit System (MCTS) has discovered as it tries to find a new location for a bus barn (Hubbuch 2020). In the FoxConn case, the promised subsidy was so large the company could also avoid most or even all of the costs of installing any new public infrastructure. How many of the workers would get back and forth from Milwaukee was a concern of neither the State nor the local municipality. If this project had really proceeded as planned, this cost would most likely have fallen on the hapless MCTS which does not include the new factory in its service area. Based on previous experience, the inability for city dwellers to reach suburban locations and vice versa would be their concern (Palzewicz 2020).

Let us assume that some politicians who express the view that picking winners is unfair are sincere and not simply doing what is most advantageous to themselves or favored companies. Then they might have a point that the taxpayers could end up supporting a white elephant. There is the risk that an industry that seems like it is going to be significant in terms of employment and the tax base never materializes. Is this not what happened with the FoxConn deal? This was a bet that consumer electronics assembly would relocate to the USA and do so in a fashion similar to mega-factories in China. Furthermore, the opponents would be right that the risks of whether some growing industry is going to bring a city a winning project are usually on the government side, not the corporate side. Recall the maintenance base prepared for United Airlines at Indianapolis airport in the 1990s. Great promises of improved efficiency were made that could justify a large government investment that would be paid back by the tenant. Interestingly the company who designed the facility has not removed the initial project description (FSB 2020) from its website. At its peak around the year 2000, United Airlines provided 3,000 jobs. They had promised it would eventually expand to 6,300. When they ended up leaving in search of cheaper labor, they could easily make this decision because there was little penalty. The airport eventually found other tenants, but with only 1,400 jobs instead and reduced economic stimulus and revenues (O'Malley 2010).

So, if this kind of incentive can fail to live up to its promises, are the proponents of not picking winners correct that the government should not do it? Not completely. The answer is to make investments instead so that they might still be worthwhile without necessarily targeting a specific private industry. In the United Airlines case, airport hangers are difficult to repurpose. If the money had gone to a public purpose like building a bus rapid transit or light rail line instead, its utility would have been less dependent upon this one company. Indianapolis happened to sorely need a better transit system. There might be some stops or stations, or perhaps a branch line to serve a major employment location, that do not meet expectations. But, by and large, the public would have something of lasting value, and the employment site that did not meet expectations at the outset remains a prime location that has infrastructure in place. Lastly, this kind of investment is not predatory against other communities. Instead, it shifts the competition between regions to a positive dynamic where they try to become more attractive as a place to live rather than a negative one where they compete to starve services in order to cut taxes to businesses.

Many politicians have an ideological bent against public investment instead of private investment because this is still picking winners. But surely the type of investment matters. Wastewater treatment needs to be done and technology options remain limited, so this argument is not pertinent and not much of an excuse for inaction. It might be pertinent when it comes to power generation, as there can be different mixes of sources. If governments help solar water heater manufacturers with purchase rebates, they may spend less on building natural gas-powered plants. So, one can expect a serious debate as both the long-term outlook of the industries and the relative effectiveness of the choices must be considered. There can also be different mixes of transport infrastructure. If government builds more bicycle lanes it might need fewer local road lanes, if it builds a metro it might need fewer freeway lanes. It would be helping bicycle and metro railcar sales and utilities supplying industrial electricity, but it would not be helping the asphalt suppliers.

The most common choice facing politicians is whether to approve roads or not. As has been mentioned in earlier chapters, other investments such as water supply, sewer, and power distribution follow logically because they are related to the road patterns. Low density sprawl with residences separated from commercial uses has come to be seen as the default choice in most of the USA. Indeed, proponents of such designs have even spoken of alternatives as "social engineering." In my career I have always wondered how this argument persists. The idea is that the public is somehow being forced to walk, use bicycles, use transit, live in apartments instead of single-family housing, and so on. Why is it not equally valid to say that people are being forced to drive or be chauffeured everywhere under auto-dependent sprawl? Some evidence of how many people feel pressured to drive is in the possession of drivers' licenses. In very rural Vermont, only 18 percent of the total population do not have licenses, whereas in very urban New York State it is about 42 percent (BTS 2020).

This was a long and perhaps roundabout argument for why most politicians do not try to paint a vision. There does not seem to be a need when there is a default path forward and not much effective organized opposition attempting to defy the status quo. The amount of money spent on advertising every year by the auto industry at all levels to remind everyone of the positives of the status quo is enormous (Furillo 2020). The car styles may change and some of the store names may change in the strip malls, but we will continue live our lives in the same fashion. Both the Flintstones and the Jetsons lived this way using private vehicles and not too much has changed since the early 1960s except in a handful of densifying central cities. It is true that there really is no "we" since no choice was offered, but it is also true that politicians do not usually get put on the spot to define this "we." Supposedly, it should be democratically decided what kinds of housing and lifestyle choices would be available.

Should a loan be accepted instead of a grant?

If one lives in the Northeast Corridor (NEC) then one might occasionally hear politicians talk about the modernization of the closest thing the USA has to a high-speed rail system. It operates between Washington, D.C. and Boston with some slower and less frequent services extending south and north. There is a certain amount of pride expressed by some politicians in the current upgrading of the *Acela Express*, the slightly faster of the two services offered. This upgrade is nothing like the previously discussed example of new freeway interchange enhancements. These freeways will be open without charge to all (who have access to automobiles). In contrast, the new generation rolling stock for the *Acela Express* upgrade was financed by a $2.45 Billion USD loan from the Feds, not a grant, like the highway departments receive (Wire, staff reports 2016). This means the loan will have to be paid back at least in part through a continued policy of very high fares. Unless the fares are very competitive with driving and taking the bus it will not move the volumes of people that the Shinkansen in Japan, ICE in Germany, TGV in France, AVE in Spain, or one of the two competing high-speed services in Italy, succeed in doing. As a consequence of its debt burden, Amtrak's role in the NEC will continue to be largely limited to competing with airlines and attracting people on business expense accounts and a few wealthy travelers and vacationers who are occasional users who can buy advanced purchase tickets.

This is quite a constraint on any vision for rail. Lowering fares and increasing service would make the NEC an instrument for reducing the tremendous volumes of traffic on Interstate 95 and all the personal costs and fuel consumption that this central artery of the east coast entails. This is not to say that beneficiaries should never be charged for upgrades that benefit them. But in this case, the benefits to the public at large from a much more frequent and affordable train connection can be quite significant and might justify the subsidy. (More details about this later.) This is just the opposite to the freeway interchange where the environmental benefits are limited and will remain limited, if there are any at all. There will be some commercial genuinely interstate traffic that benefits if the promised delay reduction occurs, but largely the beneficiaries will be local companies and suburban commuters. This is all upside down as it incentivizes choices with significant environmental "bads" and dis-incentivizes choices with significant environmental goods. To provide latitude for building a different type of city, politicians must advocate for radical change to infrastructure evaluation and funding methods to get prices right, and not settle for mere capacity or technology upgrades.

Academics and bloggers and the equilibrium-gap fillers

One must always expect that academics will speculate about the future, that is one of the things that the planning profession does, and indeed, one of the hottest topics is what the future role of Uber/Lyft and other Transportation Network Companies might be in the face of pandemics. Such studies are grounded in science and, hopefully, impartial because of peer review. These will be covered in the news media and stimulate public discussion, especially in regions where the tech sector has a large presence (Whiting 2020). Then there are the bloggers and other analysts, some of whom are quite sophisticated, who offer their visions. For example, one author speculates on the cogent issue of how much more transit cities in the USA could have if construction costs were as low as in the Nordic countries? (Levy 2019).

On the other hand, technology upgrades promoted by private commercial interests selling new products are the "equilibrium-gap fillers" in economic parlance when there is little public leadership in filling unmet needs satisfactorily. How their own technologies fit into the urban fabric in the short term and what the long-term consequences of their widespread acceptance might be are not really these companies' concern. If anything, corporations are more short term focused than they have ever been because of demands for quarterly reporting and management incentive structures.

Many of the ideas being peddled are not as new as they seem. The tiny car just being released by a French manufacturer that can be driven by youngsters and parked almost anywhere is not new, but the allure of electrification, its' "cute" plastic body and the City of Paris' effort to push out large cars, has the car industry sensing an opportune time to try again (Henley 2020). Long before the autonomous car hype, the car-based lifestyle has been promoted as a symbol of freedom and prosperity. The Model T was designed to be affordable to most people. The 1939 World's Fair pavilion sponsored by General Motors in Queens is another classic example, as is the related documentary known as "The City" (Brody 2020). Another was the gyrocopter in the 1950s that would be stored in the garage instead of the family car. "Gee, Dad, can I have the keys to the gyrocopter?" The latest Vertical Takeoff and Landing (VTOL) aircraft may be electrically powered, but they do not differ much from conventional helicopters beyond being marginally quieter and cleaner (Hawkins 2020; Pallini 2020; Spires 2020). Elon Musk has been quoted as saying that tunnels are a solution to traffic congestion. Yet, the first rail tunnels go back to 1863 in London in what is now the District and Metropolitan Lines. The exhaust portals for the coal-powered locomotives are still visible. When electric traction was perfected in the

1890s tunnels quickly proliferated. Elon Musk has had several technological angles involving tunnels all using electric cars or pods instead of larger trains. Earlier concepts included lowering and raising cars by platform hoists similar to those used on aircraft carriers which as someone who has worked on aircraft carriers I can assert are totally unsuitable for public use. The current tunnel for the Las Vegas Convention Center has manually driven Tesla cars queuing in a very large, space inefficient atrium (Lambert 2020; Walker 2020).

There are two conditions for a new technology to make it into widespread use as a public service. The first is that it must be technologically sound, that is, it can safely and reliably operate day in and day out. The second is that it must perform some tasks equal or better than the existing alternatives, otherwise it is pointless (Vuchic 2007). Concepts like the gyrocopter did not take off (pardon the pun) not because they did not fly well and could not be made even more reliable with mass production, but because they could not operate safely and quietly in large numbers with non-professional pilots. The eVTOL taxi service is very likely to fail not because it will not fly well, it probably will, but because it will still suffer from a shortage of convenient landing locations as do conventional helicopters. Musk's tunnel concepts are all unworkable not because tunnels cannot be successfully constructed, they can, but because it will cost far more

FIGURE 4.1 Home helicopter in a popular magazine – the dream of local flying trips is nothing new.
Source: http://www.coverbrowser.com/covers/popular-mechanics/12#i566

FIGURE 4.2 Modern day electric Vertical Take Off and Landing (e VTOL) version of the urban helicopter.
Source: Chesky / Shutterstock (1622663068)

to operate on a per person basis than larger trains. It does not make economic sense to pair the high infrastructure cost of a tunnel with the low capacity of four passenger cars, even if they can be autonomously queued, boarded, and dispatched on multiple loading locations seconds apart, a complex operating concept not yet proven operationally sound.

Some technologies are having a renaissance. Bicycles are making a comeback in places where the perception that riding them is safe. But they were once very popular in many countries, and not just in China. It was the combination of affordable cars after the onset of the Model T and increasing conflicts with these proliferating motorized vehicles that pushed them out of the transportation role into the recreational role. Electrification of bicycles and scooters is admittedly an important technological boost, but even electric scooters are not new inventions. It is these types of boosts that stimulate the commercial campaigns. Non-technological concepts can also have a renaissance, such as promotion of fare-free transit. One can read the same pro and con arguments made over 40 years ago (Stanger 1978). But these don't have commercial backers as ticket selling and payment control is not needed.

It is the visionary that has proven as important as the latest generation of propulsion plant, battery miniaturization, and other such technological advances, as well as concepts not so dependent upon technological change but whose time might be right. The visionary has first advocated and then pulled the levers of power to put in place the traffic engineering measures, parking and energy pricing policies that promote the safe and practical revisiting of infrastructure usage based on updated technologies. Advocacy for new visions has brought the changes in the balance of transportation modes, power sources, and environmental management techniques used in everyday urban life.

FIGURE 4.3 E scooter riden by suffragette 1916 (Public domain).
Source: https://i.pinimg.com/originals/2a/46/bb/2a46bb942a6b5917f93dd53df4b91a27.jpg

FIGURE 4.4 Bake-O-Mat brings a shop that cooks right to the neighborhood in a small truck. The idea originated from the New Departure ball bearing division of General Motors.
Source: Oh So Lovely blogspot November 13, 2011
https://ohsolovelyvintage.blogspot.com/2011/11/auto-matic.html

FIGURE 4.5 The latest rendition of the neighborhood vending truck, but this time without a driver and presumably without human assistance.
Source: Chesky - Shutterstock.

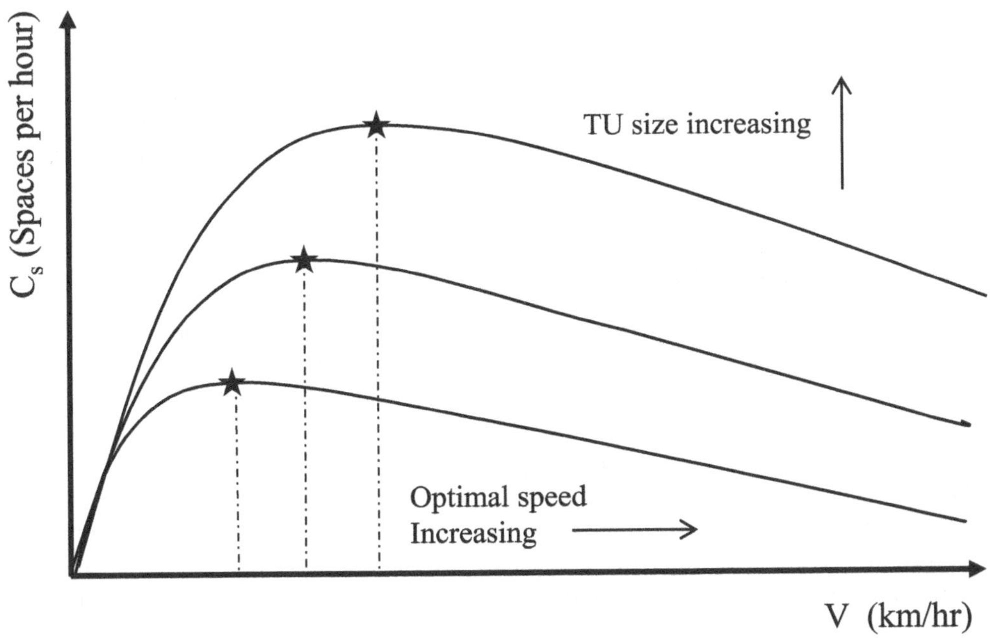

FIGURE 4.6 Speed that maximizes capacity decreases as Transport Unit (TU) size decreases.
Source: Bruun 2013.

Covid-19 shows money is there when politicians decide there is

After all of the policies that pumped billions and even trillions of dollars into the economy first through the CARES act in 2020 and then another stimulus bill in 2021, does it really make a difference any longer when a member of the Congress or one of the President's aides adopts a "can't do" attitude, allegedly because there is not enough money? Yes, if one is going to start with this assumption, then there can never be plans for the future. One must work backwards by trying to envision what the future might be and only then try to figure out what it might cost. From there one can also do some further envisioning of who might be enlisted to help pay, who has not helped in the past, and who might save money in the future. If the additional costs and the money savings both occur in the same institution, so much the better. It could reduce the bureaucratic resistance and obviate the need for statutory changes.

Visions must transcend the boundaries of current responsibilities of existing institutions. Governments have had to reorganize from time to time throughout history. The real questions are how soon and who will take the leadership? NGOs representing architectural, planning, and environmental interests have made important contributions to the discussion of what our future city will be like, but ultimately, they do not really control finances for large-scale projects. Once they have accomplished bringing new ideas to the popular imagination and politicians decide to join the chorus, new funding sources must be solicited. Other power structures beyond the influence of these same NGOs will become involved. It is the politicians who bridge the various power brokers in the various existing departments, legislate any reorganizations and who break logjams. A famous example would be Tom McCall, the Governor of Oregon from 1967 to 1975 who was no doubt an early environmentalist himself, but also influenced by vocal public and environmental activists (Thompson 2005, 2007). He decided to push for legislation that could allow the re-assignment of federal money set aside for the Mount Hood freeway through Portland. Then, in the 1980s, a successful effort was mounted for using the same funds for the beginnings of the MAX light rail network instead.

Once others saw money diversion could actually be achieved, politicians in other places quickly took note. But the process from conception through opening of the rail line instead of a freeway took at least 15 years. It would probably have taken less time to get the money if the freeway project had been submitted for Federal funds instead. But whether it would have taken longer to construct, no one knows. It would have met with intense protest and court actions by NGOs and citizen groups.

A good time to be a visionary

There is an exceptional opportunity to be brave at the moment, not unlike the environmental movement of the early 1970s. The huge tax cuts favoring the wealthiest of individuals that Congress passed at the end of 2017 showed that concern about the national debt is not real. Combine this with the more recent huge bailouts during the Covid-19 shutdowns of large corporations it is quite clear that money is there if politicians want it to be. The Federal Reserve is now a target for supplying any needed funds. Why not invest directly into public works by purchasing state and local bonds instead of buying toxic assets and numerous rounds of Quantitative Easing aimed at providing liquidity in capital markets? Buying up toxic assets and otherwise giving money to large banks is much more indirect than investing in public works projects. Every state has "shovel ready" or near ready projects and maintenance backlogs.

I have always wondered why some politicians even bother to hold a full-time office. Politicians in this context does not mean only persons elected to office but those who accept public leadership positions. Many of them could make more money in their previous professions, so that is not the reason. Some who are in various consulting services, like real estate, legal, accounting or civil engineering get access to steer projects in a certain direction and make contacts usable later for their firms, so these can also be reasons. Much has been written about the revolving door when politicians retire or are defeated and return to their previous careers. Senior appointees in the US DoT under the Trump administration are now lobbyists for Uber and Lyft (Higashide 2020) and vice versa (Giaritelli 2017) while the Secretary of Transportation under the Obama Administration joined the Board of Directors of a traffic AI company (News Staff 2020). But that still leaves many politicians who must have other more selfless motivations. It is these people who in this author's opinion are missing in action.

Public agencies including water and sewer districts, public power utilities, and so on, will release long-term plans for informing the public when major environmental impacts are anticipated and in accordance with Federal matching fund rules and their state's own statutory requirements about the right to know and participate. But with global warming and unabating congestion, transit and highways are perhaps feeling the pressure the most to develop such major plans. The Los Angeles County Metropolitan Transportation Agency (LACMTA) has been notably outspoken lately about the need for a much faster pace of development of transit than existing programs permit (Teale 2020) and improving equity in service and financing, even toying with the idea of making transit fare free throughout LA County (Hymon 2020). But this type of aggressive visioning is in the minority and they are no doubt being given a lot of slack for transit promotion and freeway lane tolling given the severity of the problems of LA County. Most public utilities maintain a lower profile, confining themselves to statements about their in-house sustainability efforts, their commitment to diversity in hiring, to a drug free workplace, and other such contributions inconsequential to their mission to society-at-large.

Public agency plans are not likely to be effectively enacted without public statements of support from elected officials. Nor should they be for the sake of democratic control. Agencies must respond to boards of directors, many members of which are merely political appointees without any passion for the mission of the agency. The General Manager/Executive Director can get mixed up in issues like labor union backing (or not) and construction contracts over which these same board members might have a passion but are peripheral to the long-term vision of the city. They may even lose their jobs over what is seen as excessive activism. The same LACMTA is already off to a rocky start for its ambitious plans. Even though this plan did not originate with them, the killing of the planned conversion of a 1.5-mile (2.4 km) section of Melrose Avenue, a popular shopping street, to one with wider sidewalks and protected bicycle lanes is popular with the local businesses but opposed by one council member and the LAPD (Linton 2020a, 2020b; Schneider 2020). Only the intervention by other elected officials can reinstate it.

Not all infrastructure upgrades and maintenance are necessarily winning issues at the polls because much of this is behind the scenes and the public might not make the connection how the results improve their daily life. A candidate dwelling on issues like this might be perceived like a nagging mother. By comparison, better transit and shopping streets can definitely be winning issues. People can visualize the before versus after and understand that these could help the life of one of their family members, even if they themselves think they would not use them. Multiple surveys indicate that a strong majority favor more transit and even for a ten-year moratorium on highway construction. These go for all age groups and across the USA, urban and rural (Agrawal and Nixon 2017; HNTB 2018; McHarg Center et al. 2020). California had a requirement for 66.7 percent supermajorities to pass tax increases but the vast majority of over 100 transit proposals still passed, even when other proposals failed (Wachs et al. 2020). Results also shows three fourths or more of the public would favor gasoline tax increases if they know it will go for maintenance instead of road expansion and half the population would already be willing to go to a distance-based fee instead of a fuel tax (Carey 2020).

It is not just transit and less car-dominated streets. If more investment into public works that will reduce global warming and, to a lesser extent, increased maintenance of existing public works are popular issues (Dennis 2020), why does so little seem to be happening compared to our peers overseas? Why does it take decades to build what only takes five years elsewhere? One widely read transit analyst thinks that the reason that LA is not succeeding in reducing car use after 30 years of investment in rail lines is because

> American politicians are risk-averse and treat all spending as risk, and this is true even of politicians who boldly proclaim themselves forward-thinking and progressive. Even when large amounts of money are at stake, their instincts are to spread them across so many competing goals that nothing gets funded properly.
>
> *(Levy 2018)*

This author agrees that politicians generally do not prioritize the fast execution of projects that would benefit their region, but this is only a partial explanation. More reasons are the subject of the next chapter.

References

Agrawal, Asha Weinstein and Hilary Nixon. 2017. What Do Americans Think about Federal Tax Options to Support Public Transit, Highways, and Local Streets and Roads? Results from Year Eight of a National Survey. Mineta Transportation Institute. Report CA-MTI-17-1728, June.

Brody, Richard. 2020. What to Stream: "The City," a Challenging Classic Documentary of Visionary Urban Planning. *The New Yorker*, August 27. Available at: https://www.newyorker.com/culture/the-front-row/what-to-stream-the-city-a-challenging-classic-documentary-of-visionary-urban-planning?utm_campaign=falcon&utm_source=facebook&utm_brand=tny&utm_social-type=owned&utm_medium=social&mbid=social_facebook&fbclid=IwAR11v0xOthbLZSwtKD_zzV-NkHLJ5UcCD_iNUs3ki7UJDfCqScGEHYzsYOo

Bruun, Eric. 2013. Chapter 3. Route and Network Analysis. *Better Public Transit Systems: Analyzing Investments and Performance*, 2nd Edition, pp. 124–144. Routledge: Abingdon, UK.

Carey, Liz. 2020. Report: 49 Percent of Americans Support Mileage Fees. July 13. Available at: https://transportationtodaynews.com/news/18879-report-49-percent-of-americans-support-mileage-fees/

Dennis, Brady. 2020. Most Americans Believe the Government Should Do More to Combat Climate Change, Poll Finds. *The Washington Post*, June 23. Available at: https://www.washingtonpost.com/climate-environment/2020/06/23/climate-change-poll-pew/

Frankfurt Short Bruza (FSB). 2020. United Airlines Indianapolis Maintenance Center. FSB. Available at: https://fsb-ae.com/project/united-airlines-indianapolis-maintenance/ (Accessed November 29, 2020).

Furillo, Andy. 2020. The Case for Reining in Car Advertising. *Mobility Lab*, October 8. Available at: https://mobilitylab.org/2020/10/08/the-case-for-reining-in-car-advertising/

Giaritelli, Anna. 2017. Trump picks Lyft employee for top Transportation post. *Washington Examiner*, April 6. Available at: https://www.washingtonexaminer.com/tag/donald-trump?source=%2Ftrump-picks-lyft-employee-for-top-transportation-post%2Farticle%2F2619612

Hawkins, Andrew J. 2020. Volocopter Now Accepting Reservations for Flights in Its Electric Air Taxi — But not Until 2023 at the Earliest. *The Verge*, September 16. Available at: https://www.theverge.com/2020/9/16/21439393/volocopter-air-taxi-flight-ticket-reservation-price

Henley, Jon. 2020. Ami, The Tiny Cube on Wheels That French 14-Year-Olds Can Drive. *The Guardian*, September 11. Available at: https://www.theguardian.com/world/2020/sep/11/ami-the-tiny-cube-on-wheels-that-french-14-year-olds-can-drive

Higashide, Steven. 2020. Uber and Lyft Are Charging Through Washington's Revolving Door. *The New Republic*, September 25. Available at: https://newrepublic.com/article/159488/uber-lyft-obama-biden-revolving-door-washington

HNTB. 2018. Survey Shows Americans Support Public Transportation Funding. *Roads and Bridges*. October 11. Available at: https://www.roadsbridges.com/survey-shows-americans-support-public-transportation-funding?utm_source=WU10.18.2018&utm_campaign=WU10.18.2018&utm_medium=email

Hubbuch, Chris. 2020. Federal Officials Want More Data On Contamination, Cleanup for Oscar Mayer Site Bus Barn. *The Wisconsin State Journal*, October 5. Available at: https://mejo.us/environmental-contamination-concerns-taint-oscar-mayer-redevelopment-plan/

Hymon, Steve. 2020. Metro To Study and Consider Eliminating Bus and Rail Fares. *The Source Blog*, August 27. Available at: https://thesource.metro.net/2020/08/27/metro-to-study-and-consider-eliminating-bus-and-rail-fares/

Lambert, Fred. 2020. Elon Musk's Boring Company Gets Green Light to Expand Las Vegas Loop with Tesla Vehicles. *Electrek*, August 6. Available at: https://electrek.co/2020/08/06/elon-musk-boring-company-green-light-to-expand-las-vegas-loop-tesla-vehicles/

Levy, Alon. 2018. Meme Weeding: Los Angeles Density. *Pedestrian Observations*, November 11. Available at: https://pedestrianobservations.com/2018/11/11/meme-weeding-los-angeles-density/

Levy, Alan. 2019. Assume Nordic Costs. *Pedestrian Observations Blog*, May 29. Available at: https://pedestrianobservations.com/2019/05/29/assume-nordic-costs/ (Accessed August 15, 2020).

Linton, Joe. 2020a. Proposed "Uplift Melrose" Streetscape Project Enjoys Widespread Community Support. *Streetsblog USA*, August 26. Available at: https://la.streetsblog.org/2020/08/26/proposed-uplift-melrose-streetscape-project-enjoys-widespread-community-support/

Linton, Joe. 2020b. Council Member Koretz Kills 'Uplift Melrose' Safe Streets Project. *Streetsblog USA*, September 10. Available at: https://la.streetsblog.org/2020/09/10/councilmember-koretz-kills-uplift-melrose-safe-streets-project/

McHarg Center, Transit Center and T4America. 2020. Voters Want a Better Transit System for America, March. Available at: https://t4america.org/wp-content/uploads/2020/03/Transit-Polling-Memo-final.pdf

News Staff. 2020. Traffic AI Startup Brings Anthony Foxx, Stuart McKee Aboard. *Government Technology*, October 14. Available at: https://www.govtech.com/biz/Traffic-AI-Startup-Brings-Anthony-Foxx-Stuart-McKee-Aboard.html

O'Malley, Chris. 2010. Abandoned United Airlines Repair Base Now Bustling. *Indiana Business Journal*, December 2. Available at: https://www.ibj.com/articles/23784-abandoned-united-airlines-repair-base-now-bustling

Pallini, Thomas. 2020. Airbus' New eVTOL That Aims to Usher in An Era of Flying Taxis Just Took Its First Public Flight – Take a Look at CityAirbus. *Business Insider*, July 28. Available at: https://www.businessinsider.com/cityairbus-makes-first-public-flight-airbus-flying-taxi-evtol-2020-7?r=US&IR=T

Palzewicz, Tom. 2020. Transportation: More Roads and Bridges Not the Answer. *Urban Milwaukee*, August 25. Available at: https://urbanmilwaukee.com/pressrelease/transportation-more-roads-and-bridges-not-the-answer/

Schneider, Michael. 2020. Why Can't We Have Nice Things in Los Angeles? *The Medium Blog*, September 11. Available at: https://medium.com/@michaelschneider_5797/why-we-cant-have-nice-things-in-los-angeles-11bbb952fd92

Spires, Josh. 2020. German Airports to Build VTOL Passenger Drone Infrastructure. *DroneDJ*. September 11. Available at: https://dronedj.com/2020/09/11/german-airports-to-build-vtol-passenger-drone-infrastructure/.

Stanger, Richard M. 1978. Fare-Free Transit: Do We Really Need a Demonstration Project? *ITE Journal*. November.

Teale, Chris. 2020. LA Metro's $400B Long-Range Plan Pledges More Transit, Less Congestion. *Smart Cities Dive*, September 28. Available at: https://www.smartcitiesdive.com/news/la-metro-transportation-plan-congestion-equity/585935/

Thompson, Gregory L. 2005. How Portland's Power Brokers Accommodated the Anti-Highway Movement of the Early 1970s: The Decision to Build Light Rail. *Business and Economic History*, No. 3. Available at: http://www.thebhc.org/publications/BEHonline/2005/thompson.pdf.

Thompson, Gregory L. 2007. Taming the Neighborhood Revolution: Planners, Power Brokers, and the Birth of Neotraditionalism in Portland, Oregon. *Journal of Planning History*, August 1. Available at: https://doi.org/10.1177/1538513206297457

US Bureau of Transportation Statistics (BTS). 2020. Table 4-2: Licensed Drivers: 2010. *US Department of Transportation*. Available at: https://www.bts.gov/archive/publications/state_transportation_statistics/state_transportation_statistics_2012/table_04_02 (Accessed August 15, 2020).

Vuchic, Vukan R. 2007. *Urban Transit: Systems and Technology. Chapter 7.4. Evaluation of Unconventional Modes and New Concepts* (p. 475). Wiley.

Wachs, Martin, Jeremy Marks and Romic Aevaz. 2020. Webinar: Ballots for Buses: Local Option Transportation Sales Taxes in California, September 17. Available at: https://www.enotrans.org/wp-content/uploads/2020/08/Ballots-for-Buses-Slides.pdf

Walker, Alissa. 2020. Somehow Elon Musk's Tesla Tunnels Are Even Less Useful Now. *Curbed*, July 23. Available at: https://www.curbed.com/2020/7/23/21334351/elon-musk-boring-company-las-vegas-tunnel

Whiting, Sam. 2020. Bay Area Mass Transit Could Start to Resemble Uber or Lyft. *San Francisco Chronicle*, August 26. Available at: https://www.sfchronicle.com/bayarea/article/Bay-Area-mass-transit-could-start-to-resemble-15500617.php

Wire, Staff Reports. 2016. Amtrak Secures $2.45B Loan. *Times Union* (Albany NY), August 26. Available at: https://www.timesunion.com/business/article/Amtrak-secures-2-45B-loan-9187588.php

5

THOMAS FRANK'S ANALYSIS OR HOW WE GOT THE DUAL ECONOMY

Thomas Frank (not to be confused with a prolific self-help video celebrity with the same name) is a widely read author who studied history at the University of Chicago. After graduation, he had a brief stint as adjunct faculty and then moved on to be a book writer. Several of his books have gone on to be very popular. *What's the Matter with Kansas: How Conservatives Won the Heart of America*," published in 2004 had a cogent explanation of why so many people seem to vote against their own economic interests. He chose Kansas, both because he is a native and because it was the hotbed of the Populist Party a century earlier, showing how far Kansas has changed. After the success of this book, he was a columnist for the Wall Street Journal for two years. More recently, he became a regular columnist for Harper's magazine, filling the slot of the legendary Lewis Lapham for a while. Another one of his books *Listen Liberal: Or, What Ever Happened to the Party of the People* published in 2016 also became a New York Times bestseller and is the one which I attempt to summarize in the first two sections of this chapter. His insights bolster my arguments in the chapters that follow.

I do not mean to say that no one else has similar viewpoints, but they are in a distinct minority and have received less publicity. One of these is Richard Reeve's *Dream Hoarders: How the American Upper Middle Class Is Leaving Everyone Else in the Dust, Why That Is a Problem*, and *What to Do About It* (2017). Another is Stephen Rose's *The Growing Size and Incomes of the Upper Middle Class* (2016). Yet another is Matt Karp who paints a dystopian future where current economic trends continue (Karp 2019). My apologies to others whose writings and speeches I could also have referenced. I would also add that similar viewpoints from other pundits seem to be increasing in frequency on political commentary shows. One can expect this trend to continue with recent political movements like Black Lives Matter that are bringing renewed attention to the history of racial segregation and inequality and with budgetary crises at the city and state levels because of reduced revenue during the Covid-19 epidemic.

How the Democratic Party evolved into a party for the professional class

Listen, Liberal focuses on the evolution of the Democratic Party from the New Deal era onwards. At the time of the Great Depression its primary mission was to promote improvement in the lot of the working people. It was very clear that Calvin Coolidge and

DOI: 10.4324/9781003245704-5

then Herbert Hoover, even after the crash of 1929, thought that the best way to manage the economy was to minimize public spending. The Democrats had to jettison economic orthodoxy, not just to help the regular people but to save capitalism from itself. The Social Security Act of 1935 established a retirement fund and the Fair Labor Standards Act of 1938 established a minimum wage and overtime pay rules, while other laws enabled unionization and other efforts to address the harshness against workers visited upon them during the depression. Companies could take advantage of their desperation. Recall FDR's quote about the bankers: "I welcome their hatred." It is also important to point out that in my opinion Frank does not overly romanticize the Democratic Party of the era, but at least one book reviewer felt otherwise (Gage 2016). Many of the laws passed did not pertain to agricultural or domestic workers (DeWitt 2010). There were few enforcement mechanisms to make sure that regulations also applied to the black community and women. After all, the Democratic Party was still dominant in the deep south.

The executive branch of the federal government generally was not too committed to integration, although there were some highlights like President Truman desegregating the military by Executive Order in 1948. Then the landmark *Brown versus Board of Education* ruling by the US Supreme Court in 1954 ended the doctrine of "separate but equal." But legally sanctioned segregation persisted at the state level. Finally, in 1957, as civil rights activists became more militant, the feds protected students entering Little Rock Central High School using the regular Army (not the National Guard which was controlled by the governor of Arkansas). Other state and local governments in the south were stubbornly refusing to comply with court rulings about integration as well. This put the southern Democrats in Congress in an increasingly tense situation with other members when it became clear that it was only a matter of time before legal protection of civil rights was going to have enough votes to pass.

As is well known, the presidency of Lyndon Johnson changed the Democratic Party irrevocably, even he admitted they had probably lost the south "forever." With the passage of the Civil Rights Act of 1964 and the Voting Rights Act of 1965, most white southern Democrats switched to the Republicans in 1968 or voted for the third-party candidacy of George Wallace, the governor of Alabama. The Democrats were also fractured by the Vietnam War. Eugene McCarthy's early primary successes based on his anti-war stance caused Johnson to give up on re-election. Vice President Hubert Humphrey became the presidential candidate in the end, after Martin Luther King's and then Robert Kennedy's assassinations and riots leading up to and during the convention. Humphrey was seen as a friend of labor, but he was seriously handicapped by his loyal support of Johnson over the Vietnam War. Furthermore, labor was also fractured, revealing it really was not a "movement" at all. This was especially apparent with the leadership of the AFL-CIO supporting the war. After Richard Nixon won the 1968 election, the Democratic Party was in disarray. Then in 1972 the anti-war wing of Democratic Party succeeded in getting George McGovern nominated. But without the traditional base of the southern vote and with labor splintered, Nixon had an easy time getting re-elected in a landslide.

The traditional Democratic coalition was gone. It was about this time that it evolved in a new direction. Labor was not the cohesive block it once was. Some segments were even quite reactionary and many supported the Vietnam war in opposition to "hippies and peaceniks." Many saw that decreases in military spending after the war ended would reduce high-paid jobs. Others still opposed integration of minorities and women into their unions. Lots of unions members were now prime recruiting material for the Republicans. Even though they fought a lot, the one thing the leaders of the Democrats agreed upon was that the legacy of the New Deal had to be overturned "with its fixation on the working class," even if perhaps not for the same reasons. There needed to be new appeals by the Demos to attract a larger number of northerners and westerners, many of whom had been loyal Republicans. The professional class, in particular, had been staunchly Republican. Nowadays, they are one of the strongest cohorts for the Democratic party, meaning that those who have been Democrats have been staying Democrats as they age.

Nixon's forced resignation over Watergate broke the strong grip the Republicans were rapidly achieving under this re-alignment. The first post-Watergate victory for the Democrats revealed their transformation. The Democratic candidate Jimmy Carter won but was quickly facing a phenomenon of stagflation where there was both slow growth of the economy and high inflation. There were several reasons for this, like the end of cheap oil economy after 1973, but workers took the brunt of the blame. They had reached a record high percentage of the total income of the US economic output. Corporations, their investors, and their upper-level employees had to divide a smaller share. Then came a second oil shock in 1979. Paul Volcker was appointed as Chairman of the Federal Reserve by Carter in the same year, where he proceeded to "break the back" of inflation by deliberately depressing the economy, causing unemployment to increase to undercut the negotiating strength of unions. This was precisely the type of person a Republican president would have chosen. Ironically, this probably helped the unequivocally anti-labor Republican candidate Ronald Reagan who took advantage of their hardships by asking "Are you better off than you were four years ago?" (Schulte 2008).

After Carter's re-election defeat by Reagan in 1980, Walter Mondale was also defeated by Reagan when he was re-elected in 1984. Michael Dukakis was defeated by George H. W. Bush in 1988. By then, it had become quite clear that labor no longer had the clout it once did under Roosevelt, Truman, Eisenhower, Johnson, or even perhaps Nixon who saw that there were union members who were pro-war and in other aspects as well part of his "silent majority." From then onwards, there were no more Democratic presidential candidates of the old school who came of age when organized labor was a key constituent of the Democratic base.

As we all know, Bill Clinton got the nomination for the Presidency from the Democratic Party in 1992. It was notable because Ross Perot got a substantial percentage of votes by US standards for a third party. Perot appealed to labor with memorable lines as in his ad "You can, in Yucatan" and "that giant sucking sound you hear is jobs moving to Mexico" where he anticipated what might occur if the North American Free Trade Agreement (NAFTA) passed. It was also notable because Clinton belonged to a branch called the Democratic Leadership Council (DLC). One of its most notable features was the minimal input from organized labor into its agenda, let alone from the disorganized working class. With the strong exception of Robert Reich as Secretary of Labor, his cabinet was heavily oriented toward the financial sector. One of his first legislative efforts was to push through the NAFTA in 1993, something that the previous Republican president could not pass. And after its passage, the moving of unionized industrial jobs in a steady stream and even the threat to move to Mexico by management would gradually further weaken the union movement, thereby also diminishing its ability to extract revenge by helping a primary competitor to Clinton. It is important to note that municipal unions were much less vulnerable, mostly impacted from increased internal competition for jobs with superior benefits.

His healthcare reform proposal had elements similar to ones that had been proposed by Republicans. It was convoluted and difficult to understand by the public and was defeated in the face of an aggressive advertising and lobbying campaign. Shortly after came the Omnibus Crime Bill of 1994 that began the mass incarceration of working-class people culminating in the USA having the highest percentage of its citizens behind bars, even ahead of authoritarian countries. Then came the dissolution of Aid to Families with Dependent Children and its replacement legislation that passed in 1996 called Temporary Aid for Needy Families, emphasis on temporary. This probably could not have been passed under a Republican president, either. In fact, there was an alliance with Newt Gingrich, Speaker of the House from 1995 to 1999, against the progressive wing of Congress.

When Clinton sought re-election, to use Frank's term, he would "body slam" people who helped get him elected for his first term, such as Jesse Jackson and Sister Souljah. This caught on as a campaign strategy for other Demos later. Obama did the same with his minister, Pastor Jeremiah Wright with the United Church of Christ (Crawley 2008). Wright had been quite outspoken about the violence the USA had brought to other countries through continual war adding that "the chickens had come to roost" through violence at home as well. The purpose of this type of attack seemed to be an appeal to potential white swing voters, while taking black support for granted.

During his second term Clinton continued with an agenda in harmony with the Republicans, the dismantlement of the last remnants of the New Deal. This included the death of the depression-era Glass-Steagall legislation passed as part of the United States Banking Act of 1933 that forced the separation of commercial banking from investment banking as a result of the Great Crash of 1929. There were warnings about why this reversal was a bad idea, and, in retrospect, these warnings proved correct. The banking crisis of 2008 would not have happened if it were not possible to put regular, commercial mortgage loans into highly leveraged investment securities.

The second term also coincided with the first budget surpluses in a long time. Clinton and his branch of the Demos took credit, of course, but the real reason seems to be a jump in productivity starting in 1995 that tailed off again in the early 2000s. To this day, people argue about the reasons for this (Uchitelle 2000). Whatever the reason, it provided an opportunity to finally start clearing the (much smaller) backlog of infrastructure repairs and start to catch up with our peer countries by modernizing airports, passenger railroads, and so on. There could have been a policy of spreading a lot more federal investment into rural areas. It did not happen.

Long story short, the Demos did not really have that much to offer versus the Republicans except that it was easy to get jobs in the late 1990s. Even this was not that impressive, because the slight increase in pay due to tighter job markets still did not bring the working class to higher pay than they had in real terms back in the 1970s. The Demos were also tainted by the impeachment of President Clinton. My personal view is that if the Demos had done more to help the working class through highly visible infrastructure investment and the associated jobs, the election that brought George W. Bush would never have been close enough for the Supreme Court to intervene. Indeed, the failure to increase public spending to counteract a destabilizing spending and borrowing binge by the private sector during the "dot-com bubble," where growth was driven in large part by investment into the internet and tech sectors, was viewed as a wise course of non-action by the elite economic advisors from the expensive schools. At the same time, the Federal surplus was viewed as a sign of fiscal responsibility instead of a warning sign of serious financial instability.

The private sector debt reached roughly 10 percent of GDP and probably caused the 2001 bust because private interests can only go into debt so far before credit dries up and new income is insufficient to cover the loans. The incoming Bush administration finally counteracted the dot-com bubble only after it burst. It used tax cuts to the upper tier, assistance to the pharmaceutical industry (remember the "donut hole" controversy?) and military/war industry spending increases for recovery instead of spending on something more popular like infrastructure. It was a repetition of history; there was also a huge binge of private spending from 1927 to 1930 that put it deep into debt before the Great Crash of late 1929. But then it was the Republicans who failed to counteract it instead and Roosevelt introduced massive spending on public works but only after a few years delay.

Jump forward to the Obama era and nothing fundamental about the Clinton-era Democratic Party had really changed. Like under Clinton, a medical reform was introduced early. It was called the Affordable Care Act and still mostly in the private sector. But this time it was based on a plan introduced by a Republican governor in Massachusetts that would require people to join existing insurance companies. It passed this time. Many of the same cast of characters who supported bank deregulation, like Lawrence Summers, were once again in prominent positions. Robert Gates, appointed by Bush, was retained as the Secretary of Defense signaling a continuation of foreign policy as well. The era saw millions of people lose their houses with almost no help. Once again, it is my personal view that if the Democrats had done more during Obama's eight years to help the working class through decent paying infrastructure jobs in the depressed rural areas, Trump's vote count would probably not have been close enough to Hillary Clinton for the Electoral College or voter suppression to matter.

Frank argues that the Obama era Executive branch would not criminally charge bankers at the "too big to fail" firms after the 2008 crisis in large part because investment bankers are not just high achievers like themselves but their classmates "in both senses of the word." "Complexity is a sign of sophistication" in banking, not a sign of fraud. Ivy leaguers dominated Obama's cabinet. Almost all of these people were "plucked from obscurity" by their educations. Attendance at fancy schools is what defines them as individuals. So, what does the Democratic Party believe in today? The "first commandment" is that the people on top deserve to be there because the USA is now a meritocracy. There is a "coalition of the ascendant." People at the top show great deference to each other. But the ones working in the lower rungs of the economy like public utilities, even with similar pedigrees, get no solidarity. This author can attest to that.

The Democratic Party today

The history that Frank presents leads to a Democratic Party that now fully "embraces the winners." It must "protect the innovative knowledge industries." The converse side is that it cannot simultaneously look out for the people who might be victimized by the protected winners. Almost 30 years since the DLC took the reins of the Party, the results are clear. The majority of Americans have insufficient savings to handle an emergency like an airline trip to a funeral and no money to take a vacation, assuming they even are entitled to one. An illness in the family can lead to a bankruptcy (Eidelson and Cannon 2020). In summary, the shift to a government managed by an elite, technocratic professional class with the right pedigree "explains everything that is frustrating, disappointing, irritating..." about the modern Democratic Party. It also partly explains the support for Space X and Hyperloop at the expense of investment in traditional infrastructure.

Even at the local level, which tends to be more competitive than State and Congressional levels, Democrats have largely abandoned the working class. The wing of the party in power, the neoliberal and professional class, tend to believe far more in incentivizing professional class businesses than in making their cities more attractive and livable for those already there. They will give tax breaks for skyscrapers and new biomedical research centers, undercutting their property tax base should this near-bribe prove successful. This means no additional money to modernize and expand their schools, libraries, parks, transit systems and other public services. Until another major wing of the party more concerned with economic inequality and sustainable development takes power, the vision of a future city that reflects increased prosperity for all in the long term is left largely to concerned citizens and NGOs, only some of which are not funded and operated by the same professional class. Because the longer-sighted citizens and NGOs do not control the purse strings, one continues to see the same complaints and the same protests over lack of progress year in and year out.

A perfect example of Frank's argument is the complete default to citizen activists by elected officials that can be seen in the recent Covid-19 crisis and its impact on the Southeastern Pennsylvania Transit Authority (SEPTA). There has long been criticism that SEPTA runs two classes of service, the Regional Rail Division and the City Division. The City Division monthly pass is not valid on its Regional trains. Most Regional Rail stations serving residential neighborhoods within the City proper have been neglected, part of the same policy of discouraging boarding and alighting in the lower income areas. In the Regional services, the aim has been to try to provide everyone travelling between Center City and university complexes with the suburbs with a seat, even if they have not been able to meet this goal. Meanwhile, in the City services, overloads are commonplace on the buses and streetcars. Even the few bus lanes that might speed up trips for the masses go largely unenforced. Speaking as an expert myself on this topic, it seems a shame that a region with one of the largest networks and such potential to be like an *S Bahn* with frequent all-day service over the whole region like Vienna or a large German city has had no such plans or even such a vision for decades (Levy 2017; Rudick 2021).

FIGURE 5.1 SEPTA REGIONAL RAIL ROLLING STOCK DURING COVID-19.
Source: Will Tung 5th Square.

FIGURE 5.2 SEPTA 38-year-old non-accessible streetcar.
Source: Will Tung 5th Square.

With the recent service cuts, some workers faced dangerous overcrowding on buses and streetcars while some of the Regional Rail trains have been running almost empty when so many suburbanites work from home. It was left to a group who name themselves the *5th Square* (a reference to the Philadelphia City Hall under the master design by William Penn) to distribute a petition demanding access to the Regional trains, trains that often run parallel to the buses and streetcars (5th Square 2020). In other rich countries, a monthly transit pass usually grants privileges based on the number of zones for which it is valid, not on the mode used. Studies that made recommendations on how to extract more benefit have been gathering dust for decades (Vuchic et al. 1993). The City of Philadelphia contributed more to SEPTA's operating subsidy than the surrounding four counties combined for a number of years, so it had negotiating leverage. Where has the Democrat-dominated Philadelphia City Council been on this issue all these years? Whom do they represent?

This example involving a petition was chosen as it is one in which I have taken an active interest both as a part-time academic who participated in these studies of the SEPTA system and a resident of the City of Philadelphia for many years. In places where initiatives are legally permissible (not in Pennsylvania), they provide another means for communities to take matters into their own hands when their representatives are missing in action. If nothing else, petitions might get publicity and embarrass elected officials who just do not seem to see the need to get involved. Why should they when they can take bus passengers' votes for granted?

Furthermore, the Democrats believe that changing demographics will naturally benefit them, of which there is some truth. States that used to be solidly Red and the Democrats did not even bother to campaign for presidential elections thanks to winner-take-all Electoral College are changing. Texas is already purple and might be blue within a decade if not sooner as a higher percentage of minorities vote. However, how Latinx people will vote is not certain, as some are more concerned with traditional LatinX/Catholic cultural values than economics. Virginia has already become blue at the Presidential level as the upper-tier Northern Virginia suburban voters heavily dependent on federal spending recognize that the Democrats are now in their corner.

Connection to the dual economy

The concept that people performing jobs needing similar skills and educational background get wildly different pay and working conditions, that governmental support for research favors certain groups, and that protection from competition is extended to certain groups is not new. Some economists have been talking about the evolution of a "dual economy" for a long time. Yet, the connection to the capture of the political system by the upper tier of the dual economy as an explanation to how government money is collected and distributed is not often made. Frank's contribution was that he doesn't talk only about the greed and influence of the 1 percent, or the ability of CEOs to multiply their salaries over the years, or about the pervasiveness of corporate lobbying, or about a patriarchy that blocks equality of women. He provides a more detailed and nuanced picture of who is on top and why. This is no doubt one of the reasons that Frank's books have proved so popular coupled with the fact that he is an engaging and often entertaining writer.

If Thomas Frank's argument that I attempted to summarize in the earlier sections of this chapter is correct and the Democratic Party has indeed evolved into catering to classes of people that increasingly resemble its leadership, this will be reflected in its economic platform and policies. A technocratic government run by an ostensibly well-educated class could, in principle, consider a wide range of needs and desires among a broad swath of the citizenry. But as the interactions narrow professionally and personally, inevitably the interests of the Democratic Party will narrow as well, even with good intentions.

The USA is still a surprisingly racially segregated society even half a century after the passage of the Civil Right Act. Despite a period of integration in the 1970s and 1980s, social classes and ethnic groups remain physically separated. In both the stratification of income levels and through zoning that creates clusters of housing in the same price range, the geographic concentrations of companies in the same business sector offering similar income levels have served to maintain these differences.

Schooling has also been re-segregating (García 2020). Whole generations have grown up in subcultures that reinforce a particular perception of the society from the lens of the class in which they exist. In the words of Stephen Rose: "Because people tend to live in communities with similar incomes, they view themselves as being near the middle because their neighbors' circumstances are similar to their own even if their incomes are significantly below or above the U.S. median" (Rose 2016). Upper middle-income students go to school with each other, they shop at the same places, they apply for the same tier of universities and rarely to community colleges or trade schools. They get their career ideas from their parents, the parents of their friends, and from their dormmates. In his description of income classes, Frankenfield (2019) agrees with me that a 20 percent versus 80 percent is a more useful descriptor than the 1 percent versus 99 percent breakdown.

Being responsive to the professional and select non-professional workers who have been able to retain sufficient political power will require policies that protect their share of disposable income and better-than-average benefits. But there are also competitive market pressures mandating a measure of cost control. Plus, there are pressures for governments to spend on urgent needs, which might require taxes to be raised at the state and local levels. Over time, these three issues – maintaining upper tier incomes and benefits, exercising cost controls, and spending on urgent needs – are juggled by elected officials and governmental managers by reducing government spending for those who lack sufficient political power to resist cuts. At the same time, for subgroups who matter, investments and services are maintained, and aspects of the labor market that threaten to force them to bear some of the downsides of an increasingly competitive, global, capitalist economy are controlled.

If the user share of the cost of some services like universities must increase as a result of cuts, this might well be acceptable to the upper tier as long as it is still affordable. Public school support cuts at the state level are not so devastating in a district with a wealthy local property tax base to take up the slack. One form of spending cuts is to convert previously full-time, unionized public school jobs into charter school jobs with lower pay and fewer benefits. New Orleans is now a nearly all charter school system with more than 90 percent of students attending (Hasselle 2019). Nationally, about 10 percent of students are charter students. This type of job conversion has happened even more spectacularly at the university teaching level. More than 75 percent of college faculty is now off the tenure track and more than half are part-time (New Faculty Majority 2020). Most openings for tenure track positions are filled by graduates from a small number of programs, and indeed most candidates cannot even get an interview even after outstanding performance at their snubbed university. Only 25% of institutions in the USA produced 71 to 86% of all tenure-track faculty depending upon the field according to one study, and whether you went to a prestigious university as an undergraduate still counts (Benderly 2016). To repeat what Thomas Frank pointed out, solidarity does not extend to people in the same profession, only to those of the same pedigree and working in certain fields perceived to be where smart people like themselves go. These places do not include local bus systems, or public school building architectural practices, or sewer planning consultancies, or naval shipyards, or other such places where one might get their hands dirty or expose themselves to industrial dangers.

The dual economy will also be evident in the evolution of laws to provide protection from competition. As an example, billing rates have not been driven down for most medical services provided by the professional class because neither the States' programs nor federally assisted Medicaid and Medicare will pay for visits to cross-border or overseas providers nor can pharmaceutical prices be negotiated for large quantities by the Federal Government, all of which could save the taxpayers massive amounts of money at the expense of the upper tier. Another example: in many places, the city financed construction work will get to be done by selected trade council members earning high hourly rates and generous overtime, with little opportunity for unskilled people in the affected neighborhoods to participate and learn a skill, even if overtime costs for the taxpayer could be reduced. If a Federal grant is involved local hiring can be difficult because there is a prevailing wage regulation meaning union rates and participation by lesser-skilled locals at a lower rate is excluded. This seems to finally be raising the ire of elected officials with talk of a Green New Deal (Castronuovo 2021).

The dual economy will also be evident in the distribution of benefits from state and local government spending. As an example, mechanisms like Tax Increment Financing (TIF) were meant to recapture some of the increased land value in the corridor where major infrastructure is installed to help defray the cost (National Academies of Sciences, Engineering, and Medicine 2020). This was only fair since higher wealth landowners were getting windfall increases in the value of the land they owned. Now TIF has morphed into a complex apparatus where wealthy neighborhoods might get a disproportionate share of investment spending having nothing to do with the initial district that generated both the costs to the taxpayer and the later increase in value. This change is not going unnoticed with the heightened concern from some public and elected officials in the face of steep revenue drop-offs as this recent example from Chicago shows where over a third of property tax revenue goes to select TIFs (Dardick 2020). Many residents of Chicago perceive the city as deliberately favoring not just current upper tier residents, but trying to recruit more of them as well as part of the economic development plans (Yamahtta-Taylor 2021).

Moreover, such zones have become a means for inventive extraction of public money for private gain for hedge funds and indirectly for others who tend to be in the upper-tier. The owners and season ticket holders of an NBA team located in Philadelphia is a prominent example with very high ticket prices. Furthermore, the Sixers wanted to pay their taxes back to themselves by building an arena for themselves in a "neighborhood improvement zone (Murphy 2020)." Something similar worked before. In 2016 they extracted $82 million in tax credits from New Jersey taxpayers for a new training space across the Delaware River in Camden, one of the poorest cities in the USA (Rose 2020).

There are many strategies to keep money flowing to the military-industrial-intelligence complex not available for public works. Continual modifications of existing military hardware, expensive feasibility studies for new generations of weapons, and once in a while a major new system that will provide cash flow for decades, like the F-35 fighter aircraft family or Gerald Ford class of aircraft carriers. Money has been distributed strategically so that there are contingents of both professional class and higher paid blue-collar workers that have a stake in maintaining military projects indefinitely. There used to be far more competition, even between public and private facilities. The 37 Sturgeon class nuclear attack submarines, the workhorses of the cold war era, were built at multiple private and US naval shipyards. Nuclear submarine capable US Navy shipyards like Mare Island (Vallejo, CA) and Charleston have closed and private yards in Connecticut and Virginia have been permitted to create a duopoly on all new construction.

As a generalization, federal funds are available for favored locations and topics in which the upper tier is involved but not for others. There is a stream of funding for pharmaceutical research from the National Institutes of Health that does not even have to be paid back if a drug successfully turns a profit, something that has received a lot of publicity with the advent of the Covid-19 vaccines. Autonomous car researchers in both academia and in private industry have received millions of dollars in Defense Advanced Research Projects Agency (DARPA). While preparing a presentation a couple of years ago about subject areas needing research related to urban transport, I discovered that the US Federal Government has given away at least 11 surplus military facilities to use as test facilities for autonomous cars and trucks. One striking example is the former inland area of the Concord Naval Weapons Station. Given its size of over 5,000 acres (2,000 hectares) and its location in the Bay Area and near a BART line, it would be worth a fortune if it were ever to be sold for housing. NASA is providing grants for electric air taxi design (Mobility21 2021). Robotics, in general, nanotechnology and biotechnology are all big winners.

By comparison, funding for research questions that cities want answered is very limited. Many remain, such as optimal conversion investment strategies to become more sustainable, what more sustainable infrastructure designs look like, more efficient and quicker construction techniques, and especially detailed recommendations how to cope with the results of private efforts that other parts of government is aggressively helping to promote that might adversely affect the daily life of residents, like autonomous cars and air taxis.

Similar trends elsewhere but not as extreme in the USA and the UK

The same phenomena can be seen in other rich countries as well, but it not as extreme as in the USA and the UK. First, having the aforementioned Lockean philosophical heritage makes these countries more pre-disposed toward "small government" and averse to public spending, at least as long as it does not inconvenience the upper tier. Second, the Democrats became the "Third Way" since Bill Clinton and the UK's Labour Party became "New Labour" under Tony Blair. The disaffected in the USA had to decide whether to go to the Republicans and in the UK either the Tories or the Liberals. In other countries, having a larger number of major political parties and proportional representation gives the disaffected more options. Party members cannot be taken for granted so easily. It is telling how many of the parties across Europe that would best be classified as "social democratic" have shrunk dramatically in recent years. They have been correctly perceived as going along with an agenda that mostly benefits an upper tier of society and so many voters have gone elsewhere like Green or ultra-nationalistic parties.

The tension is heightening between the upper and lower tiers. Low productivity increases in global competition in the "real economy" means there are not many productivity gains to share for the lower tier in most of the private sector. The media workforce is split into pundits who live in great comfort, or perhaps even The Hamptons if one is an opinion leader, and to contingent reporters. Academia is split into people living in the creative class bubble and possibly a free mansion if one is a university president and to contingent instructors. Meanwhile, the "financialized economy" of the managerial class has captured a higher share of what profits are generated in the real economy through self-delegated salaries, stock buybacks, mergers and acquisitions, and so on. The professional class in general and select unions, especially those with security clearances, are largely insulated from foreign competition. As are some unions in the public service sector, when they are aligned with political machines willing and able to negotiate annual 1 or 2 percent salary increases and provide benefits to them that are far superior to their fellow residents (more about this later). The USA is particularly harsh to the lower tier continuously hitting them with higher deductibles and medical copays, which is tantamount to pay cuts that are accompanied by a fear of personal bankruptcy.

Federal funding injection is essential to bring an equitable Green New Deal

How public spending is distributed for public works is the subject of the next chapter. How other urban public spending is distributed is addressed two chapters away. All public spending at the state and local levels is potentially in competition so one must view it in its entirety to understand the decision-making processes that result in these allocations. Spending or lack thereof in one sector also can have consequences for spending in another. Spending at the Federal level works differently, as the USA has a sovereign currency and does not need to balance its budget. There were huge federal tax cuts skewed toward the top during the same period when the Iraq War was initiated with little concern for the national deficit. The federal spending that benefits those living the good life only selectively requires compensating downward pressure on spending elsewhere. Concern for the deficit get invoked when there is talk of a national infrastructure program.

Stagnant or declining incomes in the lower tier are making it harder for state/provincial and local/regional governments to tap them for needed charges and tax subsidies to cover increasing operating costs of public services. Public capital investment is also harder to finance. The upper tier is generally much better represented at both the state and local level and has long been harder to tap for public works unless it is of perceived benefit to them. The result has been a dynamic of decline where public services stagnate and get cut for the lower tier. School budget cuts can hit everybody, but less so for the districts of upper tier citizens as their local tax base is better. In districts with weaker tax bases, upper tier parents can avoid increasing class sizes through private schooling options. Fees increases like university tuition also hit everybody but the upper tier can better handle loans if they even need them, and typically qualify for financial aid if they earn less than $100,000 per child. For example, an average income physician earning $199,000 per year with two children qualifies for aid (Financial Samurai 2021).

Capital investment will be wholly inadequate unless there is a massive contribution from the federal government. State and local governments, to the extent they even choose to invest, will be slow to increase taxes on the upper tier and are likely to use bonding that further transfers wealth to the tiny minority that own most of the bonds. Furthermore, since operations and maintenance are currently largely or totally covered at the lower levels of government, this reluctance to increase taxes means any maintaining and operating of the products of public investments required by the Green New Deal will be hard to afford and a reason cited for inaction. Unless there is a political realignment at state and local levels and/or federal strings are attached to new funding demanding more equity and better scientific justification, what does get done will continue to reflect existing power and economic relationships like Frank describes instead of what is most effective to simultaneously address urgent environmental and social problems.

References

5th Square. 2020. SEPTA: Restore Service and Lower Fares on Regional Rail. Available at: https://www.5thsq.org/rr_petition?utm_campaign=newsletter_121&utm_medium=email&utm_source=5thsq (Accessed August 15, 2020).

Benderly, Beryl-Lieff. 2016. How Prestige Shapes the Professoriate. *Science Magazine*, March 2. Available at: https://www.sciencemag.org/careers/2016/03/how-prestige-shapes-professoriate?fbclid=IwAR2XEnYffQMqfT9sIJhdCYae_ZsRGd0iPHy76OUCeZYHcnSJskO2WZwn8ww

Castronuovo, Celine. 2021. Mayors Join Calls for Biden Administration to End Ban on Local Hires in Federal Infrastructure Projects. *The Hill*, March 2. Available at: https://thehill.com/homenews/state-watch/541189-mayors-join-coalition-urging-biden-administration-to-end-ban-on-local

Crawley, Ashon. 2018. Jeremiah Wright Knew What America Was Becoming. The Obamas Can't See What It Is. *Huffington Post*, December 19. Available at: https://www.huffpost.com/entry/michelle-obama-jeremiah-wright_n_5c182d2fe4b08db99056c8a7?guccounter=1&guce_referrer=aHR0cHM6Ly9kdWNrZHVja2dvLmNvbS8&guce_referrer_sig=AQAAAIUm3sNnzQWJSHKAZSrhp0GBMGAJSIJtG93N2zZfVkNU7gVhVSbjU-pID-TKPMM7fDs0um3sHtSuCbhs8k4vB4oLfhHYF3-s8d-fWgmuue50J8IzWJuBR0j2C-dmbTgvc99wLL0ck9r4FthG6BJzonBg5smGcsQeJyXNt5n93epE7

Dardick, Hal. 2020. Record $926 Million Flows into Controversial Chicago TIF Districts, More Than a Third of City Property Taxes. *Chicago Tribune*, August 6. Available at: https://www.chicagotribune.com/politics/ct-cook-county-chicago-tif-district-report-20200806-7wh5hc7mxzctfackoi4nkefjsq-story.html

DeWitt, Larry. 2010. The Decision to Exclude Agricultural and Domestic Workers from the 1935 Social Security Act. *Social Security Bulletin* 70(4): 49–68. Available at: https://www.ssa.gov/policy/docs/ssb/v70n4/v70n4p49.pdf

Eidelson, Josh and Christopher Cannon. 2020. How the American Worker Got Fleeced. Bloomberg *Businessweek*, July 2. https://www.bloomberg.com/graphics/2020-the-fleecing-of-the-american-worker/

Financial Samurai. 2021. How To Get Financial Aid Making Multiple Six Figures A Year. *Financial Samurai*, January 30. Available at: https://www.financialsamurai.com/financial-aid-when-making-multiple-six-figures/ (Accessed June 3, 2021).

Frankenfield, Jake. 2019. Which Income Class Are You? *Investopedia*, November 20. Available at: https://www.investopedia.com/financial-edge/0912/which-income-class-are-you.aspx

Gage, Beverly. 2016. 'Listen, Liberal' and 'The Limousine Liberal. *The New York Times*, April 26. Available at: https://www.nytimes.com/2016/05/01/books/review/listen-liberal-and-the-limousine-liberal.html

García, Emma. 2020. Schools Are Still Segregated, and Black Children Are Paying a Price-Economic Policy Institute, February 12. Available at: https://www.epi.org/publication/schools-are-still-segregated-and-black-children-are-paying-a-price/

Hasselle, Della. 2019. Now An All-Charter District, New Orleans Schools Experiment Still Faces Questions. *Times Picayune/New Orleans Advocate*, August 12. Available at: https://www.nola.com/news/education/article_30fbef6e-b476-11e9-a3b5-57480c7a30f7.html

Karp, Matt. 2019. Is This the Future Liberals Want? *Jacobin*, October 14. Available at: https://www.jacobinmag.com/2019/10/future-liberals-want-matt-karp-populism-class-voting-democrats

Levy, Alon. 2020. Analysis: How SEPTA Can Turn Regional Rail in Philly into High-Frequency Rapid Transit. *WHYY Radio*, October 10. Available at: https://whyy.org/articles/analysis-how-septa-can-turn-regional-rail-in-philly-into-high-frequency-rapid-transit/

Mobility21. 2021. NASA Enlists Universities, Companies to Help Design Flying Taxis. Available at: https://mobility21.cmu.edu/news/ (Accessed April 7, 2021).

Murphy, David. 2020. In Proposing a Taxpayer-Funded Arena for the Sixers, Josh Harris and David Blitzer Are Running a Race They Know How To Win. *Philadelphia Inquirer*, August 30. Available at: https://www.inquirer.com/sixers/sixers-new-arena-funding-josh-harris-david-blitzer-20200830.html

National Academies of Sciences, Engineering, and Medicine. 2020. *Tax Increment Financing for Transit Projects*. The National Academies Press. Available at: http://nap.edu/25985

New Faculty Majority. 2020. Facts about Adjuncts. Available at: https://www.newfacultymajority.info/facts-about-adjuncts/

Reeves, Richard V. 2017. Dream Hoarders: How the American Upper Middle Class Is Leaving Everyone Else in the Dust, Why That Is a Problem, and What to Do About It. *Brookings*. https://www.brookings.edu/book/dream-hoarders/

Rose, Kennedy. 2020. Kenney mum on Sixers' proposed arena plans at Penn's Landing. *Philadelphia Business Journal*, August 27. Available at: https://www.bizjournals.com/philadelphia/news/2020/08/27/kenney-stays-silent-sixers-arena-penns-landing.html

Rose, Stephen J. 2016. The Growing Size and Incomes of the Upper Middle Class. Urban Institute, June. Available at: https://www.urban.org/sites/default/files/publication/81581/2000819-The-Growing-Size-and-Incomes-of-the-Upper-Middle-Class.pdf

Rudick, Roger. 2021. Will Philadelphia Ever Get its S-Bahn? *Streetsblog USA*, February 25. Available at: https://usa.streetsblog.org/2021/02/25/will-philadelphia-ever-get-its-s-bahn/

Schulte, Bret. 2008. Ronald Reagan v. Jimmy Carter: "Are You Better Off Than You Were Four Years Ago?" *US News and World Report*, January 17. Available at: https://www.usnews.com/news/articles/2008/01/17/the-actor-and-the-detail-man

Uchitelle, Louis. 2000. Economic View; In a productivity surge no proof of a new economy. *The New York Times*, October 8. https://www.nytimes.com/2000/10/08/business/economic-view-in-a-productivity-surge-no-proof-of-a-new-economy.html

Vuchic, Vukan R., Shinya Kikuchi, Eric Bruun, et al. 1993. A Plan for SEPTA's Regional Metrorail System. University of Pennsylvania Scholarly Commons. Available at: https://www.researchgate.net/publication/331651602_Plan_for_SEPTA_Regional_Metrorail_System#fullTextFileContent

Yamahtta-Taylor, Keeanga. 2021. What's at Stake in the Fight Over Reopening Schools. *The New Yorker*, February 9. Available at: https://www.newyorker.com/news/our-columnists/whats-at-stake-in-the-fight-over-reopening-schools

6

DUAL ECONOMY AND THE PUBLIC WORK SECTOR

To repeat from the previous chapter, the dual economy is a widely recognized phenomenon. It means that, even within the same industry and similar jobs, there can be two different levels of base pay, benefits and permanence. And the upper tier is where the people who have similar class affinities "in both senses of the word" reside. It consists of the professional class who went to elite universities, but there are also some upper-tier jobs for people who went to Ho Hum State U and jobs not requiring degrees within select manufacturing, construction, and government service sectors. This chapter focuses on how it manifests itself in public works, with particular attention to transportation-related examples as transportation drives the urban form and hence the costs of most other public works as well.

The duality has gradually spread through larger swaths of the economy, for several reasons. Globalization has put severe competitive pressure on some industries that are labor intensive and can draw on multinational production sources. For example, in the heyday of Detroit, the US auto industry had a much higher health insurance overhead than other rich countries. This could be solved in part by outsourcing much of the component manufacturing to the non-union southeastern USA. This kind of logistic system is based mostly on trucking instead of railroad and dispersing the industry across the countryside. The Figure 6.1 based on Glen Weisbrod's (2015) research shows the corridors and provides some statistics about the volume of business being conducted by the auto industry. This evolution converts many previously high overhead positions to lower-tier jobs, while most of the industry's upper-tier positions remained in places like the more prosperous suburbs or Central Business District of Detroit that are attractive to the top management and their cohort of professionals.

There are others who see this dual model of the separation of workers from each other and from top managers of the production food chain as the creation of "automotive manufacturing powerhouse" and it has been promoted with government and university assistance as a positive means of increasing the competitiveness of U.S. industry (Colucci 2017). I think this was misguided. First, it is transferring existing jobs to the rural south after people moved to the urbanized north to find manufacturing jobs in the automotive industry and all the infrastructure duplication and disruption that entails. Second, there is no "powerhouse" in the economic sense known as the agglomeration effect, meaning that both companies and workers benefit from having many similar companies near one another. Instead, facilities are widely dispersed

DOI: 10.4324/9781003245704-6

largely away from cities and across multiple states by design. It is more like what Kurt Vonnegut called a "False Karass," akin to being a Hoosier if one comes from Indiana.

In sectors not pressured by international rivals, consumers too bear some responsibility. If they keep buying from one lower-cost competitor, it becomes fast expanding, so other companies follow. The airline industry is a good example. Regional airlines replacing service using larger planes might have the livery of a major airline, but they are very much lower-tier employers. The pay is often so low that pilots deadhead from cities with cheaper housing and crews pay into a "crash pad" they share when they overnight. Even after 2009 crash of Flight 3407 in Buffalo, New York, where exhaustion was a major factor the primary focus was on pilot training (jumppilot 2012). One federal reform was that training hours would be further increased, making the personal cost of getting into a lower-tier job even higher (Silk 2016). No labor law reforms were forthcoming demanding that overnight schedules include paid motels. Regional lines no longer only provide connections to small towns, their original mission, but also often replace larger airliners still staffed by higher-tier employees to provide continual pressure on wages.

Fairness demands that it be said that some industries did need a shakeup. Already in 1994, the TV show *The Awful Truth* did a skit showing how a dark-skinned movie star could not get a lift in Manhattan, but a light-skinned person with a mile-long prison record and a person dressed as a clown both got picked up promptly. Racial discrimination in the taxi industry remains widespread if Los Angeles is typical (Brown 2018). Uber and Lyft are sometimes filling gaps that needed addressing, serving districts of cities where taxis will not go, where one had to wait several hours, or even reserve 24 hours in advance. By comparison, the informal transit, for

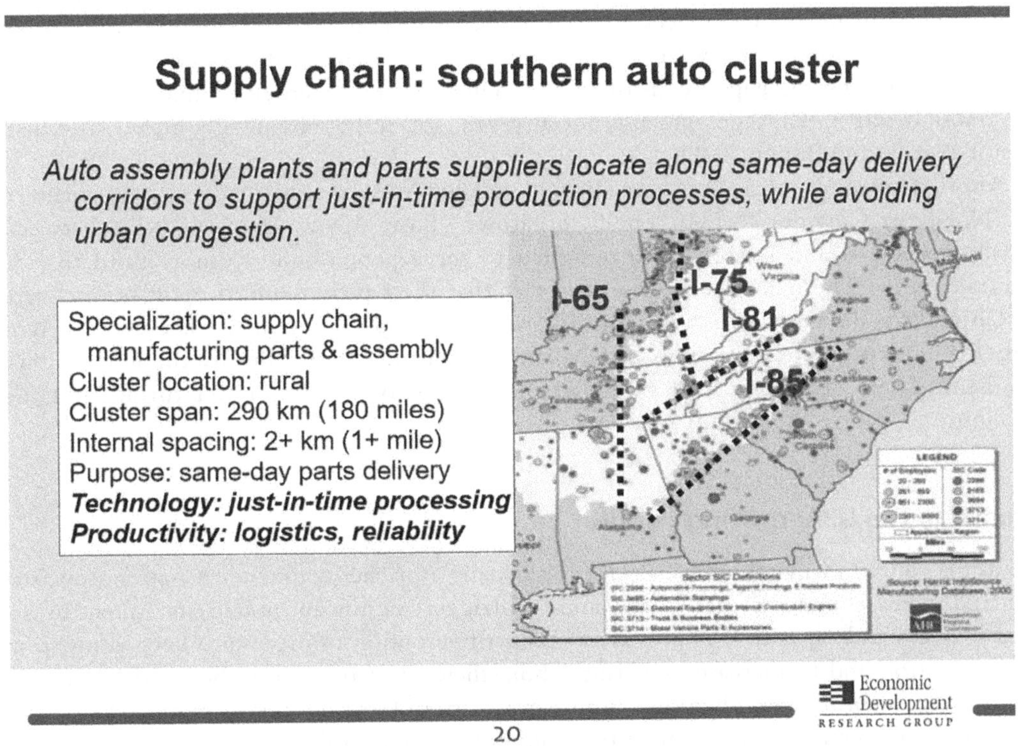

FIGURE 6.1 Dispersal of the auto industry to a less sustainable and less union friendly design.
Source: Glen Weisbrod (2015).

FIGURE 6.2 Person dressed as a clown successfully hailing a taxi in NYC (from Michael Moore's *Awful Truth* TV show).

FIGURE 6.3 Yaphet Kotto, movie and TV star, trying to hail a taxi in NYC (from Michael Moore's *Awful Truth* TV show).

example, in the Flatbush district of Brooklyn where they are known as dollar vans, arose already decades ago (Reiss 2020) and have been an ongoing subject of regulation, or not (Boyle 1994). They offer local employment reflecting the ethnic characteristics of the neighborhood and low fares while containing costs by serving only shorter trips (Orlove 2018). Not to overstate and give the impression the gaps are all filled now, Uber and Lyft were not found to be serving the transit deserts in Chicago, which is not surprising given the substantially higher fares than transit (Barajas and Brown 2020).

Another example of a sector needing a shakeup was intercity passenger services in the Northeast Corridor (NEC). The "Chinatown" buses operating in the NEC between Washington, DC and Boston were designed to serve people who cannot afford to ride Amtrak trains. The name stems from the fact that their pickup and dropoff points were in Chinatown districts with few or no intermediate stops. They have since evolved into larger, more corporate operations due to enforcement of safety rules by the federal government. There are many such gap fillers providing for the lower tier throughout the economy.

Transit in the USA: moving people

Transit is viewed as a vital public service in virtually all richer countries. As cities grow, the demand increases and trips get longer, and this triggers significant public investment to increase speeds and capacities, to provide a competitive option to driving to keep congestion under control, and to increase operating labor efficiency. Larger cities began these investments over a century ago when they built elevated train lines and increasingly tunnels with the advent of electric traction. But this is quite expensive to finance, so unless demand is very high, it is more common to run lines parallel to roads but sharing intersections. These are called Light Rail Transit (LRT) and Bus Rapid Transit (BRT) to differentiate them from old-fashioned streetcars and buses that operate in mixed traffic. Over twenty-five (25) cities in the USA have installed at least one LRT line and at least five (5) have implemented at least one BRT line since the early 1980s. Starting more recently, at least ten (10) cities have built lower-performance streetcars for the purpose of urban revitalization at least as much as for transportation (Spieler 2018).

The UK as a public transport outlier

In the UK, outside of the London metropolitan area, it is treated as just another retail product not requiring much infrastructure construction at public expense or service planning by a government-controlled agency. This places it in the company of poorer countries without the ability to manage the commercial use of their streets or funds to develop planned transportation systems. It has also privatized other public services to a far greater extent. The UK is thus a subject of separate attention in several places.

Where have most new transit extensions gone?

Transit investments influence land values by making access to jobs easier, and when capacity is expanded, enabling high-rise buildings. Office complexes over a rapid transit station are of much higher value nowadays than a suburban office park as, to once again use Richard Florida's term, creative class workers migrate back toward the central city. This increased value is sometimes recognized by "tax-increment financing" or other formulas so that commercial landowners along new lines must help pay through part of their windfall gains. Existing non-commercial properties also increase in value. Houses in walking distance from regional trains especially are worth more. If homeowners stay, they can opt out from the stressful auto commute. If they leave, they can cash out and buy houses away from the neighborhood whose character is going to change if densification is allowed. All of this makes investment a political issue of interest to the financial sector, land developers, and higher income neighborhoods. The lower income parts of the city or struggling post-industrial towns surrounding the city that might want an economic boost are facing a power struggle with these interest groups. The local Metropolitan Planning Organization (MPO) and transit agency may well have performed studies showing that there is more "bang for the buck" in upgrading existing high-ridership corridors or in improving access to depressed areas, but their input is strictly advisory. When public funds are requested or a vote to raise funds is required, elected officials will decide.

On the one hand, there is competition for receiving investment. Many major transit investments have been opportunistic to keep costs down. The first San Diego LRT line that started the wave in 1981 (along with Edmonton and Calgary in 1978) used an existing corridor, as did the Blue Line LRT between downtown LA and Long Beach. Portland used an existing freeway corridor. But many more corridor choices reflect political power. The first line in the Minneapolis-St. Paul region that opened in 2004 went to the southwest, the most prosperous part of the region. People in the Bottineau corridor with a lower average income are accusing elected officials of only half-heartedly supporting them as they still don't even have a design let alone an operational line (Moore 2019, 2020). One of the first lines the Bay Area Rapid Transit District (BART) built was a line to Concord, necessitated by the need to provide something to all counties in the BART District. This opened up higher income commuter housing opportunities due to the very high cruising speed of BART, a hybrid between rapid transit and regional rail. More recently, Washington Metro's Silver Line, also part of the hybrid Metrorail system is going deep into the "hunt country" near Leesburg, Virginia.

Promoting sprawl was not supposed to be one of the goals for transit investment; that was supposed to be the domain of freeways. But if one announces years in advance without a corresponding requirement to zone for dense development along the line, sprawl promotion will be its result.

On the other hand, there may also be opposition to transit improvements from existing property owners who stand to lose. In the mid-1990s, the owner of Bellevue Square feared that LRT from downtown Bellevue to downtown Seattle would reinvigorate the latter as a regional shopping destination. More than one major public university (Minnesota, Maryland, and Washington) protested that the vibration from the trains will affect their labs. Recently, Duke University Health System, a private ostensibly non-profit organization, managed to kill an entire LRT project in the Raleigh-Durham area. After years of negotiation, it still cited a list of unresolved concerns: "....Duke University's, legal, ethical and fiduciary responsibilities to ensure the safety of patients, the integrity of research, and continuity of our operations and activities." Many other hospitals around the world have adjacent rail lines (Grubb and Vaughn 2019; Stancill 2019). Airport operating authorities were notorious for trying to block rail access as it would reduce revenue from parking, which in a common scheme of airport financing, requires airlines to make up this difference. In a few cases, like Philadelphia and Los Angeles, very large airports are city owned and turn a modest profit. Airports are major employers of lower-tier workers nowadays. Faster rail transit would make it easier to attract such workers, but this was trumped by concerns for revenue sources. Better commutes for lower tier workers hardly factored into the equation. Although there is more concern for workers now, there is still concern about attracting the wealthy traveler like one very recent Earth Day ad promoting long term parking at Boston's Logan Airport shows (CBSBoston Staff 2021).

When budgets are not growing, how is transit being re-organized?

Most transit agencies have budgets that grow only with the inflation rate. Some have not even recovered from the 2008 to 2009 cuts. Service expansion is out of the question for most of them. Operations are heavily publicly subsidized, with smaller agencies covering only about 10–20 percent through the "farebox." Even the big city agencies with much higher demand levels only cover at most 40–50 percent. In the last few years, diminishing ridership has been the topic of many news articles. Reporters at *The New York Times* (2018) and *Atlanta Journal Constitution* (2018) have even been questioning whether rail transit might become obsolete with the advent of autonomous cars. Spoiler alert: no.

One of the reasons offered for the ridership loss is people switching to Uber and Lyft. This is at most a partial explanation. In places like Manhattan and central San Francisco, these services are indeed attracting some affluent people away from transit, but even though they are cheaper than taxis they are still too expensive to use every day for most people. Lower fuel prices are also offered as a reason, but one must still be able to afford to own and, in many cases, to park a car. Ask a transit planner instead of a tech guru, and you get other explanations for diminishing ridership. The increasing congestion causes transit vehicles to slow down. This is a double whammy: first, it raises costs as a given vehicle can make fewer trips per day, and second, the deteriorated service makes people seek other options, which in turn lowers revenue and can lead to even more service cuts in a dynamic of decline. This is exactly what happened that precipitated the public takeover of transit in the 1960s and 1970s. But this time they would already have been moved to the public sector.

Another significant and often more important reason is the relocation of much of the back-office, warehousing, light manufacturing, and other lower-paid work to low-density suburbs with cheaper rents and poorer or even no transit options. Higher paid jobs where transit is better but rent is higher are displacing them. Thus, the purchasing of more cars is also a symptom and not just a cause of transit decline. There is not just the oft-cited love affair with the car, there is also the shotgun marriage.

It is premature to say what the impact from Covid-19 will be in terms of demand and financing of transit services. Of course, there is some legitimate fear of being in close proximity to others. So far, the response in many communities has been to cut transit service which endangers the lower-tier essential workers through overcrowding. This can be out of all proportion to fare losses as fares are a small portion of operating support at most agencies. If upper tier workers stay away should working from home become permanent, this could cause a repeat of the historic downward spiral of transit as permanent service cuts lead to people seeking other travel options. On the other hand, many of the people who could work from home traveled during the peak hours to and from the city centers. This raises the cost of operations because much of the capacity is used only for a few hours per day requiring more buses and drivers, or more rail rolling stock to lengthen trains, all of which are used only a few hours per day (Bruun 2005). Reducing the number of drivers is one of the justifications for conversion to rail technology for commuter-oriented services. If some of the savings from reduced peak hour demand could be retained within the agency, this could translate into increased frequency during off-peak periods and extension of service into the sprawling perimeters where there is latent demand.

Should a transit agency have to choose whom to serve?

A few cities have dealt with their ridership loss, like Houston, by re-organizing their transit systems to increase service on popular routes at the expense of less popular routes. This is good news for people for whom these routes work, and certainly eases congestion and provides environmental benefit to the city by attracting some people out of their cars. But it is bad news for the transit dependent who have been sacrificed. There will probably be little to gain by advocating for these people by City Council members when there are so many other competing priorities. Moreover, these priorities are often set by organizations that vote as a block or give campaign donations or both. Before the re-organization there were already some large service gaps and nothing was done about them, proving the point that improving transit so that no part of the city is deprived is not the highest priority. But not always. The Norfolk, Virginia, City Council recently voted down such a re-organization because it would hurt the transit dependent in minority communities (Murphy 2021). Should concern for economic and racial justice have to be in conflict with environmental benefit maximization?

Big city unions versus the gig workers

In a few cities there have been some attempts to add some smaller buses that would fill the gap between taxi/Uber/Lyft and forty-foot-long buses. To do so, cities either need more operating funds or must cut some existing services. In theory, smaller buses can be an affordable alternative because of the cost sharing among multiple public and private parties. In practice, this idea runs up against the forces of the dual economy. The bigger city transit unions typically demand the same hourly rate and benefit terms for a small bus and will fight any attempt to outsource. A current example is in Bucks County, one of the suburban members of the Southeastern Pennsylvania Transportation Authority district, or SEPTA, which negotiated a night time and fare free service using small buses branded as Owl Link. It is needed and desired by many workers in this auto dependent area as there is no local bus service after ten at night (Sofield 2021). The drivers, vehicles and operation are outsourced. These are not gig employees, they are wage employees albeit at lower wages and benefits than those who drive the large buses. It was done without cooperation with TWU 234 who have now filed an unfair labor practices complaint with the State of Pennsylvania (Fitzgerald 2021). They had an upcoming opportunity to once again strike in October 2021 so they have strong bargaining power. If they prevail, there is likely to be no service at all, let alone a free one. Many other communities have wanted something similar all along the SEPTA Regional Rail network for many years now.

Thus, we have a situation where the unionized drivers are paid about $35 per hour plus virtually free healthcare with almost no copays and prescriptions capped at $10 (TWU100 2020). As a result of this cost structure, management pays overtime instead of hiring more drivers. Some drivers can be earning in the six figures with overtime and before benefits. Compare this to the Uber/Lyft driver who has no health insurance, pays for any care with after tax income, gets no overtime and probably earns in the realm of $10–$15 per hour. There is nothing in between in many places and the SEPTA example shows why.

Comparison with Finland on transit

Compare also US big city transit costs to those in Finland. In the USA, labor can represent from 60 up to even 70 percent of operating and maintenance costs. In Finnish cities, labor is only about 50 percent. This would be similar in most of the European Union. Providing healthcare similar to Nordic countries is very expensive and is imbedded in the cost structure and passed along in the fare and to the taxpayer. This means healthcare that is virtually free for your entire family without copays or surprise billings, but at US prices that are roughly twice as high. Hourly wages in large US cities are also higher. Bus and metro train drivers in Helsinki are not making a base pay of approximately $70,000 per year. Moreover, the high overhead of each employee in a US system with such a contract means it is often cheaper to pay overtime rates than to hire additional workers. Hence, my argument that these are jobs that put these workers in the upper tier in the USA but not in Finland.

As a member of the EU, Finland has been pressured to put out the operation of most public services like bus transit for public tender. It is not considered a vital service like police or fire. And perhaps it need not be considered as such when there are multiple private companies responsible for different routes. If workers go on strike against one for-profit company, others might still be operating. In a bigger city in the USA, if a public sector transit union goes on strike, there are no profits to reduce or CEOs earning millions of dollars to punish by this strike. But it can cover the entire region working great hardship on the transit dependent and do permanent damage to the economy. If all services are provided by one agency, it might not be too strong to say that the union can hold the city, region or even a nation hostage, providing great leverage against public officials. This remains the case not only in the USA, but in the EU as well, for example, some national railways. Despite low productivity growth in the rest of the economy, they can be demanding 1 or 2 percent annual pay increases when other workers have stagnant wages (Benanav 2021). Since green investment will target strongly organized sectors, there are certain to be conflicts over whether to give more work to existing unions or to new organizations that perhaps pay less but provide more employment.

There have been disputes about whether the European Commission (EC) procurement rules have gone too far in their ideological commitment to privatization and blocking subsidy as was discussed about transit in Chapter 2. As a compromise, local governments can retain full control of some of the public property, including operating labor, but they must be careful not to not to hide costs in other departments or overbill the city residents, that is, turn a profit. The city of Helsinki has retained operating control of the metro line and all the streetcar lines. But stay tuned, as there is pressure to turn city departments into corporations as services extend across municipal borders.

US government role in the transit manufacturing industry

Federal procurement laws also contribute to replacement of well-paying jobs. Manufacturing has largely migrated to the non-union south, places like Tennessee, Kentucky, and Alabama. Companies might even get new factories built with public subsidies from state economic development funds and through tax abatements, but not the cities, for the investment and operating fund needs for transit systems in their own cities used by their own residents. Under Buy America regulations, transit agencies are not allowed to compensate in the price comparisons for the unfair subsidy that a manufacturer receives from taxpayers in other states. Buy America further requires that any capital investment that uses federal matching funds must have at least 60 percent US content (increasing to 70 percent by the time you read this) but it is not allowed to specify local content. Often there are existing facilities that might have to be shut down that could have been put back into use.

One ironic result of these various restrictions on grants from the federal level and incentives from the state level that seems to be unfolding is the emergence of CRRC, a Chinese government owned company, as a dominant manufacturer. It received subsidies to build a new plant in East Springfield from the state of Massachusetts, which was legal since the state cleverly did not involve federal matching funds, which helped CRRC to win the order for new subway cars for Boston. There will be delivery delays (Dwinnel 2020; Ryan 2020a) but this is not unusual for the USA since a few cities orders different equipment at infrequent intervals instead of buying designs based on modular platforms as is the European procurement approach. Kawasaki, with large subway car plants in Yonkers, New York and Lincoln, Nebraska was seriously pondering leaving the industry as it is becoming so hard to make a profit (Isawa 2018; Staff 2018). Elsewhere, a new assembly plant for regional railcars will be built as a condition of winning an order out west while one in Philadelphia and Illinois closed down. So it goes.

Given the slow pace of regional transit investment, and almost non-existent market for intercity passenger railcars, the industry for both the bus and railcar manufacturing is quite small for such a large country. Transit bus purchases are roughly 5,000 per year and only a few hundred per year for intercity and regional railcars outside of the New York City region. The order volume is too small for efficient mass production methods, especially if states are being played off against each other for tax breaks and outright subsidy to attract factories. If and when investment was to increase substantially and Buy America restrictions were removed, legacy U.S. companies that do pay decently and don't freeload could get more work for their existing plants. So would European companies that also pay taxes and union wages. Even with higher wages, purchase costs might still come down as truck assembly line methods would be used instead of what is largely building by hand today.

As with rapid transit cars, a Chinese electric-bus manufacturer is making breakthroughs thanks in large part due to restrictions in Buy America. Los Angeles communities are being given promises of training and well paid local, unionized jobs if they forego Federal matching funds and contract directly through them instead (PR Newswire 2020). The company's main factory for other customers is in Lancaster in the Inland Empire known for low wages. Another Chinese manufacturer located its factory in Greenville, South Carolina, copying the rest of the automotive and transit industry moving to the non-union south.

New York City: out-of-control costs and a subway system operating slower than 50 years ago

The New York City metro area has a transit system largely frozen in time. There are still no coordinated connections or joint fares with New Jersey Transit. In defense of New York City Transit (NYCT), mayors and city councils over the years have not been overly supportive of measures that favor transit. The last few years have seen the advent of a few "select bus" routes that are faster, but bus transit remains very slow with few priorities over cars added over the years. There was the 63rd Street tunnel and a few new interconnections roughly 30 years ago, but not a single new subway line and only about 11 stations out of about 472 in over 50 years. The recent extension of the 2nd Avenue subway tunnel by a few stops is estimated to be the single most expensive transit construction on a per mile basis in history.

The New York Times did a cost comparison with the Paris Metro that needs similar diameter tunnels and station lengths in granite and found it costed four times as much (Rosenthal 2017). There seemed to be very little competition with only two bidders. The other recent extension of the 7 Line to the Hudson Yards (Jacob Javits Center) was also quite expensive. But who should be surprised when the station has a full-length mezzanine such that the construction cavity is large enough to place several Sistine Chapels in a row. And the atrium below the station entrance looks big enough to perhaps lay the Sistine Chapel on its side inside? In the Mayor and City Council's defense, they do not have the last say in wage negotiation or major procurements. These are the purview of the NYCT's parent company, the Metropolitan Transportation Authority (MTA). The city of New York selects only 4 of the 17 board members.

There are a couple of megaprojects underway, one being Eastside Access connecting Grand Central Station with Penn Station and it is about to open. It is many years delayed and costs have escalated dramatically. This is not unusual (FlyvbJerg 2007) and probably not specific to

FIGURE 6.4 Size of station cavity for the line 7 extension at Hudson Yards (Jacob Javits Center) instead of more modest tube without mezzanines.

Source: Metropolitan Transportation Authority / Patrick Cashin.

the NYC area given how it is also tied into an aqueduct replacement and must be built under Midtown Manhattan with all of its dense infrastructure and without closing Grand Central Station. But this ongoing megaproject plays a role in keeping wage rates high since it increases demand while the unions have a lot of control over supply.

FIGURE 6.5 The completed 34th Street-Hudson Yards (and Jacob Javits Center) subway station showing the enormous size of the two-level station.
Source: Epicgenius Creative Commons Attribution-Share Alike 4.0.

FIGURE 6.6 Hudson Yards (Jacob Javits Center) Station atrium under construction in 2013.
Source: Metropolitan Transportation Authority / Patrick Cashin.

The other is the Gateway project and its delay is probably much less excusable. This has been a serious and neglected issue for decades. There are only two NEC tracks under the Hudson river, shared by Amtrak and New Jersey Transit. Already very old and further eroded by Super Storm Sandy, the power system and maybe the tunnel itself could fail at any time. A second tunnel is needed anyway to increase capacity. There was one attempt about a decade ago, derisively known as "The train to Macy's basement" by persons who noted, this author included, that it would have very limited capacity since it would be a dead-end terminal. It was killed early in New Jersey Governor Christie's administration. Gateway remains to be funded. Many fingers point at the US Federal Transit Administration claiming a politically motivated low recommendation rating. Perhaps, but the truth is that none of the states along the NEC Corridor had stepped up with an investment plan not based on loans with an as yet-to-be-determined repayment plan. This is somewhat surprising, as trains using it are very much of importance to the upper tier living in the New Jersey suburbs and traveling to other large cities on business.

Much of the NYCT subway network still has a slower operating speed than it did 50 years ago with far too many slow speed sections, despite rolling stock with equal or better braking performance. There were temporary slowdowns after a collision in 1995 that were never lifted (Gordon 2018a, 2018b). Signaling systems on most of the lines are ancient and is finally being addressed on a significant scale, thanks in part to increased availability for work due to Covid-19 service reductions (Nessen 2021). NYCT places much of the blame on their unreliability on budget cuts from the State of New York over the years. But part of the blame for the unreliability of the signals must surely reside with the labor costs. Hourly rates and benefits are so generous that NYCT simply could not afford to hire the number of technicians and mechanics needed. It has actually been cheaper to pay some workers overtime when there are major component failures (and hope there aren't too many) than to hire more staff on a permanent basis to try to bring the system into a more reliable state. The head of the NYCT transit union says that his system is in better condition lately and yet the top 10 employees still earned an average of over $122,000 extra in 2020. The MTA as a whole spent over $1.1 Billion on overtime (Lieh 2021). The MTA is a creature of the State of New York spawned in an era when the State had better finances than NYC. The transit unions, as well as many of the private construction unions, are closely allied with the Governor of New York.

Seattle and its glacial construction pace

This author is a native of Seattle and has thus followed its transit saga especially closely. For a city its size, Seattle was quite late to the game of major transit infrastructure investment. It necessitated a local funding vote as the State was unwilling to help. It is chronically broke as there is no state income tax. There was a vote in 1995 that would have built rail lines extending from King County where Seattle and Bellevue, the "edge city" on the east side of Lake Washington are located, to Pierce County where Tacoma is located and to Snohomish County where Everett is located. Long story short, there was public opposition from some elected officials who felt short changed and an intense campaign by anti-tax groups. The proposition won in King County where the bulk of the system is located, but it lost slightly in one of the others. As a result of a requirement that at least two counties get a majority, it would be built nowhere. Another vote in 1996 funded a shrunken and clearly inadequate system that got less opposition. In 2008, yet another vote was held to enlarge it again. It is taking until 2021 to get to Northgate at the north end of the city, a distance of only 8 miles from downtown Seattle, and until 2023 to reach Bellevue, Many of the people who voted for better transit will be retired by the time these segments are completed and people are looking for answers (Baruchman 2019). And the further extensions might be slowed down again, due to a downturn in the local economy from Covid-19 and reduction in tax revenue intake (Groover 2020; Ryan 2020b). Traffic is already horrendous, and the population is growing fast.

The situation is ridiculous. First, if states in the USA would collect a gasoline tax high enough to at least cover the direct cost of building and maintenance of roads, like every other rich, industrialized country, the states might have money to contribute. Currently, cities in Washington State must help to maintain and operate most of their roads, which therefore puts roads in competition with schools, universities, homeless shelters, libraries, water treatment and other vital functions. To help solve this under taxing of auto users, an annual "car tab" tax was passed. This tax has been rescinded by a yes vote on an anti-tax initiative. Gasoline tax increases are still vociferously opposed by many politicians and anti-tax crusaders. Second, there are many multibillionaires paying less than 3 percent in state and local taxes in Washington State (ITEP 2018). Any one of them could pay for the entire construction project and still have most of their money left.

Los Angeles also very slow and with similar problems

The situation with Los Angeles is similar. It would need its rail projects completed yesterday due to monumental traffic and population growth. The rapid transit Red Line down the Wilshire Boulevard Corridor is taking over 30 years to reach UCLA in the west end. It has to be built in segments due to intense competition for federal matching funds and because it too has had to jump hurdles. After natural gas leaked into the initial segment of the Red Line in the early 1990s, a law was passed banning new construction of transit tunnels that had to be overturned that delayed construction. Tax cuts required only a simple 50 percent vote in the California state legislature. But passing tax measures later on by local governments to replace lost revenue would require a two-thirds (66.7 percent) popular yes vote.

There are currently efforts to speed up construction of already approved projects, but not necessarily for the sake of the residents or the environment. It has been publicly argued many times that projects must be sped up because the Olympics are coming in 2028 and the Board of Directors submitted a recommendation list of 28 projects (Executive Management Committee 2017). The Governor of California has expressed his willingness to provide State support for what are now "critical" transit projects (Zahniser and Nelson 2021). Who will benefit from this are almost certainly people in the upper tier. There remain many important links that are badly needed but still in the early planning stages, like a line connecting the San Fernando Valley with the rest of Los Angeles, in an extremely busy corridor that are probably decades from completion.

Philadelphia: no transit expansion in 37 years (but two new stadiums and convention center)

One last snapshot of the transit industry in larger cities. At least Los Angeles and Seattle are installing transit infrastructure. Philadelphia has seen no expansion in 37 years. Its streetcars date from 1981. They are not compliant with the Americans with Disabilities Act of 1990. Like other long-time residents, I totally stopped imagining any expansion. And why would anyone? Neither the City Council nor any of the Mayors made it a priority in a long time. The transit stations and stops as well as the vehicles are decidedly down-scale, more reminiscent of a transit museum than a modern transit system. Things get replaced only when truly dilapidated, like the overhead structure of the extremely busy Market-Frankford rapid transit line which is very important to some lower income sections of the city. The only expansion in the works is not really a service improvement, per se, but a purchase of some double-decker regional rail cars to relieve overcrowding. Headways will remain at 30 or 60 minutes, quite substandard for a region of about 5 million people.

I guess the elected officials of Philadelphia did not get the memo that creative class workers appreciate these kinds of things. Nor did the suburban legislators. Then again, they may have given up as well, as the Commonwealth of Pennsylvania legislature is rural dominated and refuses to properly fund almost anything urban. What would this city do with the money even if it got it? After some probably empty threats late in 1984 by the Eagles to relocate, the city promised and then built 50 luxury skyboxes in Veterans Stadium of which the Eagles got to keep the revenue, plus some other improvements at a cost of $10 million (Cipriani 2018). To sweeten the deal, the city also deferred the Eagles' rent of more than $800,000 per year for 10 years through 2011 which included time in the brand-new stadium as well.

Unlike the residents of Los Angeles County or Seattle's King County, the Pennsylvania legislature won't grant residents the right to tax themselves through voter initiatives or referenda (NCSL 2021). Again, demonstrating their priorities for public spending, in the late 1990s both the city of Philadelphia and the state of Pennsylvania each found their one-third share of the money to replace the supposedly obsolete dual-use Veterans Stadium with separate football and baseball stadiums, a fad that other cities have followed as well. Let us not forget the PA Convention Center needlessly replacing the historic Philadelphia Convention Hall and Civic Center and then a further expansion destroying further historic buildings and allowing casinos along the Delaware River instead of park space. The Buildings Trades Council can be counted on to back any project simply because it provides them with employment, even if is contrary to the majority of residents, adding pressure for the Mayor and City Council to go along.

A brief history of the airline industry up to deregulation

Airlines in the USA were privately owned, one of them, United Airlines, was owned by Boeing and then spun off due to antitrust rulings. Many other airlines, especially in smaller countries, were owned in large part or totally by national governments. By the time of the jet-powered airliner in the late 1950s, costs had decreased so much that the industry took off (pardon the pun). It brought the demise of virtually all ocean liners, and in the case of the USA, almost all intercity trains. The airlines were regulated by the Civil Aeronautics Board, or CAB, as to the routes they could serve and capacity they could offer. They were obligated to continue to serve some unprofitable places in return for having lucrative trunk routes with high demand. By the late 1970s, many economists and politicians felt that the industry was being held back and deregulation legislation was passed. Indeed, the US airline industry did grow but there were many casualties along the way: companies, employees, and many mid-sized cities, that saw major employers close their hubs. Others saw the number of flights and destinations dramatically decrease.

Cutting to the present, the US industry has evolved into an oligopoly as antitrust enforcement is not what it once was. There can be intense competition among major airports, and this is what the boosters of deregulation focus upon. But people and businesses in smaller cities see it another way. They can be captive to one or two airlines that will fly only to their nearest hub. And it can be quite expensive. A flight from Philadelphia to State College can cost as much as to Los Angeles. This can mean outmigration of businesses dependent upon a lot of flying, loss of tourist trade or conventions, residents who can no longer afford seeing relatives and friends, and other such blows. Cities that used to be hubs like Cincinnati, Pittsburgh, Memphis, and St. Louis can testify to that (Dayen 2017).

The European airline industry also saw some consolidation and mergers after national governments began to divest themselves. They also went through a wave of deregulation, both internally and within the European Union. But competition by lower cost airlines has not been extinguished to the same extent as in the USA. Several very large airlines operate out of the numerous smaller airports enabled by the higher population densities and closer spacing of cities. But their future is uncertain as some national governments are considering bans on flights well served by high quality rail services, beginning with France (Reuters 2021). This would be fitting as it was the first to start building a high-speed network 40 years ago, the *Train à Grande Vitesse*, or *TGV*. It has already received massive public capital investment so why not try to obtain further environmental benefits? This is throwing down the gauntlet to the EC who do not seem to share this logic, as they are likely to oppose it as a restraint on competition based on their past opposition to smaller airports receiving "state aid." Replacement of airliners with high-speed rail is most certainly not going to happen in the USA in the near future, as the next section should make clear.

Serving the US dual economy: Essential Air Service but no essential bus service

There was some recognition of hardships that can occur because of the freedom of airlines to enter and withdraw from airports at will. Thus, there is an Essential Air Service (EAS) program where the federal government supports selected flights. But the question can then be asked, why not an Essential Bus Service or Essential Train Service program? Intercity buses and trains have also disappeared over the years including recently, albeit with a few locations that have had some services restored (Schwieterman and Kupets 2014; Schwieterman et al. 2021). The answer has a lot to do with their clientele and the political clout they bring. Buses are stigmatized as serving lower-tier socioeconomic groups. The most efficient solution, if everyone were to count equally, would be to support whatever transport modes are appropriate based on equitable criteria for the particular origin and destination pairs. Some pairs would need an airplane to keep travel time down; others would not.

It would be a mistake to assume that the situation is better in Europe for smaller cities. Essential Air Service is not a concept that would be easily approved in today's Europe. There was a case recently where the EC's watchdogs demanded a city in southern France stop giving "state aid" to its local airport based on an ideological position that pressures lower levels of government to borrow money from private sources and government loans using a market approach to improve their facilities if they want to attract airlines and passengers. According to this view, if airlines or passengers are given subsidies then it can be seen as subsidizing a feeder network to big airports instead of a means to hold onto businesses and young people. To the extent that rural areas do not have fast and affordable transport links to their central towns from the bigger cities, it is a problem. Young people and some businesses actually do leave.

The extent varies, but if it is important to stop depopulation anyway for other reasons, it is also important to see if it can be reversed with increased investment in rural areas and small towns. The EC expects small cities to try to attract businesses and attract passengers through public investment in stations, terminals, airports and so on and then raise user charges, making things worse. But if companies are already close to losing money on a specific service and hit with higher costs, like airlines, they will leave.

The approach of always being against airplanes is short sighted from an environmental perspective: It just means that bigger cities will grow instead as towns shrivel. Bigger cities require new infrastructure as the populations relocate in search of new livelihoods. Meanwhile, old infrastructure and housing stock is abandoned. Environmentalists might applaud closing of airports, but they too might be short-sighted. Public policy needs to be based on a look at the bigger picture and the longer term in the specific decision circumstance. After researchers studied three smaller cities in Italy trying to attract or maintain low-cost air carriers, they recommended "to strengthen their role, airport policies need to be carefully defined and be included in a wider strategy aimed at promoting destinations and local development, rather than simply promoting air traffic." (Laurino and Beria 2014).

The Northeast Corridor: trains for a minority, buses and cars for the rest

California is the only place constructing true high-speed rail, but at a quite slow pace, leaving the USA further and further behind its peers. The NEC is by world standards a "higher speed rail" system, not true high speed. But it is the closest the USA has at the moment. Amtrak provides two classes of service, the very expensive *Acela Regional* and the extremely expensive *Acela Express.* There are several major cities in a row and Amtrak can fill its current limited fleets of trains at these fare levels, so it might have an excuse to not be affordable to lower-tier workers. But it has no intention of evolving into something for everybody. The recent past president of Amtrak was Richard Anderson, previously the CEO of Delta Airlines. His entire vision was that of a business class train. Appointing an airline executive is reflective of the goals of Congress and a row of Presidential administrations and is merely a continuation of public policy that this public-owned corporation should try to turn a profit. In a recent interview, William Flynn, the current CEO of Amtrak, was specifically asked about the high fare on Amtrak compared to other countries and did not seem to see this as problem, arguing that there are currently some low-cost advanced purchase fares, but these compete with airlines not with driving (Grabar 2021). So the lower tier remains non-existent in their plans. Amtrak management and Congress over the years have been much less committed to continuing the long-distance trains that serve as a form of Essential Train Service to many smaller cities. All lines under 750 miles (1200 kms) must now be supported by states, which puts small towns at the mercy of possibly reactionary governors and legislatures that must be willing to cooperate with one or more of their adjacent counterparts. There is one important recent change. There is renewed interest by Amtrak in restoring some long-distance services with the discussion of funding of a Green New Deal and in connecting towns with *Thruway* buses.

Amtrak is replacing its merely 20+-year-old *Acela Express* fleet before it even placed an order to replace the 45+ year old *Acela Regional* equipment. The fact that Amtrak accepted a loan (not a grant) for $2.45 billion guarantees that fares must stay very high (LATF USA 2016; Wire, staff reports 2016). If there had been concern for the entirety of society and a desire to extract the environmental benefit of reduction of car travel along Interstate 95, a better policy would be to replace all trains with rolling stock of the same speed. The mathematics of scheduling is such that capacity is reduced if trains operate at different cruising speed. Mimicking the *TGV* in France, Amtrak could buy some double-decker "duplex" trains to increase seating, offering peak and off-peak fares rather than two entirely different services. Amtrak is now finally moving ahead negotiating an order that would make it hard to undo a two speeds, lower capacity approach (Rash 2021). Difficult, but not impossible, since orders take several years to fill and later deliveries could be modified.

Meanwhile, the only affordable alternative for most route segments in the NEC is to ride buses, on a few segments there might be a more local train service with a price somewhere in between. If there is no such train, do not count on getting home for Thanksgiving as capacity is limited on the buses. Also, to save money and avoid the stigma of bus stations, there are no intercity bus terminals for the newer companies in either Philadelphia or New York City, only curbside or parking lot pickup. In Washington, D.C., community complaints in their Chinatown caused Union Station to create a bus station in the auto parking garage. It is not exactly in the spirit of the Americans with Disabilities Act (ADA) to have no seats or shelter for the elderly or disabled. And having to stand outside in a humid summer or freezing winter seems to this author like replacing one stigma with another. There are different worlds in which train and bus travelers live.

The UK: High Speed Rail 2 (HSR2) and substandard regional transit

The UK Central Government has similarly been contemplating a proposal for a few years now that is clearly aimed at building a railway for the upper tier while ignoring the lower tier. The HSR2 project is supposed to go from London to Birmingham, and then later to Manchester and Leeds. There will be heavy dependence upon autos to access the stations as connecting transit will be uncoordinated and of widely varying quality outside of London. There have been many reports, both official and unofficial, criticizing this project from a cost standpoint. Parliament is divided. With a price tag escalating over £80B, the opportunity cost of not first helping to upgrade city and regional systems first should be far more seriously considered. The UK Central Government has been very stingy when it comes to helping cities and regions, even though the *Department for Transport* (DfT) has lots of evidence of public dissatisfaction, including its own reports (DfT 2006; DfT 2012; Taylor and Sloman 2014). Moreover, if HSR2 proceeds, the results can be perverse. Moshe Givoni and Hector Martinez Sanchez (2009) figured out that near the stations in Birmingham, it will be quicker to commute to some parts of London than from the London suburbs. Providing the highest-income people with yet more housing choices facilitated by riding in a luxurious environment should not be a high priority, not when urban traffic is severely congested and commuting costs have become severe burdens for many, both in money and time.

The UK: A380 retirement is a mistake; airlines assumed Heathrow will get a third runway

The long-haul intercity market also competes for public investment. Even if an airport is self-financing (a debatable point), the landside transport connections and environmental impacts are not. An extreme example is the proposed third runway at the slot-restricted Heathrow mega-airport. It appears that the airline industry has assumed that they will win out against the environmentalists and public at large and be able to use the same smaller aircraft that are increasingly being used to spread their network to smaller airports. Otherwise, they would not be retiring their huge and more efficient (at high load factors) A380s, 747-8s, and other huge airplanes. The entire point of them was to serve airports that were slot restricted. Given the low interest rates at which airlines can purchase aircraft, they will just try to fly more and smaller aircraft into other nearby airports in the meantime. For example, even with several other airports already encircling London, the closest in one, London City, just completed a major expansion with a new taxiway and eight new gates. This will allow diversion of some airplanes from Heathrow to liberate more slots (Bates 2020). When the third runway becomes available at Heathrow, they will use it too with even more flights.

Each of these huge beasts cost over $400M, yet airlines seem willing to retire them with a minimum of ten years of life yet. Good for the airliner manufacturing industry, but quite revealing about the levels of waste that are acceptable in the private sector serving the upper tier. By comparison, many cities in the UK have substandard transit due to lack of public support. This they have in common with cities in the USA cities like Cincinnati (Malaska 2011; Simes 2011) struggled to get a mere $100 million to build a beginner streetcar line and Kansas City struggle for $50 million for an extension that will serve for many decades (Kite and Stork 2020).

Proponents for airport expansion make a big deal out of the fact that airport terminals are becoming carbon neutral. But they also have visions of a future of continual growth in long-distance travel demand. This is not going to be carbon neutral (Bates 2021). Airliners will likely be the last motorized transport to use non-fossil fuels on a big scale. Currently there is no tax on jet fuel used for international travel to avoid advantaging one country's airlines against all the others. One possible way to restrain growth in air travel would be at the expense of frequent air travelers. There is the so-called "hockey stick" curve showing that about 20 percent of the population do about 80 percent of the flying. Because travel has stringent ID requirements, it would be easy, technologically speaking, to impose a carbon tax on the individual instead of on the fuel, according to how often she/he flies. The person who has never seen their overseas family or seen a mountain range in person need not be shamed into not flying. Expect this type of solution to be a tough sell when the policymakers are among the targeted population despite its fairness and progressivity.

The USA: Hyperloop, maglev, and other fantasy alternatives to trains

There is some fascination with alternatives to trains. These seem to arise every time new or better intercity train services are proposed. The Missouri governor wants hyperloop between Kansas City, Missouri and St. Louis rather than a conventional train. The hyperLoop remains unproven but is taken seriously apparently because Elon Musk proposed it. Professor Friedrich Lehner (1900–1979) developed equations for the study of capacity as a function of speed decades ago in exhaustive detail (Vuchic 2007b). Assuming the vehicles were to have a mere 30 spaces of the currently envisioned hyperloop vehicles, a back-of-the-envelope calculation I performed using Lehner's equations demonstrates that there would have to be elaborate terminals with multiple loading platforms with departures less than 1 minute apart all merging into a steel tube in a near vacuum in order to provide enough capacity to be meaningful in comparison with airline service, say 1,000 spaces per hour. Could vehicles stop safely from high speeds in case one vehicle failed? What if there was a vacuum leak? How would riders be rescued mid-tube in a system failure? To be charitable, there are many grounds to be very skeptical.

Maryland's Governor Hogan, rather than bolster the existing state-owned MARC trains, supports a privately led proposal for Magnetic Levitation (MagLev) trains and the federal government seems to be taking contributing toward it seriously as well (Phillips 2021). MagLev technology makes no sense in the context of connecting the Baltimore Central Business District (CBD) with somewhere in the Washington, D.C. center. The time savings for such a short trip is minimal, and the infrastructure would be totally incompatible with existing trains, thereby negating the advantage of these higher-speed trains being able to merge with other trains at existing terminals thereby saving great construction time and expense. Even if it were affordable, where would one place new terminals that would have to be entirely grade separated in the built-up central areas so that convenient connections could be made to existing transportation modes?

Then there is the aborted higher-speed rail project from the early days of the Obama Administration that was to connect the numerous medium sized cities in the Midwest. It was part of the stimulus package of 2009 (Naylor 2009). This one had a chance of success as it involved moderate speed increases using existing technology and, amongst other things, would have created a network centered on Chicago with a hub around Columbus. Governor Kasich of Ohio opposed it as did Governor Walker of Wisconsin and Governor Bransted of Iowa. So too, for Governor Scott for Florida's genuine HSR proposal and for Governor Jeb Bush in an earlier incarnation. The regional planning authority for Columbus is now seriously looking at a hyperloop alternative and I am embarrassed to say that the US DoT seems to be taking the concept seriously as well:

> Virgin is working with the Mid-Ohio Regional Planning Commission on a system that would connect Pittsburgh to Chicago via Columbus in about 56 minutes at a cost of about

> \$93. The agency has completed environmental and feasibility studies for the system, which likely would be built in sections from west to east and take about 30 years to complete.
> *(Blazina 2020)*

Thirty years to complete? Surely this project does not have greenhouse gas reduction as one its goals. The more modest proposal from 2009 would have been completed by now.

These types of standalone solutions reflect the lack of coherent vision for intercity transportation at the federal level. The Interstate highways surely had a formula that incentivized cooperation. Compare this to the current lack of an institutional framework to connect together the three regional rail services connecting a string of cities through Virginia and Maryland passing through Washington, D.C., all of which are totally separate in schedules and fares (Gordon 2021). Instead, there could be diametrical lines running across the entire region at one fare instead of new segments like the proposed MagLev train. Or an unofficial proposal for a coordinated intercity network for the San Francisco Bay Area instead of one based on service districts, counties, and individual cities. It would be internal to California, just as much of the Interstate Highway project (Bay Area Council Economic Institute 2021).

The promise of being able to connect into a larger network might yet dampen enthusiasm for non-conventional technologies. Then again, the separateness of the service from the lower tier might be the appeal. It certainly seems to be the case for the Tampa St. Petersburg area, where an electric air taxi and aerial gondola have been discussed by elected officials long before the region has established regular, decent quality bus or rail connections between the primary cities in the three county region (Johnston 2021; McManus 2021). The air taxi fares are estimated to be "only" twice the cost of an Uber or Lyft ride for distances of 25–50 miles (Johnston 2020).

Logistics and supply chains: from historical logistics to modern supply chain management

Logistics is an old-fashioned term that means the planning and conducting the movement of materials. This could range from lower value but heavy bulk cargoes like coal down to very high value and light cargoes like diamond rings and high fashion clothing. There can be raw materials, intermediately finished materials, and finished products. Analyses would examine the trade-offs between the cost of transporting, the costs associated with managing orders, price reductions for larger orders, the cost of tying up money in unsold inventory, and costs of running warehouses/ distribution centers. With globalization and evolution toward Supply Chain Management (SCM) the important decision of internal versus external production was added to the trade-offs. A formula that determines the so-called Total Logistics Cost determines the combination of choices that balances all these costs in order to minimize the total cost. Then there are some adjustments. How much extra inventory to hold would then be decided depending upon the consequences, minor to severe, of "stocking out" and the degree of randomness of consumption. Historically, one department might manage these operations with minimal consultation with other departments.

> Total Logistics Cost = Internal production costs + Annual inventory costs + Ordering costs for all external orders placed + Holding costs for all external orders placed+ Annual transport costs + Annual in-transit costs (e.g. refrigeration, hazardous).

As industrial logistics has evolved into SCM, companies re-organized the departments involved such that production batches can be larger or smaller and delivery speeds faster or slower depending upon even the particular customer and product type. An outside company could get higher or lower levels of service at different prices. Thus, it became a collaboration to optimize the supply chain. Globalization could be justified by noting that the much lower production costs could more than offset the much longer shipping distances and additional cost of holding inventory in "slow moving warehouses." On the other hand, longer trips can have wider variance in delivery times. As a result, several important variables can change, and SCM has come to mean continual adjustments as relative shipping costs and times, manufacturing costs, and exchange rates change.

Lengthening supply lines reduces both costs and sustainability

Different industries have different supply chain priorities. For example, the running shoe industry is labor intensive so when wages started to climb it migrated away from China and toward Vietnam where the government still had a more Stalinistic bent toward independent labor unions or, more recently, the low-margin bicycle industry moved to Cambodia after President Trump instituted Section 301 tariffs on imports from China. The dirtiest industries like steel manufacturing design their supply chains to find cheap power plant fuels, to avoid costly exhaust scrubbing and waste product disposal. Electroplating industries can avoid the costs of properly disposing of toxic chemicals. As countries begin to compete for higher end product manufacturing, as raw materials availability shifts, and transport costs go up or down, the SCM will change too. These decisions go to the highest levels of corporations nowadays. It is no longer a decision for the shipping office. Trying to force companies out of patriotism to return manufacturing in general or some specific industry that used to be the mainstay of some region will not work, not when their competitors are without loyalty. Nor will the returning work necessarily pay what it once did. But changing their overseas production and transport costs will definitely make companies revisit their SCM decisions.

The polluter pays principle, if invoked, will force the beneficiaries of products like steel to pay. A pollution tax added to the price purchasers pay can help clean the smokestack exhaust or clean the water and landfills. A requirement to take back old appliances and vehicles in what is known as "reverse logistics" can incentivize longer product lives and less material use and this already exists in Germany and other places. A carbon tax for adding CO_2 to the atmosphere will make companies reconsider whether to relocate. (More about this in the last chapter.) Many industries would never have the left the USA in the first place if they had to pay one way or the other. And it is only fair for the beneficiaries of products borne of high energy intensity and pollution to bear the costs by imbedding it in the price instead of shifting the cost to people whose health is deteriorated and their communities despoiled without the financial means to mitigate it.

The USA: Inland Empire case study

Inbound logistics is concerned with receiving inventory and then distributing it to where it will have further value added within one's own organization. Outbound logistics is concerned with passing inventory along or delivering it to where it will be sold. Both have been dramatically transformed since the 1950s. Containerization has greatly lowered the price companies must pay to move products long distances. Ships carry containers overseas, while intermodal trains and trucks carry them on land. Ships are now bigger than aircraft carriers, intermodal trains can be over one mile long with only two crew members, and trucks have gone from 40 to 50 foot containers, although the trucking lobby has not succeeded so far in making truck weight limits even heavier, a move that would work against a GND by moving freight back from rail to truck.

All of this is to reduce operating cost through fewer and cheaper workers, many of whom were historically unionized, such as the Longshoreman's Union and the Teamsters. Meanwhile, the public is pressured to pay the capital costs of deepening and lengthening seaports as shipping lines purchase ever larger "Post Panamax" vessels thanks to the recent wider lane available through the Panama Canal. There is no guarantee they can recover these costs as these global company decisions typically happen without prior consultation with public agencies.

There is a place in the supply chain, however, where employment has grown: warehousing and distribution. Depending upon the product, containers must be opened and the goods sorted before further travel. The ports of Los Angeles are Long Beach are a giant container port complex, one of the largest in the world. Because there is not enough room for all the warehousing and sorting, containers are rushed to a place in the semi-desert near Lancaster and Palmdale known as the Inland Empire. Land is relatively cheap and there are lots of people willing to work for low wages. From there, the supplies will move onwards to further distribution centers if the final destination is not the greater Long Angeles area. These destinations too are likely to be concentrations of lower-paid work. Amazon has distinguished itself by achieving such a high market share of retail that it has huge distribution centers, excuse me, "fulfillment centers" across the USA. Walmart is huge as well, of course, but to date Walmart delivers a much higher percentage of food products than Amazon, which requires different supply chains than more durable goods.

Does it really make sense to ship food from across the continent or the globe when conditions are suitable for it to be grown within the same region, maybe adjacent to the same city? Does it really make sense to ship raw materials across an ocean and then back again as finished products? Apparently, yes it does, from a monetary cost standpoint. One must admire the efficiency achieved from a single-minded focus on cost cutting. From a sustainability or livable wage standpoint, and for citizens who would like thriving, local/regional commerce, it does not. To reverse this trend will require intervention in the supply chain that incentivizes companies and government agencies to change their SCM. Covid-19 may well have opened the eyes of a lot of people of the downside of "lean" supply chains that do not stock inventories of goods not used at a steady pace but might be essential for a medical emergency or unanticipated manufacturing demand, like semiconductors. Such items are only available on short notice in competition with companies and institutions in other countries.

The blocking of the Suez Canal by the colossal Post-Panamax container ship Ever Given has also highlighted the vulnerability of supply chains that are both lean and long. Will industry change its practices as a result on their own and, if not, can they be pushed? To understand what would be most effective requires a systems approach. What might be most effective is not necessarily the easiest to achieve institutionally, however. Taxes are anathema to many industries and politicians, regardless of how much they might be justified. For others, taxes are not the most important factor but why not go for "free" money? Companies have been shrewd in their tactics playing locales off against one another for weaker environmental regulations and lower taxes, higher subsidies, and to weaken labor's negotiating strength.

To return to an earlier example, the relocation of automotive parts manufacturing to the southeastern USA has scattered industry largely into greenfields. As a result, supply chains are also largely redesigned around non-union trucking instead of unionized railroads. As a result of this dispersal of job sites, workers often no longer have more than one company from which to pick from nearby such that there might be upward pressure on wages when the industry has an upturn. Sustainability will require reversing some of these trends and reconsolidating similar industries in more optimal locations. There used to be a concept for such concentration, benefit of agglomeration.

Amazon and other recent developments are clogging the streets and sidewalks

When I used to teach a course on SCM, several students per semester would pick the subject of home delivery for their term paper. They could pick the type of product(s) they wanted to investigate. I would learn from their research, too. Is this better for the environment? The answer is: it depends. There are so many considerations including how many other drop-offs there were nearby, what the urban form was like, how wide of a time window for delivery, does someone have to physically receive the goods, how big is the delivery vehicle, and so on. Furthermore, is it practical? One can see that the Amazon delivery solution is most certainly not when packages stack up on sidewalks and trucks block streets. This is a cost imposed on other traffic, other businesses and pedestrians. And it can be imbedded in the price of things where no delivery is requested.

Moreover, the competitive delivery cost is enabled by low wages considering the pace of work involved. Amazon requires the use of a smartphone application for so-called stops which can actually involve several deliveries to different locations and walking across busy streets in a hurry due to tight scheduling (Gurley 2021). There is little incentive for Amazon to design safe routes as "independent" contracting firms would be responsible in case of an accident.

And the search to lower costs further goes on, with companies like Amazon seeking to replace people in warehouses with ever more robots and ground delivery vehicles with drones. Drones clearly already represent a noise and visual intrusion plus a myriad of further safety and environmental hazards if they were to be used on a large scale (McKinnon 2015). Despite awareness of the need for the public sector to regulate their commercial use little preparation seems to have occurred so far except to keep them away from airports. This follows the recent pattern of non-regulation of delivery windows and curb use in most of the USA. In older times, lack of government oversight would be an issue that unions would at least partly address. But there currently are no unions in Amazon to fill this regulatory void.

Do people really need next day delivery? This used to be reserved for particularly valuable or urgent items. It was part of the business model for companies like UPS to charge more for that. It promoted efficiency, as companies could even out less urgent distribution over several days to the benefit of all shippers. And keep in mind that trying to replace in-person shopping with virtual online shopping is not a smart goal. There is a place where everything is delivered to you, it is called prison. Most people, including those with mobility impairments, want to participate in life and it isn't doing them a favor by delivering absolutely everything to them. Making retail

FIGURE 6.7 Drone delivering a package - autonomous logistics.
Source: Mopic / Shutterstock.

FIGURE 6.8 Parcel pickup from multiple companies at a neighborhood store in Helsinki.
Source: Eric Bruun.

businesses fail and boarding up the high streets has already happened in rural areas. Extending it to more urban areas is depriving even more people of a social life.

Comparison to Finland: *Matkahuolto* with pickup lockers in local stores as a comparison

There are alternative ways to deal with packages. First, don't order things you can get when you know you will be going shopping anyway in a place that has what you want. Second, pick up what you ordered at one of your local stores. Instead of delivery vehicles from a variety of companies driving to and fro, each with a handful of deliveries, have them all deliver to a nearby store where the clerk can hand it to you or you can pick it up from a locker by typing in a code from a text message. One such service is *Matkahuolto*, which translates to "courier service." It is especially notable because it is a creature of a consortium of intercity bus services such that deliveries can be made to over 1,200 points in Finland, including remote towns. In this way it also helps bus operators by giving them steady income using their belly space, helps to slow down the disappearance of passenger services, and provides business for stores.

Power, water, parks, and their connections to transportation/land use decisions

Most types of public works have their own experts and are generally discussed by different government departments, academic departments, conferences, and trade magazines. The size in square miles of a district that is required to support a given number of residents and commercial space is largely determined by the modes of transportation used, the types of buildings and lots used for housing, the number of people living per square meter in this housing, and land set aside for parks or is otherwise impractical or impossible to build upon such as flood plains, steep hill sides, and so on. The lower the density, the more asphalt and concrete needed for the roadways. Critically, more support infrastructure will be required at a higher capital investment per person. Longer mainlines are needed for water delivery, longer sewer pipes, longer electric power cabling, more natural gas pipes, more streetlights, and so on. Then there are the operating costs. There is more roadway to maintain. Longer pipes mean more water leaks, more gas leaks, and more maintenance. And as a result of longer distances to travel, there are also higher costs for school bus service, more fire stations to operate, etc. How the expenses for all of this are covered (or not) is discussed in the next chapter.

Costs increase with lower density on the private expenditure side as well. For people who don't have large yards that permit children to play, it is a longer distance to go for green space. And, of course, the distances required to reach stores and jobsites increases, at some point making purchase of an auto necessary with all that entails. There is solid evidence that the total cost of transport, both public and private expenditures, decreases with increasing mean density of a metropolitan region. Jeff Kenworthy, Peter Newman, and their team collected this information at great difficulty in their Millennium Cities Database (Vivier and Mezghani 2001). It must always be kept in mind when politicians rant about wasteful government spending that there can be private spending reduction offsets to increased taxes for public services like transit.

More local parks are needed if children are to be able to reach them without an auto. Like other public services, parks are often poorly maintained and inadequate (Hahn 2020). Land acquisition can be quite expensive if park space has not been preserved in public ownership. New or expanded parks must compete with other uses, many of which could make money for the upper tiers so it makes a difference where this proposed park is located.

A good example once again is the city of New York due to its size and large numbers of families without cars. Despite parks proving to be especially important as a safe refuge for people spending too much time in their residences during the Covid-19 epidemic, NYC's park budget was actually proposed for a 14 percent cut right in the middle of it. Some of the cost of monitoring would be shifted to the police department instead of park employees, absolutely the wrong thing to do in a time of especially high tension between minorities and the NYPD (Whalen 2020).

Water supply becoming the most urgent resource issue of all

Perhaps the single biggest infrastructure issue, even more than investments that will reduce GHG generation, is water supply. The USA has been hit by severe droughts. And in the west, mountaintop snow and glacier melt as a source of water supply is expected to diminish further. Pressure is on to divert more water even from rivers with endangered species. Perhaps not surprisingly given the dilapidated state of so much of transportation infrastructure, spending to conserve and better manage water has also been far from adequate. Water distribution is mostly handled by interstate agreements. At the federal level, capital investment support has diminished over the years which reduces their leverage for nationwide long term conservation planning and for promoting equity

There is some low hanging fruit requiring only minor investment. Leaking delivery pipes that are easily accessible at low cost need to become a thing of past. There is overlap with the need to replace lead delivery pipes into houses for safety reasons, which is not affordable to most of those affected and who have already paid a big price through poisonings, so a case can be made to combine this all under the public purse. Later, the more difficult to reach pipes should be inspected, replaced, and repaired using the principle of diminishing returns.

Public education campaigns can point out to consumers that products like almond milk are not environmentally responsible even if they are vegan, that meat consumption should be reduced, not to drink bottled water if you have safe tap water, to install water conserving commodes, and so on. Many of these are likely to encounter intense opposition from the affected companies concerned only about short-term sales.

There are further steps requiring regulatory or statutory changes. Certainly, water should no longer be priced such that water-intensive crops like rice are grown in a semi-desert like the Central Valley of California. Same with other water-intensive crops like cotton and almonds. The struggle to reform pricing and water allocation has been going on for decades. Remember the famous line "Forget it, Jake. Its Chinatown?" The movie Chinatown was over the intrigue behind water allocation in Los Angeles. This remains today a very tough battle in the western states that is spreading eastward (Uyeda 2021). Water is being wasted in huge volumes though poor agricultural management, leaks, and evaporation. Dilapidated piping, obsolete combined flood control/wastewater, and treatment systems need replacement. Supply also is going down because of decreased summer mountain runoffs and depleting aquifers. Is it any wonder that safe drinking water needed by residential consumers to sustain their daily lives is becoming more expensive, even unaffordable to some? *The Guardian* newspaper sponsored some research on the US water supply and found that prices have gone up 80 percent on average during the past decade in a survey of 12 cities (Lakhani 2020).

One hears about houses with small children that have had their water shut off. Places like Flint still have not had their lead service pipes replaced. In other sectors, we hear about schools that have roofs that leak when it rains, people who are spending two hours to commute to work as transit is so inadequate, hardship upon hardship. Can enough money be found so to address these hardships, quickly and in cooperation, instead of being played off against one another for limited funds? A resolution was introduced in the US House of Representatives to address this on the national level but the US Senate has not taken action (Lawrence 2019). It requires a national plan as watersheds, aquifers and rivers do not respect state borders.

Synergy between infrastructures, not simply the sum of the parts

One often reads reports or hears speakers claiming that X percent of greenhouse gas or Y percent of energy is consumed by use of vehicles or by buildings. This is very simplistic and cannot be a guide for building out new districts or retrofitting existing ones. Urban forms that use high-rise buildings mean that a higher percentage of trips will be performed by transit, bicycling, and walking. Furthermore, for any given population size, a more compact district also means that the car trips will be shorter. Buildings also become more efficient as shared walls insulate better than exposed walls of single houses. And being more compact means that there is more land nearby for farming and forestry, thereby also potentially shortening logistical supply lines. Thus, infrastructure investment is synergistic, not the sum of the parts, both for capital investment and subsequent operating and maintenance costs.

The idea that that one has to choose between different crises should never be accepted without further study. This is just another manifestation of public works being in silos. For example, San Antonio recently had a vote to put more money into its underfunded transit system but some officials expressed concern that funding would come out of aquifer and linear creekway projects (Garcia 2020). Maybe crises can be addressed simultaneously. There are more sophisticated solutions for redeveloped areas that consider transportation, electricity, and waste and drinking water together as a system that can consolidate support and provide new opportunities to alleviate threatened interests (Urban Blue-Green Grids 2021).

Can the money be found to address both the longer-term maintenance backlogs and new efficiency-increasing public works investments? Or will we be seeing the return of water tanks on the roofs of buildings and gasoline-powered generators in the backyard like a developing country? Can urgently needed regulatory and legislative changes happen? Based on Martin Gilens' and Benjamin Page's research (2014) on the behavior of the US Congress from the last few decades, there will continue to be a power struggle between interests in the upper tier, the outcomes of which might coincidentally happen to be beneficial for some aspect of the environment and perhaps to some of the hapless people in the lower tier. So, the answer to all these questions is most likely a no. And it will stay that way until the majority get effective political representation. Furthermore, public infrastructure is not all of the spending to be considered. Additional public services compete for both investment and operating and maintenance support. These are the subject of the next chapter.

References

Badger, Emily. 2018. Pave Over the Subway? Cities Face Tough Bets on Driverless Cars. *The New York Times*. July 20. Available at: https://www.nytimes.com/2018/07/20/upshot/driverless-cars-vs-transit-spending-cities.html

Barajas, Jesus M. and Anne Brown. 2021. Not Minding the Gap: Does Ride-Hailing Serve Transit deserts? *Journal of Transport Geography* 90: 102918.

Baruchman, Michelle. 2019. Could Light Rail Be Built Faster? 5 Take-Aways from Traffic Lab's Transit Event. *The Seattle Times*, July 17. Available at: https://www.seattletimes.com/seattle-news/transportation/could-light-rail-be-built-faster-5-take-aways-from-traffic-labs-transit-event/

Bates, Joe. 2020. London City Airport Completes Major Airfield Expansion Projects. *Airport World*. December 18. Available at: https://airport-world.com/london-city-airport-completes-major-airfield-expansion-projects/?dm_i=2XWC, 13YP2,1EVKIL, 49YH4,1

Bates, Joe. 2021. Huge Investments Needed in Airport Infrastructure to Meet Future Demand Airport World. 30 June. Available at: https://airport-world.com/huge-investments-needed-in-airport-infrastructure-to-meet-future-demand/?dm_i=2XWC, 168CV, 1EVKIL, 4J2R2,1

Bay Area Council Economic Institute. 2021. The Megaregional Case for a New Transbay Rail Crossing, San Francisco. January. Available at: http://www.bayareaeconomy.org/wp-content/uploads/2021/01/ES_NTRCmegaregion_1.27.2021.pdf

Benanav, Aaron. 2021. Automation and the End of Work? Labor Market Dynamics between Innovation and Stagnation. *Humboldt University of Berlin*. See Presentation from About 57 Minutes. Available at: https://www.youtube.com/watch?v=y9bEKFGMebQ Accessed June 4, 2021.

Blazina, Ed. 2020. U.S. Department of Transportation Posts Hyperloop Framework. *Government Technology*, July 27. https://www.govtech.com/transportation/US-Department-of-Transportation-Posts-Hyperloop-Framework.html?utm_term=U.S.%20Department%20of%20Transportation%20Posts%20Hyperloop%20Framework&utm_campaign=COVID-19%20Nearly%20Killed%20the%20Economy%3B%20It%20Didn%27t%20Kill%20Traffic&utm_content=email&utm_source=Act-On+Software&utm_medium=email

Boyle, Daniel K. 1994. Jitney Enforcement Strategies in New York City. *Transportation Research Record* 1433: 177–184. Available at: http://onlinepubs.trb.org/Onlinepubs/trr/1994/1433/1433-023.pdf

Brown, Anne Elizabeth. 2018. Ridehail Revolution: Ridehail Travel and Equity in Los Angeles. *UCLA Electronic Theses and Dissertations*. Available at: https://escholarship.org/uc/item/4r22m57k

Bruun, Eric. 2005. Bus Rapid Transit and Light Rail: Comparing Operating Costs with a Parametric Cost Model. *Transportation Research Record* 1927: 11–21.

CBSBoston.com Staff. 2021. 'This Has To Be A Joke': Logan Airport's Earth Day Tweet Sparks Criticism. *CBS News Boston*, April 19. Available at: https://boston.cbslocal.com/2021/04/19/earth-day-tweet-logan-airport-parking-garage/ (Accessed April 29, 2021).

Cipriani, Ralph. 2018. How Vince Fumo Saved the Eagles from Moving to Phoenix. *Big Trial*, January 28. Available at: https://www.bigtrial.net/2018/01/when-vince-fumo-saved-eagles-from.html

Colucci, Jose. 2017. Strengths, Uniqueness and Synergies across the Southeast. *National Institute of Standards and Technology*, January 27. Available at: https://www.nist.gov/blogs/manufacturing-innovation-blog/strengths-uniqueness-and-synergies-across-southeast

Dayen, David. 2017. Unfriendly Skies. *The American Prospect*. November 3. Available at: https://prospect.org/power/unfriendly-skies/

Dwinell, Joe. 2020. MBTA Defends Work at Chinese-Owned Rail Plant in Massachusetts. *Boston Herald*. October 14. Available at: https://www.bostonherald.com/2020/10/14/mbta-defends-work-at-chinese-owned-rail-plant-in-massachusetts/

Executive Management Committee. 2017. Board Report: Twenty Eight by '28 Project List – Transportation Investment Guide in Tandem with the 2028 Olympic and Paralegal Game.: Los Angeles County Metropolitan Transportation Authority. *Board of Directors*, January 18. Available at: http://media.metro.net/projects_studies/resources/images/28x28_board_report_jan_2018.pdf

Fitzgerald, Thomas. 2021. Transit Workers Union Files Complaint against SEPTA for Hiring a Contractor to Operate New On-Demand Shuttle Service. *Philadelphia Inquirer*, May 27. Available at: https://www.inquirer.com/transportation/transit-septa-owl-link-shuttle-night-shift-workers-bucks-20210527.html

Flyvbjerg, Bent. 2007. Policy and Planning for Large-Infrastructure Projects: Problems, Causes, Cures. *Environment and Planning B: Urban Analytics and City Science* 34(4): 578–597. Available at: https://doi.org/10.1068/b32111

Garcia, Gilbert. 2020. VIA's Difficult Path to An Easy Election Win. *San Antonio Express News*. 7 November. https://www.expressnews.com/news/news_columnists/gilbert_garcia/article/Garcia-VIA-s-difficult-path-to-an-easy-15708847.php

Gilens, Martin and Benjamin I. Page. 2014. Testing Theories of American Politics: Elites, Interest Groups, and Average Citizens. *Perspectives on Politics* 12(3): 564–458. https://doi.org/10.1017/S1537592714001595

Givoni, Moshe and Hector Martinez Sanchez. 2009. The Accessibility Impact of a New High-Speed Rail line in the UK – A Preliminary Analysis of Winners and Losers. *Journal of Transport Geography* 25. DOI: 10.1016/j.jtrangeo.2011.09.004

Gordon, Aaron. 2018a. A Ride on the Subway Speed Limit Test Train. *Curbed*, December 19. Available at: https://ny.curbed.com/2018/12/19/18146933/mta-new-york-subway-speed-limit-test-train

Gordon, Aaron. 2018b. The Trains Are Slower Because They Slowed the Trains Down. *The Village Voice*, March 13. Available at: https://www.villagevoice.com/2018/03/13/the-trains-are-slower-because-they-slowed-the-trains-down/

Gordon, Wyatt. 2021. Plans for a Regional Rail Vision Solidify with the Goal of Better Connecting Virginia, Maryland, and DC. *Greater Greater Washington*, January 27. Available at: https://ggwash.org/view/80231/a-regional-vision-that-connects-virignia-dc-and-maryland

Grabar, Henry. 2021. The CEO of Amtrak Thinks Americans Are Ready for Trains Again. *Slate*, March 15. Available at: https://slate.com/business/2021/03/amtrak-ceo-interview-trains-coronavirus.html?fbclid=IwAR18G9lvpb1c3h1rML9yiYIAt7TAZHd3dFcD5-lXs9-pSs7fbf6LxaPaGAY&eType=EmailBlastContent&eId=0c82232d-2e49-4572-b97c-a3251b191f82

Groover, Heidi. 2020. With Coronavirus and Car-Tab Hits, Seattle Pitches Scaled-Back Tax for Bus Funding. *The Seattle Times*, July 7. Available at: https://www.seattletimes.com/seattle-news/transportation/with-coronavirus-and-car-tab-hits-seattle-pitches-scaled-back-tax-for-bus-funding/

Grubb, Tammy and Dawn Baumgartner Vaughan. 2019. Duke Won't Back Durham-Orange Light Rail Project. 'Major Setback,' says GoTriangle. *The (Raliegh) News and Observer*, February 27. Available at: Available at: https://www.newsobserver.com/news/local/article226887264.html#storylink=cpy

Gurley, Lauren Kaori. 2021. Amazon's Cost Saving Routing Algorithm Makes Drivers Walk Into Traffic Vice. June 2. https://www.vice.com/en/article/5db95k/amazons-cost-saving-routing-algorithm-makes-drivers-walk-into-traffic

Hahn, Jessie Feller. 2020. Crisis funding for public parks: A Conversation with Adrian Penepe. *Meeting of the Minds*. June 23. Available at: https://meetingoftheminds.org/crisis-funding-for-public-parks-33818?mc_cid=86904a61f6&mc_eid=c97d92650f

Institute on Taxation and Economic Policy (ITEP). 2018. Who Pays? A Distributional Analysis of the Tax Systems in All 50 States, 6th Edition. Available at: https://itep.org/whopays/

Isawa, Masashi. 2018. Kawasaki Heavy Weighs Exit from Money-Losing Train Business. *Nikkei Asia*, October 31. Available at: https://asia.nikkei.com/Business/Companies/Kawasaki-Heavy-weighs-exit-from-money-losing-train-business

Johnston, Caitlin. 2020. Air Taxis and Gondolas: Tampa Bay Looks to the Skies for Next Transit Options. *Tampa Bay Times*, December 4. https://www.tampabay.com/news/transportation/2020/12/03/air-taxis-and-gondolas-tampa-bay-looks-to-the-skies-for-next-transit-options/

Johnston, Caitlin. 2021. Tampa Bay Riders to Wait 10 Years for Regional bus Transit Line. *Tampa Bay Times (TNS)*, January 25. https://www.tampabay.com/news/transportation/2021/01/22/tampa-bay-riders-to-wait-10-years-for-regional-bus-transit-line/

jumppilot. 2012. FAA Pilot Training Rule Delayed 6 Years. *Airline Pilots Forum*, June. Available at: https://www.airlinepilotforums.com/safety/68823-faa-pilot-training-rules-delayed-6-years.html

Kite, Allison and Cortlynn Stark. 2020. Decades in the Making: Kansas City gets $50M to Extend Streetcar South of Plaza. *The Kansas City Star*, August 28. Available at: https://article.wn.com/view/2020/08/26/Decades_in_the_making_Kansas_City_gets_50M_to_extend_streetc/

Lakhani. Nina. 2020. Revealed: Millions of Americans Can't Afford Water as Bills Rise 80% in a Decade. *The Guardian,* June 23. https://www.theguardian.com/us-news/2020/jun/23/millions-of-americans-cant-afford-water-bills-rise

LATF Staff. 2016. Amtrak Upgrades High-Speed Trains With $2.45 Billion Investment. *LATF USA,* August 28. Available at: https://www.latfusa.com/article/2016/8/amtrak-upgrades-high-speed-trains-with-2-45/

Laurino, Antonio and Paolo Beria. 2014. Low-Cost Carriers and Secondary Airports: Three Experiences from Italy. *Journal of Destination Marketing & Management* 3: 180–191.

Lawrence, Brenda, Rep. 2019. *House Resolution 1417 Water Affordability, Transparency, Equity, and Reliability Act of 2019.* U.S House of Representatives. Available at: https://www.congress.gov/bill/116th-congress/house-bill/1417/cosponsors?searchResultViewType=expanded

Lieh, Kara. 2021. Big MTA Earners Got More Than $200,000 in OT in 2020 — But Overtime Closer to Budget Than Before. *New York Daily Mail*, March 13. Available at: https://thenewyorkmail.com/local/big-mta-earners-got-more-than-200000-in-ot-in-2020-but-overtime-closer-to-budget-than-before/

Malaska, David. 2011. After Setback, City Mulls Smaller Streetcar System. *CityBeat*, March 30. Available at: http://www.citybeat.com/cincinnati/article-23004-after-setback-city-mulls-smaller-streetcar-system.html

McKinnon, Alan. 2015. *Distribution by Drone: In Green Logistics Improving the Environmental Sustainability of Logistics.* 3rd Edition, p. 448. Kogan.

McManus, Tracey, Kirby Wilson and C. T. Bowen. 2021. St. Petersburg Republican Wants to Derail Regional Transit Agency. *Tampa Bay Times*, February 12. https://www.tampabay.com/news/transportation/2021/02/11/st-petersburg-republican-wants-to-derail-regional-transit-agency/

Moore, Janet. 2019. Supporters Push for Bottineau Blue Line Light-Rail Project. *Star Tribune,* July 17. Available at: https://www.startribune.com/supporters-push-for-bottineau-blue-line-light-rail-project/512849812/

Moore, Janet. 2020. Move to Again Engage BNSF Railway on Bottineau LRT Project Fails. *Star Tribune,* August 13. Available at: Available at: https://www.startribune.com/move-to-again-engage-bnsf-railway-on-bottineau-lrt-project-fails/572103502/

Murphy, Ryan. 2021. Overhaul of Norfolk's Bus System Rejected Over Concerns about Effects on Poor and Black Residents. *The Virginian-Pilot*, March 16. Available at: https://news.yahoo.com/overhaul-norfolk-bus-system-rejected-173000636.html

National Conference of State Legislatures (NCSL). 2021. Initiative and Referendum States. Available at: https://www.ncsl.org/research/elections-and-campaigns/chart-of-the-initiative-states.aspx (Accessed June 24, 2021)/

Naylor, Brian. 2009. Stimulus Puts High-Speed Rail On The Fast Track. *NPR Morning Edition*, February 24. Available at: https://www.npr.org/templates/story/story.php?storyId=101073906&t=1602433956345

Nessen, Stephen. 2021. Subway Trains Are Going Faster As MTA Upgrades Century-Old Signals. *The Gothamist*, March 23. Available at: https://gothamist.com/news/subway-trains-are-going-faster-mta-replaces-century-old-signals

Orlove, Raphael. 2018. There's Finally a Song About Dollar Vans and It Slaps. *Jalopnik*, December 31. Available at: Available at: https://jalopnik.com/theres-finally-a-song-about-dollar-vans-and-it-slaps-1831399515

Phillips, Zachary. 2021. Feds study Baltimore-Washington Maglev Train Route. *Construction Dive,* January 28. Available at: https://www.constructiondive.com/news/feds-study-baltimore-washington-maglev-train-route/594131/

PR Newswire. 2020. Press Release: Labor and Community Groups Sign Landmark Community Benefits Agreement with Proterra. December 23. Available at: https://www.prnewswire.com/news-releases/labor-and-community-groups-sign-landmark-community-benefits-agreement-with-proterra-301197935.html

Rash, Wayne. 2021. Amtrak Names Siemens Mobility Preferred Bidder for New Train Equipment. *Forbes*. April 21. Available at: https://www.forbes.com/sites/waynerash/2021/04/21/amtrak-names-seimens-mobility-preferred-bidder-for-new-train-equipment/?sh=39f80907f7b3

Reiss, Aaron. 2020. New York's Shadow Transit. *The New Yorker.* Available at: https://projects.newyorker.com/story/nyc-dollar-vans/

Reuters. 2021. French Lawmakers Approve a Ban on Short Domestic Flights. April 11. Available at: https://www.reuters.com/business/environment/french-lawmakers-approve-ban-short-domestic-flights-2021-04-11/

Rosenthal, Brian M. 2017. The Most Expensive Mile of Subway Track on Earth. *The New York Times*, December 28. Available at: https://nyti.ms/2pR3IlH

Ryan, Greg. 2020a. MBTA's new Orange, Red Line Cars Face Another Big Delay. *Boston Business Journal.* October 5. Available at: https://www.bizjournals.com/boston/news/2020/10/05/mbta-orange-red-line-cars-face-another-big-delay.html

Ryan, Dan. 2020b. Center City Connector on Hold Again Amid Fresh Funding Gaps. *Seattle Transit Blog.* June 25. Available at: https://seattletransitblog.com/2020/06/25/streetcar-on-hold-again/

Schwieterman, Joseph P., and Jessica Kupets. 2014. Back on Track: Initiatives to Restore Rail Service to U.S. Towns and Cities 2004-2020. *Chaddick Institute Working Paper.* September 29.

Schwieterman, Joseph, Brian Antolin and Crystal Bell. 2021. On the Brink: 2021 Outlook for the Intercity Bus Industry in the United States. *Chaddick Institute.* January 30.

Silk, Robert. 2016. Training rule blamed for pilot shortage. *Travel Weekly*, January 19. Available at: https://www.travelweekly.com/Travel-News/Airline-News/Training-rule-blamed-for-pilot-deficit

Simes, Randy A. 2011. Cincinnati to Break Ground on Smaller Streetcar Starter Route this Fall. *UrbanCincy,* May 3. Available at: https://www.urbancincy.com/2011/05/cincinnati-to-break-ground-on-smaller-streetcar-starter-route-this-fall/

Sofield, Tom, 2021. On-Demand, Late-Night Public Transit Coming To Lower Bucks County. *Levittown.com*, May 6. Available at: http://levittownnow.com/2021/05/06/on-demand-late-night-public-transit-coming-to-lower-bucks-county/

Spieler, Christof. 2018. *Trains, Buses, People: An Opinionated Atlas of US Transit.* Island Press.

Staff. 2018. Report: Metro Carmaker Kawasaki Could Exit Rail Business. *Trains*, November 5. Available at: https://trn.trains.com/news/news-wire/2018/11/05-report-metro-carmaker-kawasaki-could-exit-rail-business

Stancill, Jane. 2019. Thanks to Duke, Durham' Light Rail Dream Is All But Dead. *Bloomberg CityLab*, March 14. Available at: https://www.bloomberg.com/news/articles/2019-03-14/why-duke-killed-the-durham-orange-light-rail-project

Taylor, Ian and Lynn Sloman. 2014. Building a World-class Bus System for Britain Extended Summary Report. *TfQL Community Interest Company*, March 16. Available at: http://www.transportforqualityoflife.com/u/files/160314_Building_a_World-class_Bus_System_extended%20summary%20report_FINAL4_for_web.pdf

Transit Workers Local (TWU). 100. 2020. Prescription Benefits at TA/OA/MTA Bus. Available at: http://www.twulocal100.org/story/prescription-benefits-taoamta-bus (Accessed December 1, 2020).

U.K. Department for Transport (DfT). 2006. *Putting Passengers First: The Government's Proposals for a Modernised National Framework for Bus Services*. December. Available at: http://webarchive.nationalarchives.gov.uk/20090806013054/http:/www.dft.gov.uk/pgr/regional/buses/secputtingpassengersfirst/pdf-puttingpassfirst.pdf

U.K. Department for Transport (DfT). 2012. *Reforming Our Railways: Putting the Customer First*. Presented to Parliament by the Secretary of State for Transport, March. Available at: https://www.gov.uk/government/uploads/system/uploads/attachment_data/file/4216/reforming-our-railways.pdf

Urban Blue-Green Grids. 2021. Hammarby Shöstad, Stockholm, Sweden. Available at: https://www.urbangreenbluegrids.com/projects/hammarby-sjostad-stockholm-sweden/

Uyeda, Ray Levy. 2021. A Bleak Future for Water. *The Baffler*. February 18. Available at: https://thebaffler.com/latest/a-bleak-future-for-water-levy-uyeda?utm_source=Baffler+Readers&utm_campaign=9e6bbb552f-TYS_02202021&utm_medium=email&utm_term=0_3541d01f8a-9e6bbb552f-46816556

Vivier, Jean and Mohamed Mezghani. 2001. The Millennium Cities Database: A Tool for Sustainable Mobility International Association of Public Transport (UITP) and European Council for an Energy Efficient Economy (ECEEE). Available at: https://www.eceee.org/library/conference_proceedings/eceee_Summer_Studies/2001/Panel_3/p3_5/

Vuchic, Vukan R. 2007b. *Urban Transit: Systems and Technology. Chapter 4. Transit System Performance: Capacity, Productivity, Efficiency, and Utilization* (pp. 149–201). Wiley.

Weisbrod, Glen. 2015. Estimating Wider Economic Impacts in Transport Project Prioritisation from Ex Post Analysis. *International Transport Forum-OECD*. November 10. Available at: https://www.itf-oecd.org/sites/default/files/docs/weisbrod_presentation.pdf

Whalen, Andrew. 2020. NYC Cuts Parks Budget by 14% When People Say They Need Them Most. *Newsweek*. July 2. *https://www.newsweek.com/nyc-budget-cuts-parks-department-new-york-city-council-mayor-de-blasio-1515160*

Wickert, David. 2018. Atlanta Gambles on Expansion Amid Declining Transit Use. *Atlanta Journal-Constitution*, June 12. Available at: https://www.ajc.com/news/local-govt—politics/atlanta-gambles-marta-expansion-amid-declining-transit-use/df7NwwbopQmkuueHHJm40I/

Wire, staff reports. 2016. Amtrak Secures $2.45B Loan. *Times Union* (Albany NY). August 26. Available at: https://www.timesunion.com/business/article/Amtrak-secures-2-45B-loan-9187588.php

Zahniser, David and Laura J. Nelson. 2021. Newsom Offers $1 Billion to Complete 'Critical' Transit Projects Before 2028 Olympics. *The Los Angeles Times*. May 15. Available at: https://www.latimes.com/california/story/2021-05-15/newsom-billion-dollars-2028-olympics-la-transportation

7

DUAL ECONOMY AND INSTITUTIONS COMPETING WITH PUBLIC WORKS

The bigger picture of how funding decisions are made is that there are multiple competing claims on the public resources besides public works and services that are dependent upon major investment in public works. This chapter describes the context in which urban elected officials and public institutions under their guidance choose and prioritize their budgets.

Urban planning in the USA: A product of party duopoly

Just as with all other aspects of governance in the USA, the reality for urban politics is that there are only two significant political parties. Roughly speaking, the Democrats control most of the levers in the big cities, except for sometimes the important exception of the mayor. Meanwhile, the Republicans control many smaller satellite cities and surrounding county governments. This makes regional plans quite challenging. Then to further complicate planning, there may be more than one state government involved, not just in bigger cities like New York City, Philadelphia, and Washington, D.C., but medium-sized cities like Portland, Oregon and Kansas City, and some smaller agglomerations like the Quad Cities. The state government may be dominated by Republicans but that does not mean that those who represent rural interests are aligned with fellow Republicans with suburban concerns. (Because of the recent 2020 Census the undemocratic domination of state governments by rural Republicans is expected to intensify.)

In recognition of the unwieldiness of planning in the face of such limited cohesiveness, the federal government required the creation of the new institution of the Metropolitan Planning Organizations (MPO) With the passage of the Federal Aid Highway Act of 1962 in which candidate projects were required to be placed on the MPO's Long-Range Transportation Plan (LRTP). To enforce better long-term planning, a requirement for the MPO to develop a Transportation Improvement Program (TIP) was instituted in 1975 as part of FHWA-UMTA Joint Regulations on Urban Transportation Planning. Without this, it would not be possible to get matching funds or access specific formula programs. This forced a certain degree of cooperation, at least in principle. MPOs would be granted authority to do independent, official analyses using mathematical models on questions such as whether a new project saves enough travel time or reduces congestion. With the landmark National Environmental Policy Act of 1969, further concerns would continually be added to the list of items to be studied. Particularly contentious were questions

DOI: 10.4324/9781003245704-7

like whether a finished project would degrade air quality or aggravate congestion. This was not necessarily limited to a transport or other publics work project, *per se*, but applied to any project that might strain the existing infrastructure. A mall with huge parking lots, for example, might not only overload intersections but cause flooding due to large impervious surfaces.

These analytic results are inputs into Environmental Impact Statements (EIS) and cost versus benefit computations used to justify a project. Over the years, procedures used have been enhanced to include more factors in the EIS and to broaden the cost versus benefit analysis to try to take into account factors that cannot be monetized, that is, expressed in monetary terms. There are also public participation requirements in response to anger over freeways rammed through thriving neighborhoods starting in the 1950s. "Environmental justice" must now also be considered, in response to some communities getting most of the negative impacts but not many of the positive ones, waste incinerators located in the poorest cities being a good example. But environmental justice compliance can be a hard thing to measure and agree upon and thus difficult to litigate, especially if federal funds are not used. Think of Chester, Pennsylvania where in further proof of the vulnerability of some communities, there are no sound walls along Interstate 95 that severs it, but there is a huge waste incinerator adding to the emissions of the freeway.

Metropolitan planning organizations (MPOs) and their impotence

As a result of the evolving regulations, there are tools to block or at least mitigate some of the most egregious proposed public works projects. But whether MPOs can actually help to promote a more equal distribution of worthy projects is a different question. Much of what is on the TIP might be no more than a wish list. State governments receive approximately $50B in Federal formula funding for transportation every year, and more with the new infrastructure bill. They can simply refuse to pass money along. One reform that has been sought over the years by many alternative transportation and environmental advocates is the direct apportionment of these federal formula funds to a region defined by an MPO rather than to a state government.

There are some highly publicized cases such as Governor Kasich of Ohio where he returned $375 million the previous Governor obtained from the 2009 infrastructure initiative to build a rail passenger line connecting Cincinnati, Columbus, and Cleveland (Editorial Board 2021). He also succeeded in diverting $52M won by the city of Cincinnati in a competition with other cities to a rural bridge instead (Vock 2011) even though the starter streetcar line for Cincinnati was ranked higher by a state-sponsored commission. But these kinds of blatant examples miss the bigger point. The State has an effective veto over projects on an MPO's list and the list is edited accordingly. Better to get some money at least for rebuilding a dilapidated freeway that traverses the region than to get nothing if one insists on, say, a Light Rail Transit (LRT) line or bus lanes instead.

Case study: Larry Hogan is very popular despite blatant racism and anti-environmentalism

Republican Governor Larry Hogan is quite popular with an approval rating of over 70 percent at the time I wrote this in late 2020 (CBS Baltimore 2020). This despite Maryland containing the large city of Baltimore and Prince Georges County, a suburb of Washington. Both have large percentages of African-American residents. This also despite that by no imaginable criteria can he be considered a good steward of the environment, something that so many of those working in "symbolic analyst" jobs, to use Robert Reich's term, in the prosperous suburbs of D.C. and Baltimore claim to value. For instance, Hogan has been promoting widening sections of Interstates 495 and 95, better known as The Beltway, by two lanes in each direction, also widening Interstate 270, the spur heading toward Frederick, by one lane in each direction (Rowlands 2018). These are already very wide rights-of-way and will certainly need condemnation of property and major modifications to the crossing roads.

FIGURE 7.1 View south along Interstate 270 (Washington National Pike) from the overpass for the ramp from southbound Interstate 270 to eastbound Interstate 370 in Gaithersburg, Montgomery County, Maryland.

Credit: Famartin - CC BY-SA 4.0.

FIGURE 7.2 Freeway through San Francisco – building tall instead of wide.

Credit; Jeffrey Kenworthy.

Highway widenings are clearly seen as a net benefit to Hogan despite the ire they were sure to raise from a significant part of the population. Transit, on the other hand, is seen mostly as an expense. When Hogan came into office in 2015, he tried for a brief while to cancel the Purple Line, a recently planned LRT line that would travel tangentially from Bethesda in Montgomery County through Silver Spring and the University of Maryland and on to New Carrollton in Prince Georges County and interconnect three Metro lines. He did succeed in cutting the State's contribution to the budget by shifting more of the cost to the counties, but he did not have the political muscle to really kill this project.

The communities looking forward to the Red Line in Baltimore were not so lucky. It was a long line at over 16 miles (26 kms) that could have been transformative to many of the residents. Baltimore lacks a reasonably fast way to go east-west across the city. Buses are slow and it is therefore hard to access jobs without a car. The project involved some tunneling in the central area which raised the construction expense, but this was carefully studied (Campbell 2020). There was no other way to maintain a competitive speed though a built-up central area with tall buildings. It was most certainly not a "boondoggle" like Governor Hogan claimed. Almost $300 million had already been spent on public hearings, feasibility studies and preliminary design, and a funding agreement promising matching funds of $900 million from the Feds had already been signed. The fact that the governor had the power to unilaterally cancel such a project that was already so far along based strictly on a personal, unsubstantiated opinion reveals the impotence of the MPO process as well as all of the elected officials and community groups that invested years in to what they thought was an official process that had been successfully executed.

There was some effort by the NAACP Legal and Educational Defense Fund and others to fight this decision. A complaint charging racial discrimination was filed with the US Department of Transportation in late 2015 (Legal Defense Fund 2015). The incoming Trump Administration dropped the investigation in 2017. This was always going to be a shaky proposition. It is perfectly legal to deprive a city of investment for decades because people are poor or because they vote Democratic, which is what the constituency most adversely affected by cancellation of the Red Line also were in addition to being racial minorities (Levy 2017). Which brings us back to why someone like Hogan could be so popular. He has the traditional rural Republican constituency who have been promised more roads with the saved money, and there was the traditional suburban/Republican and city/Democratic divide around the city of Baltimore. Hogan won by a 21-point margin in the Baltimore suburbs. But to get to 70 percent statewide means that many in the affluent Washington suburbs within Montgomery County approve of him as well. Higher density housing is something that many of them oppose in their own backyard (Appelbaum 2019) but would be essential if population were to be absorbed based on increased transit use instead of bigger freeways.

Ben Jealous, the former National President of the NAACP, ran against Hogan for Governor of Maryland, advocating for more racial and environmental justice in public investment. Hogan was re-elected at the end of 2018, against the tide of other Republicans who lost their governorships. Some of Hogan's popularity was no doubt due to his anti-Trump stance. But if so, it only proves the hypocrisy of the ostensibly liberal members of the upper tier who overlook his extreme anti-environmental and anti-central city policies and proposals.

Sprawl requires Ponzi scheme financing

Financing of the infrastructure that enables development across green fields involves two levels. The higher level is the major arterials, pipelines, and power lines that will require participation by publicly directed construction agencies and utilities. On the lower level comes the individual housing projects, office parks, shopping malls, and so on. Much of the upfront cost of the lower level is imbedded in the sales and rental prices of the private developers. Impact fees and other such charges by governments to developers for infrastructure connections and for environmental remediation must also be imbedded.

This might seem like it follows the user pays principle, but it really doesn't. The missing ingredient is the ongoing operating and maintenance costs. These become the responsibility of the local government. As sprawl continues for decades, the number of lane-kilometers, the length of water mains, the length of sewer pipes, the number and capacity of wastewater treatment plants, and so on, keeps increasing. But ongoing monthly charges for utilities is inadequate to catch up with the backlog of aging property. Meanwhile, the gasoline and diesel taxes are usually charged on a per gallon basis instead of percentage of value like most taxes, so the true purchasing power goes down substantially when politicians refuse to raise this tax for decades. The Federal gasoline tax is unchanged at 18.4 cents per gallon since 1993. At the nationwide level, only between 40 and 50 percent of the direct costs of highway and road system construction, operations and maintenance are covered due to the low taxes compared to other countries with similar income levels. Quite a few states also went for decades without tax increases as well, in fact ten (10) did not for over 30 years (Davis 2020). Thirty-six (36) have increased their gasoline taxes only in the last ten years when the pressure from various industries became overwhelming and it was clear that Congress was not going to act. Even the reactionary National Chamber of Commerce has long been supporting an increase in the national gasoline tax.

This pressure to raise gasoline taxes included the players who need more development areas to be opened up by new and widened arterials. The highway and construction lobbies also clamor for more paving and pipe laying. The gasoline tax collected at the state level is frequently used for further expansion to make new suburbs rather than maintaining what is already there. In the period from 2009 to 2014 the amount spent by state-level governments on road repair was almost identical to that spent on road expansion at \$21.4B versus \$21.3B (T4America and Taxpayers for Common Sense 2019). Then the impact and other such fees and part of the utility charges collected enable the next neighborhood to be connected into the network rather than plough it back into maintenance and remediation of what already exists. As discussed in an earlier chapter, there is still a widespread belief that highway users cover their costs which no doubt helps what Charles Marohn of *Strongtowns* has described as a Ponzi scheme (Marohn 2011; Herriges 2018) to continue and explains why the maintenance backlog is not clearing.

Alternative transportation advocacy groups like *Transportation4America* (T4America) have been trying to get a provision into the latest federal transportation spending authorization related bills mandating that repair is prioritized over new construction with no success. Similarly, organizations are trying something similar for some of the state governments. In fact, it is hard to change since this whole suburban funding mechanism is a well-entrenched one that benefits many interests. One can see the central importance of new construction to the modern economy by "New Residential Construction" as an indicator of economic health in the Census Bureau statistics. The economy is expected to see to the ongoing care and feeding of developers, architects, engineers, construction companies, and so on, occasionally interrupted by a recession. Elected officials avoid having to do anything unpleasant like declaring that taxes are too low or that sprawl needs to be stopped as it is unaffordable. These backlogs and land consumption are long-run problems for others to handle. In the meanwhile, a "sprawl-construction complex" continues to work well for a professional class and select workers who migrate from project to project for decades on end.

Some victories have been scored by parties who are trying to contain sprawl, create more affordable housing, and improve the viability of using transit, walking, bicycling and so on. One strategy is to try to divert new housing construction back into the existing city. Portland,

Oregon was long a leader due to its regional government that could better manage the conflicts between the cities in the three member counties. It could also enforce an urban boundary. Other cities like Philadelphia and Seattle have managed to remove minimum parking requirements which were making small apartment blocks using vacant lots unviable. Minneapolis has removed all single-family zoning (Trickey 2019). Very recently, Portland, Oregon maintained its leadership by making it legal to build up to four residences on one lot that used to have only one single family unit (Andersen 2020). But it is not clear that these victories will continue. There was a new vote scheduled for November 2020 for the first time in 30 years that would permit a major transit expansion across Metro Portland. It would increase the payroll tax and was attracting "against" campaign donations from major corporations in the suburbs with many upper-tier employees and auto-dependent lifestyles. It lost (Maus 2020).

Existing cities that succeed in changing their zoning rules can then encounter new problems because densification means there will be more cars, a lot more, if there is no improvement in transit and non-motorized options. Cities generally do not have the financial means to make the commensurate capacity increases in transit and non-motorized facilities. They are probably already using some of the new property tax revenue to maintain roads since the gas tax is so low. There is a lot of competition for use of the property tax revenue as schools, sewers, parks, etc., are also dependent upon them. Transit expansion and upgrades will usually instead need an increase in the local sales tax or property tax, indeed essential in a state that has a legislature that refuses to help transit, walking or bicycling. Even if the state is willing to help, matching funds from the Feds can take a long time and will not contribute to quick relief.

A lot has been written about how existing property owners are selfish NIMBYs. Perhaps some are, but many also have legitimate grievances. Many of them have no other wealth than their house and understandably do not want anything nearby that will devaluate it. (In many cases, they misunderstand the situation and do not realize that more density but with better transit and walking options might increase their house value.) Their concerns about increased traffic and lack of places to park are not imaginary either when there has been no investment for decades and none announced. More density where schools may already be overcrowded with no expectation of additional classrooms understandably engenders opposition. Solutions to these problems in the existing city are not always forthcoming. Indeed, it seems that many elected officials prefer the old ways of donors and developers coming to them for zoning variances and special requests, known as aldermanic or councilmanic privilege (Grabar 2021).

The upper-tier residents have options; if they cannot get satisfaction, they can move to another more agreeable location, send their children to private schools, or, if they really like the enclave where they are, they have the means to pool resources and put up a determined and effective opposition. This can be behind the scenes but is sometimes visible through the creation of concerned citizen groups. The city government of prosperous Chevy Chase, Maryland opposed the previously mentioned Purple Line (Bowen 2013; Action Committee for Transit 2020) for a multiplicity of reasons, including that the "rails to trails" right-of-way should not go back to rails. The also prosperous Beverly Hills Unified School District spent $1m of the school budget opposing the Metro tunnel to be built under Beverly Hills High School (Linton 2020). A notice for an opposition meeting for the new Brightline intercity railroad in south Florida boasted that the retired CEO of American Airlines would be in attendance (Sorentrue 2018). Indian River County along this corridor spent taxpayer money opposing this line on the grounds that it was an improper use of federal bonding assistance to help a private investor. The Supreme Court refused to hear it (Solomon 2020). If a lower court sides with this County, it could yet prove to be a severe blow to the idea of private investment in public works. This could make the Public-Private Partnership (PPP) approach to public works dependent upon the laws of individual states and engender more delays for any required legislative changes if not outright cancellation in particular states.

Once in a while, there are simultaneous efforts to promote a highway and a transit expansion at the same time. Usually, they are entirely different efforts with entirely different funding sources and timelines. This deprives the public of a chance to make a comparison and a vote that involves alternative uses of their own taxes. Such is the case with the Austin Project Connect in November 2020. Like the aforementioned Nashville case, the transit alternative required a vote on a local tax increase combined with federal matching funds (Egan 2020; King 2020; Jankowski 2020a). And like Nashville it had a lot of endorsements including the major newspaper (American Statesman Editorial Board 2020). The Austin transit project ended up winning by a 58 percent majority (Oldman 2020; Jankowski 2020b). Meanwhile, the Texas DoT was also promoting the widening of Interstate 35 through the heart of town but it would not require a funding vote. Based on what usually happens it will get a higher percentage of federal matching funds (80 percent) than the transit project (50 percent), should it go forward.

Opposition to the transit proposal was well organized. They will have had two opportunities to stop transit – once before the vote and now with lawsuits. The highway project can still go forward with the legal backing of the state to defend their EIS with a few revisions, even if the transit project does too. If so, the highway opposition will most likely have only privately funded lawsuits and receive little legal help at public expense, barring some massive overturning of the Texas state legislature.

Expansion consumes sources of nearby supplies

Further costs are created in the logistical system by the continual expansion of the urban boundary, if one can even use that term when there is no official recognition of such a concept. Average pickup and delivery distances become longer, raising the Total Logistics Cost for many industries. Sources of supply must shift outwards for many food and forestry items that used to be quite local but disappear as roads and houses cover farmland and forests. Many cities were located in particular regions precisely because they had exceptionally fertile soils and they also needed little or no irrigation. So, displacement outwards also might create the need for larger plots of less productive land, more fertilization and perhaps even some irrigation. Some of this land might be hundreds or even thousands of miles away, converting what used to be day trip deliveries to long excursions on large semi-trailer trucks and trains from places like the Central Valley in California.

One interesting research question is whether it would be worthwhile to convert some suburban and exurban sprawled development back into farms and forests but interspersed with people who want to stay where they are. It might well be that the costs of demolishing and replacing so much housing stock are more than offset by the gains. The conclusions would depend not just on the monetary costs and benefits that can be enumerated, but by the environmental and recreational benefits that are harder to quantify. For wetlands, the case will be strong for undoing any infill as wetlands are nature's flood control and water treatment systems that can obviate the need for artificial constructions.

Comparison to Finland about urban planning

Helsinki has undergone quite rapid population growth for the last decade. A lot of housing space was made available by relocating the two container ports to one consolidated port on the eastern edge of town. In one of the newly liberated locations, an existing streetcar line was extended before the first apartment building was completed as a signal that new owners could depend on transit. The other location had a metro line running through it, over which skyscrapers were allowed. Bus lines were extended beyond the current build out point, once again signaling the permanence of transit service. And the new metro extension to the western suburban town of Espoo and new regional train loop to the northern suburban town of Vantaa and the airport were both designed based on focusing the building of apartments at their new stations. Development opportunities are distributed to all regional municipalities and transit funding is linked. In fact, these rail transit projects can only be justified assuming that the new housing will create demand.

Land consumption on the perimeter is minimized by focusing most new housing starts along the new rail lines. The local municipalities have a monopoly on urban planning within their own boundaries. They are much less likely to respond to pressure from developer interest in sprawl inducing locations because a national Building and Land Use Act forbids the construction of major developments away from existing and planned highway and transit corridors. The municipalities can and have been sued by the national government over poorly located projects.

Comparison to the UK about urban planning

The UK is an interesting case by European standards as it has an exceptionally powerful Central Government. There are some regional planning organizations, but their powers are quite restricted with the exception of Transport for London (TfL) which retained the right to plan and price its network of public transport offerings. The Central Government can enforce its will on cities and the shires because of the lack of formula programs to distribute infrastructure funds to regions. It has outright denied cities permission to build rail transit because it would compete with private bus companies, let alone help to finance it. Northern England is a stark contrast to the Southeast. The UK Central Government has largely declined to do some of the things that other countries have done to try to slow the depopulation of depressed areas, such as relocating teaching hospitals and research universities and investing in their regional transport. To the contrary, the deregulated intercity train and bus services have made it quite expensive to travel, further incentivizing the relocation of businesses toward London and isolating family members from each other.

There has been some recognition by the government of the dissatisfaction with local transit offerings outside of the Southeast under the current regime of a mostly unsubsidized and unregulated business. There are a few exceptions for services deemed socially necessary implying that transit in general is not. Quality Bus partnerships is an example of making minor infrastructure investments that competing private operators are not inclined to do because of the well-known "free-rider" problem (rider meaning competitor not passenger). But this is a pittance compared to the one place that has received massive support in the last decade, the London metro region. By some measures, *CrossRail* has been the single largest public works project in the world. It is nearing completion after many delays (Smith 2020) with its centerpiece being the new Elizabeth Line that will finally relieve the Central Line as a rapid means across central London and open up reduced commuting possibilities in many areas both east and west of London. It has been needed for many decades. A cynic might think the real reason for finally financing this line was to increase the value of land along the corridor, not improving the functioning of the city. The last time there was a major new line, the Jubilee Line extension which opened in 2000, it cost the taxpayers £4B but increased the value of land by £13B, none of which was recaptured by the taxpayers (Riley 2001). The HSR2, discussed in the previous chapter, given the very modest support of urban transit projects that would connect to it, seems best explained by land value increases and perhaps by construction interests salivating over the huge cost at least four times *CrossRail*. If the Central Government took opportunity costs into consideration, there are quite a few projects that would clearly provide better value for money.

The UK does bear some resemblance to the USA in its overconcentration of economic activity. At least in the USA there are several hotspots with different climates for those who are trying to find better paying jobs. In the UK it reaches an extreme level with primarily the Southeast (greater London area) and the Southwest booming and much of the rest of the country depressed. The planning deficit is leading to a wasting away of existing housing and infrastructure in much of the country while there is a chronic affordable housing shortage and severe congestion around London. A systematic analysis of how the relative value of land from one region to the next is connected with housing pricing is provided by Ryan-Collins et al. (2017) in the context of the UK, in particular.

Public schools in the USA – a large topic in itself

There must be some generalizations made in order to keep the length of this discussion in line with the remaining sections. One must really investigate one's own state's history, particularly the funding connection between the state and local level if one wants an accurate picture of how much money is distributed and with what purposes in mind.

Overreliance on local funding

Public schools are one the largest expenditures for the taxpayers of urban areas. The schools may not necessarily correspond exactly with municipal boundaries. They may be organized in districts which include cities and unincorporated areas, so direct comparisons of budgets between cities can be misleading. Furthermore, the mix of funding from the state and local governments varies (Maciag 2020; The Share Team 2020). But if a generalization can be made, it is that much of the funding is local, reaching over 50 percent of the total in some cases. In 2014, the nationwide average for local funding was 47 percent, but it should be noted that some state governments inject far more additional funds to struggling local districts than others and in some cases local funding is dominant. Another generalization is that total government commitment to education spending has not always recovered from the 2008 crash budget cuts even if the state economy has recovered (Pew Trusts 2019). This heavy reliance on a local tax base is not the case in most of the richer countries and explains the large differences in per capita funding often seen between schools in the same metro area. Property taxes are a key source of local funding, putting the schools in competition with other basic public works needs.

Most of the cost is in day-to-day operating labor, the instructional and support staff. In some of the bigger cities, like New York, it can reach almost 70 percent. In this way, it is quite similar to transit. The very high cost is in part because of the healthcare benefit. Like transit, an educational agency is paying for something that another public agency would cover in countries with national/provincial healthcare systems. But it is only covering it better for some government workers. It simply is not correct to make the generalization that teachers are underpaid. It varies a great deal from state to state and location to location within a state. And it can vary by seniority, with high turnover of beginning teachers who are not paid as well. There is often an upper-tier constituency of teachers who can vote and give campaign donations as a block while other school employees receiving poorer benefits are not part of this machine.

While the nucleus of schools is the teachers and their assistants, there is a significant need for periodic repair and upgrade and replacement of facilities. The US Government Accountability Office (GAO) did a survey in 2020 including site visits in six states and found that over half of the school districts they visited needed major work on Heating Ventilating and Air Conditioning (HVAC) systems and have needed it for years. The students, faculty and staff are now really paying the price for this neglect during the Covid-19 epidemic. School buses do not get the same level of technical support from the federal government as transit. If they did, they would combine emissions reduction in a systems approach. They are also in need of upgrades to protect student health. More on this in the chapter on suggestions.

Other repairs, upgrades and building replacements are needed too, but the GAO did not compile a monetary estimate for the nation. Most states do not even compile such data, demonstrating a lack of interest in developing a state plan (GAO 2020). But it clear that the amounts involved are clearly far beyond their ability to clear their backlogs.

In the bigger cities, this type of large-scale project work will be bid out to the private sector and is likely to be done almost exclusively by building trades workers who are also in the upper tier. In some states or rural areas in the same state, the construction pay level might be quite low instead. In North Carolina, it is actually illegal for government agencies to contract with unions (something I thought would be unconstitutional). Because of the wide range of teacher salaries and other labor costs, one of the most common indicators, spending per pupil, can be deceptive. A better rough indicator of school system quality might be average class size for each grade. Furthermore, the lower the grade level, the smaller the class size should be.

Charter schools – diversion of average cost per student instead of marginal cost

Charter schools were originally intended as experimental schools that were given more latitude in their curriculums. Over time they have evolved into what are often very large-scale operations. While they are ostensibly non-profits, they can get around this by contracting with for-profit companies. The amount of money in play with public education being so large, penetration by for-profit firms is inevitable if given the chance by statutory or regulatory changes. Twenty-five (25) states still have not restored funding to pre-2009 levels (Partelow et al. 2019) and lobbyists can say that charter schools obviate the need to fully restore it. Pressure remains to find replacements for traditional teachers due to chronic shortages. It can be quite expensive to hire full-time "brick and mortar" public school teachers in many locations due in large part to them getting better than average health benefits (Allegretto and Mishel 2019). Labor savings can be found by switching from "brick and mortar" schools to online charter schools. Results have generally been inferior to date (Woodworth and Raymond et al. 2015; Longreads 2017). More will be learned about online teaching quality as the analyses of the Covid 19 online teaching surge become available.

The insidious effect of charter schools on public finance is that money is drawn from the public system faster than the costs go down every time a student is transferred over. The marginal cost reduction is minimal until enough students transfer to save one teacher of one subject in one grade. After that, there may be no cost reduction in the fixed costs such as building operations and maintenance even after large numbers of students have transferred out. Yet the full average cost per student might be deducted instead of the marginal cost, thereby rapidly decreasing the spending per remaining student. For the people who remain in public schools taxation is the same, but quality goes down due to larger class size.

Equalizing the quality and tax rates between school districts can mean reductions in quality for some but increases for others. Compensating particular public schools for funding diverted to charter schools will remain largely off the table under existing political alliances since this mostly benefits students in the lower tier whose parents are not influential. So it would be much easier politically to increase total funding for all public schools. But replacing this tax revenue lost to charters and even supplementing it is still going to be hard given the other competition for state funds and local property taxes. If it does succeed, it might be at the expense of the fire department or the parks or public health clinics, or transit, or the libraries, or.......

Academia in the USA: large endowments but paying no property taxes

Universities are heralded as a great thing for a city to have in this era when large scale and heavy manufacturing has left the cities. They are cleaner and involve a lot of creative-class and symbolic analyst jobs. They also do not have the shift changes that clog the streets or the noisy trucks and trains. Furthermore, campuses can serve as surrogates for parks when they have created pedestrian zones which the city itself finds so hard to do. They can improve the housing stock nearby by bringing in students and faculty of better than average means to town as well as research centers that attract even more of this creative class and symbolic analysts.

What is not to like? Well, there is most certainly one big thing. Most of them do not pay property taxes. This is not a small amount of money to forego when they hold large parcels of land in central areas. The historical argument is that they are non-profit organizations providing a vital public service in advancing knowledge that should be encouraged by keeping costs low. Well, there was a time when this might have been true, but low cost is not how one would characterize the services provided by private universities today. Tuition for student education and charges for acute medical care at their medical complexes, two of the most important services, have been increasing faster than the average inflation rate for decades. Both are among the most expensive in the world. Harvard University is nowadays voluntarily paying something in lieu of property taxes to the city of Cambridge, Massachusetts, but it is an exception, no doubt because of the embarrassment of having the world's largest endowment. Which brings us to the next item.

Another thing not to like is that multibillion-dollar endowments are exempt from corporate income tax, again on a historical claim that universities support the advancement and dissemination of knowledge. In a high profile OpEd, Victor Fleischer (2015) brought attention to five universities he researched where fund managers received more money than students received in tuition assistance: Yale, Harvard, Stanford, Princeton, and note the last one, the University of Texas, a public university.

An endowment does indeed permit some new investment in facilities and can be of benefit to more than just those working or studying at the university itself. Nevertheless, many universities clearly look like they could spare some money toward the cities and regions that host them. I noted on a recent visit back to West Philadelphia, where I lived for many years, that a new skyscraper dedicated to medical research for children had sprouted up across the river from the Penn Campus. The iconic Philadelphia Convention Hall and Civic Center is also gone replaced by other research buildings and a landscaped boulevard with a string of parking garages encircled by one way boulevards. These serve to separate the medical workers from the rest of the campus. If this complex had been situated on the Continent somewhere, it would probably long ago have been connected to the subway to integrate the complex into the city fabric and the rest of the Penn campus. The terminus of the PATCO rapid transit line is only 18 short-sided blocks away. (The PATCO system has been neglected at the New Jersey suburban end as well. Veteran planner and rail historian William Vigrass explains that 21 studies or surveys have been performed over 80 years to branch this line to either Burlington or Gloucester and all but one recommended construction (Vigrass 2014)).

Indeed, there were several research centers near to the Children's Hospital of Philadelphia and the adjacent University of Pennsylvania Hospital complex that were not there when I started my studies. The completion of each one came with promises of great advances in medical treatments. Some are only in the research stage, so we do not know if this is true or just hyperbole yet. But some like proton therapy are already available and marketed to those in the upper tier fortunate enough to be able to participate in the University of Pennsylvania Medical System.

FIGURE 7.3 Penn research complex replaces the Philadelphia Conventional Hall and Civic Center. *Credit*: Michelle Rifken.

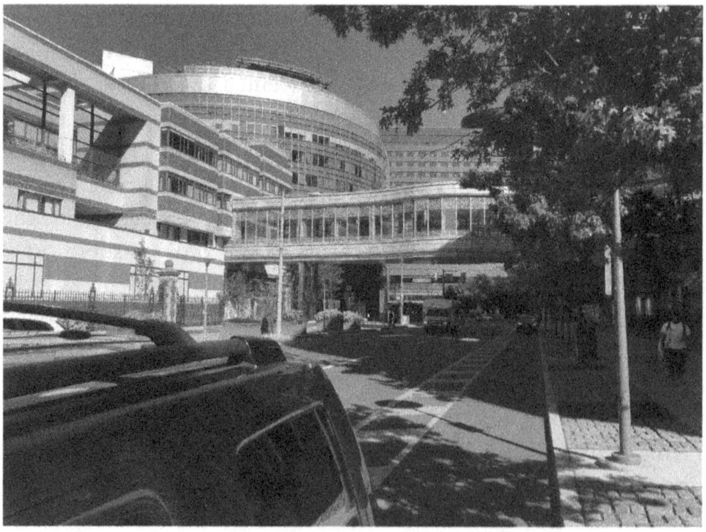

FIGURE 7.4 Connecting parking garages with overpasses and sidewalks to the Penn medical complex. *Credit*: Michelle Rifken.

FIGURE 7.5 Philadelphia Convention Hall and Civic Center at the beginning of demolition circa 2005.

Credit: William Keller.

By comparison, the Philadelphia School District has had a struggle in recent years to keep nurses in its elementary schools due to chronic underfunding. The City was depending upon a local tax base of largely low-income residents thanks to non-paying institutions and tax abatements combined with limited assistance from a stingy legislature. This is not an unusual case, as a visit to New Haven, home of Yale University, or Providence, home of Brown University, or so many others, makes clear. Universities are a case of private affluence beside public squalor, as John Kenneth Galbraith described already in 1958 in his popular book *The Affluent Society*.

Low productivity of tenured and tenure track faculty versus adjuncts

As with transit and public schools, public universities took severe cuts after the 2008 crash. Even before then, there was a long-term trend for state legislatures to trim back their contributions. Given this trend, universities claim they must use more adjunct faculty if they are to limit tuition increases. This is, of course, part of the explanation. Much has also been made of the phenomena of "deanlets" where administrative teams are brought along with an imported Dean and that administrative overhead has been increasing. In response, an official statement from the American Association of University Professors does not deny it but defended this on the grounds of necessity:

> The relative decline in state support for public higher education over the past two decades has contributed to the bloat—the disproportionate increase in nonacademic positions. As universities increasingly compete for students, they invest in various nonacademic positions, activities, and facilities in an effort to attract high paying "customers" (and potential

donors). As these institutions try to increase fund-raising, external grant, auxiliary unit (e.g., residence halls and food services), and technology transfer revenues, they increase positions in these realms.

(AAUP 2010)

Tenure track and tenured full-time faculty are stereotyped to be toward the left politically and indeed one will often hear claims of support from some of them for the plight of adjuncts; it does not seem right that adjuncts must teach multiple courses on multiple campuses without benefits or even knowledge whether their courses will be repeated the next year. So, expressing their concern, full-time faculty generally support increasing public spending on higher education. They see less blame for themselves in this ongoing saga of restructuring where adjuncts and part time faculty now teach about 75 percent of all courses in public universities in the USA (New Faculty Majority 2021). This was based on 2009 statistics and is probably worse now. But have a look at the productivity of the tenured. Depending upon the discipline, full professors earn from $90,000 to over $150,000 for nine months, plus consulting on the side and summer gigs. At the more prestigious private and flagship public universities, faculty typically teach only "2-1" or "2-2," meaning the number of courses over the two semesters. One of these courses is probably a boutique course and another a survey course both of which they have done many times and require little preparation. They will justify this limited teaching load compared to K-12 school teachers and adjuncts by saying they must have time for research. Depending on the field, the reality, however, is that they are spending a good portion of their time looking for research money in a huge national waste of effort competing against each other. The most senior and distinguished researcher is likely to be wasting the most time of all as she/he must be concerned with the care and feeding of his/her laboratory workers or research team.

FIGURE 7.6 Philadelphia Convention Hall and Civic Center showing a cross section of the distinctive arched roof.

Credit: William Keller.

If the tenured were not so comfortably absorbed into the upper tier, they might offer to increase the number of courses they teach and thereby make more full-time faculty slots affordable. After all, they usually have a faculty senate where they could pass such declarations. They could simply say on a vote that we will no longer spend more than X hours per month in a futile effort to obtain research money when there just is not enough to go around. Some could further declare that they have given up finding money for primary research (like almost everybody in my academic fields, for instance) and will use their non-teaching time doing research using secondary data. These are just examples. They are smart people. They could propose measures appropriate to their situations.

Few incentives for urgent interdisciplinary studies for sustainable infrastructure

The incessant search for research money has also meant that the university is drifting away from roles it supposed to play in the community that justify its tax-free and non-profit status in the first place. These include research that has no possibility of commercialization but is urgent and the education of future practitioners in socially necessary fields. I noted a current advertisement for an opening: "PROJECT RESEARCHER (fixed term) in sustainable last mile logistics 01.09.2020–30.8.2023 (part time)," in one of the single most urgent urban research topics with the proliferation of bike sharing, scooters, and online retailers across the world. Alas, it was both part time and only for three years and one must have a PhD. This was at a business school in Helsinki, no less, a city with a reputation for being progressive in urban transport. Another example of an urgent but interdisciplinary topic is urban development modeling that can guide cities on what kinds of urban form for infill and for expansion areas, for regulatory changes, and what kinds of supporting public investment would move them in a more sustainable direction. An example of needed professionals would be experts on public works asset management to preserve public property and to optimize future expansion and replacement plans. These are the kinds of fields that fade away as faculty retire when universities choose their faculty openings based on research funding availability and prestige.

Learning to use software on such topics is probably not a replacement for theoretical instruction. A great pedagogical experiment is underway. Transit system engineering is replaced by autonomous car development, wildlife biology is replaced by molecular biology, mechanical engineering becomes bioengineering and nanoengineering, etc., etc. This author went to AcademicTransfer.com in September and October of 2020 to try to match my background based on my transit-heavy CV with what was currently available with over 450 listings in the Netherlands (CV Match 2020). I was given only two openings that prove my point: "PhD Position Game-Theoretic Control for Multi-Vehicle Automated Driving" and "PhD Position Sustainable Production and Value Chains for Maritime Biofuels."

The intensified chase for money and prestige means that universities have moved toward hiring micro-experts who publish in their micro-journals. Granting of tenure and promotion depend upon becoming a top expert published in the right places and reliably attracting funds. Since I studied mechanical engineering and know the traditional subfields it used to entail, like energy conversion to mechanical work, fluid flows, heat transfer, stresses in components, vibrations, and other issues related to machine design, I picked this discipline to find examples of the kind of academic jobs currently available. *Highered.com* had a small percentage of actual open full-time positions with latitude to work in one of the traditional fields and quite a few that were not openings at all, but just sign-ups on a list for possible openings in the future. Some are close, like two openings at the same school for an assistant professor, but closer inspection suggests it would be better classified as bioengineering (HigherEd Jobs 2020a). Many do not really belong in this discipline but are unrelated specialties put there for budgeting and staffing appearances. One postdoctoral fellowship was to study "human-robotic swarm interaction," much closer to computer science (HigherEd Jobs 2020b). Another postdoc required a PhD in neuroscience, ecology, or biology and "will focus on the use of optogenetics to study free flight odor plume tracking in fruit flies" (HigherEd Jobs 2020c). Several were for development of a very particular type of battery, a field which has no shortage of private capital. This raises another issue which could be a book in itself: where should the line be drawn between university and corporate research?

This movement of universities toward a high degree of specialization is a tragic paradox, as most of the urgent socioeconomic and environmental problems of the world where the brain power of the university could make itself most useful are highly interdisciplinary such as more sustainable yet still democratic cities and agricultural regions. There is a combination of pure science, engineering, human behavioral response, and other social science expertise needed for generating implementable policies. The modern university is poorly suited to this. Aspiring faculty may not get any prestigious academic papers in "high impact" journals out of such projects. Nor are there very many calls for interdisciplinary research proposals instead of silos in the first place. Any search to find money will have even lower probability of success than within their own specialties. Is there any real pressure to change coming from within the full-time faculty itself when it is so difficult to buck the status quo in what are ostensibly sustainability programs? There are some thoughts on how to increase the pressure (Consensus Study Report 2020).

Comparison of academia with Finland and the UK

Despite the supposed heightened concern in Europe for environmental problems, they too have gone in a similar direction of increased specialization. Historically, PhD studies generally have to be funded beforehand without the latitude or requirement for candidates to select and defend their own topic as in the USA. This places restrictions against even the most brilliant students who might otherwise discover an important issue to be researched on their own and propose it. The USA still has more latitude once one is admitted, but one must compete for the few slots in relevant departments that actually have traditional types of funding.

My experience in Finland with the European Commission's Horizon 2020 research program was that it was mostly about technologies with commercial potential, so greener logistics means things like lighter materials for trucks and greener transit means things like alternative fuels. The Finnish national research program under the previous conservative government was similar: premised on the ideas that technological development is what is needed and we can solve most anything if we just unshackle the markets.

During my stay as visiting professor at Aalto University, there happened to be four million Euro newly available from a terminated program that was placed into a competitive Aalto Energy Fund. This seemed promising. For the first round, I assembled an interdisciplinary team from multiple specialties in buildings, power, and public works design and construction, something rare in proposals, even when all are in the same school of engineering. The idea was to study the costs and environmental impacts from infrastructure as a total system that changes as a function of what type of form the city took. We provided evidence that this area was largely unexplored and that there were compelling uses for such a model, such as extensions to cities, contemplated removal and replacement of urban structures, and as a teaching tool. We did not even make the short list. One of the reviewer comments suggested that we should have involved more departments outside of our university. Music or graphic design, perhaps? For the second round of funding, I walked out of the kickoff meeting as this time there was not even a category to which we could apply. Not that I could have reconstructed the team anyway after the embarrassment of asking so much effort from others to no avail.

A few researchers can and do obtain funds from some progressive city governments or public agencies, but this is never going to be adequate as a replacement for large research fund pools distributed by peer review. Local governments and public service delivery agencies do not see themselves in this role. Besides the competing uses for these funds, there is the free rider problem. Why should one city pay for research beneficial to many others as well?

One problem that doesn't exist in Finland is tuition unaffordability. Most students can study free of charge and even get stipends and low interest loans for living expenses. But whether the disciplines they would like to study will be available after permanent faculty are retired and temporary faculty are laid off is a different story. It is a small country and one cannot assume that there will be another school with the program a student wants, unlike the USA. If the policy of basing faculty hiring on prestige and ability to find research funding persists, students might have to leave the country to study a socially needed discipline elsewhere. They may never return.

It is also interesting to note that decades ago, when Finland was not the prosperous country it is today, a student had to pay back part of their subsidy as a percentage of income. It may be unpopular to advocate it, but there is some merit. More people can be admitted to universities for the same budget. It is more equitable since people who do not get the monetary benefit of attending university would not contribute as much financially. This assumes that the university educated will earn higher incomes, something that is not always as true as it once was. It would also provide relief for people willing to work for less since they would have to pay back less. This could incentivize people to do jobs they believe are more socially useful but less remunerative. Or to be more willing to stay in a smaller town that has lower salaries. This can be quite helpful to stem or even reverse migration to larger cities and the social and environmental costs that entails.

The UK is somewhere between the USA and Finland. It used to have free tuition but now charges all students about £9,000 per year, certainly much lower than U.S. private universities and similar to tuition at many public universities. But this amount is the same whether one goes to Oxford, Cambridge, University College London or one's hometown university or trade school without regard to the actual cost of providing the education. This is truly a subsidy to the children of the upper tier of society and acts to reinforce their class system.

Lack of vocational schools

For people who are not going on to college or university educations, there need to other options. Many people would like to work in the building trades or the medical sector, for example. Many others face pressure to get specialized skills even if they are not sure what is they would like to do with their lives. For this, public-owned vocational schools could be a good solution. Private vocational schools seem to work fine for some skills, like pilot training, but have a spotty record in general, leaving students with huge debts. The USA spends about ½ of 1 percent on assistance to adults seeking employment, one-fifth the average of the Organization for Economic Cooperation and Development (OECD) member average. These limited programs tend to be targeted only to specific sub-populations and not open to anyone who happens to feel the need or anticipate their field will fade away (Goger 2020). High permanent unemployment due to a plant closure is not the only logical time and place for retraining.

Vocational schools have increased in their importance as the number of unions that have apprentice programs has diminished. The unions that remain have survived for a reason. They have the ability to do severe damage through a strike, or they have become part of an interest bloc through organized campaign donations and voting, especially during primaries, and/or their skills are not easy or even impossible to outsource to other countries. It should also not be assumed that unions would be interested in up-scaling their apprenticeship programs, as doing so will only drive down wages and reduce overtime opportunities. Indeed, they may be an obstacle to the ramp up of workforces.

Vocational training is one area that has not been competing effectively for public tax expenditures. State supported community colleges remain quite affordable with low tuitions and provide a cost saving path to an eventual university degree and they sometimes have substantial vocational offerings as well. On the other hand, state-level training grants are sometimes just disguised aid to big corporations perhaps as part of a deal to poach companies from elsewhere. Federal formula grants have reduced from about $7 billion to $4.5 billion over the last 20 years, such a tiny amount for a nation of 330 million people (Spiker 2019). This decline has probably not been of high importance to the upper tier as their children don't go to such schools as frequently, while some of the more prosperous unions have their own avenues for training for their own members. And it should be noted that the US Government has some apprentice programs of its own, like machinists for the US Navy, but their retention rate is very high.

If there will be a major increase in spending on public works, and especially if there is a really large-scale effort like the Green New Deal, there will have to be a parallel effort that is

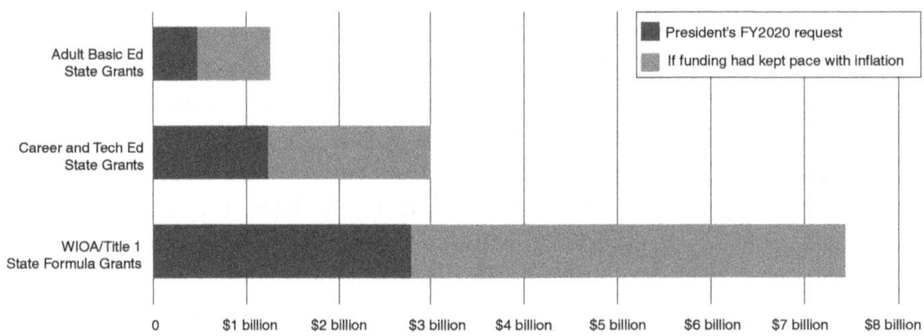

FIGURE 7.7 Federal budget skimps on workforce and education programs.
Source: Spiker (2019); National Skills Coalition.

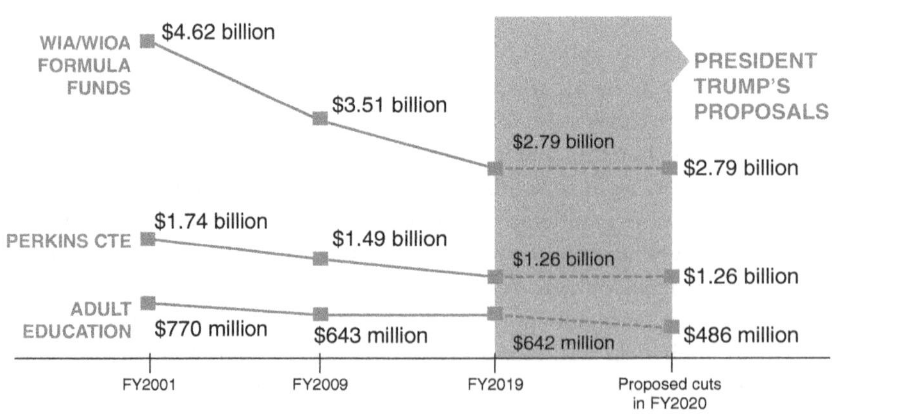

FIGURE 7.8 Three lines showing a steady decline in Work Innovation and Opportunity Act (WIOA) formula funds, Perkins Career and Technical Education (CTE) grants and other federal adult education grants over the last 20 years.
Source: Spiker (2019); National Skills Coalition.

FIGURE 7.9 Two would-be scholars making a statement about their working conditions
Source: Dr Garry Potter; Contract Faculty: Injustice in the University https://www.youtube.com/watch?v=yOB_vUF5Dic&fbclid=IwAR26AIJwGNG1Wu6L-Lamw0SonBxZTuUhlg3Yw7xp5lBdHArrqfMe6nTEhgo

commensurate to provide the work force. Otherwise, the timeline for construction will be too slow to address GHG generation, there will be a huge inflation in construction costs, or both. Because development is over-concentrated in a few metro areas, these areas already have private construction booms and little or no spare capacity. Meanwhile, Federal funding contributions to public sector investments typically place prohibitions on the hiring of locals who are willing to learn at a lower wage, thereby aggravating the capacity shortage. As mentioned in a previous chapter this law is being challenged.

Much will depend on whether concern over deficits continues to hold sway whenever public works spending is discussed at the Federal level. Unlike state and local governments there is no need to balance budgets and the policy paralysis that entails. Modern Monetary Theory (MMT) holds that the accumulated debt of countries with sovereign currencies is irrelevant, that the national deficit is of little concern when interest rates are low, and these same governments can spend up to the point that inflation starts to grow to unacceptable levels (Kelton 2020; Mosler 2010). If MMT begins to gain traction, rather than continued focus on where the money will come from, the real question will be how staffing can be up-scaled on a short timeframe before reaching capacity of the stimulated sectors.

Healthcare in the USA: neither market nor government price regulation

Medical costs in the USA are by far the highest in the world by any measure. One of the most common is as a percentage of the GDP. The USA is now at over 17 percent, most other rich countries are below 10 percent. It is a medical non-system where neither competition nor government regulation is working effectively to control costs. Cost competition does not work when the need for care is urgent. Nor does it work for the consumer when your employer picks your insurance company. The federal government does exert some regulatory pressure on Medicare billing rates and through control of the Veterans Administration, but almost none in the remainder of the medical non-system. Congress has specifically forbidden it to negotiate for the prices of pharmaceuticals it purchases in large volumes, a strategy employed almost everywhere else. This is cited as strong evidence that the majority public interest is not being defended, either because government does not have the power or the will, or a bit of both.

The private portion of US medical expenditures is not perceived as a tax in most comparisons with peer countries. But it has the same effect of reducing disposal income (for those not doing the charging). Both copays and drug prices have been increasing faster than the general rate of inflation for many years. The upper tier tends to have coverage that better shields it from these increases. And professionals working in the medical sector are paid at higher levels than people in other sectors. Quite a few people scoffed when presidential candidate Biden talked about people who like their health insurance, but it was a dog whistle to people who realized they had better coverage and were not paying extra for it.

Lack of effective policy and cost control in the medical sector cuts across how all other public services are provided by both raising the cost structure and by limiting funds available for competing priorities. There is a lot of focus on insurance and pharmaceutical companies as the villains. But these are an incomplete explanation for the ongoing and relentless cost growth. There are others who benefit besides large corporations. Physicians in the USA are paid roughly double what they earn in other peer countries with the average income of general practitioners climbing to $200,000 per year. Dentists have reached an average of $150,000 per year. Specialties range from $240,000 to over $500,000 per year (Tank 2020). The pay is often defended by loan debts, but at these income levels it is not hard to pay them back. And why wouldn't this justify very high pay for the adjunct faculty who spent eight to ten years at the University? They also often have huge debts. Researchers and sales people at pharmaceutical companies can be very well compensated. Their firms can receive National Institutes of Health research funding but also get the benefits of monopoly pricing when the patent is awarded to their firm instead of the government if a drug proves to be a big seller.

Also, true to the dual economy, within the medical system one finds among the lowest paid workers, like the home healthcare assistants who average about $24,000 per year (BLS 2020). Without a national healthcare agency to set staffing standards and wage levels and without professional licenses, their bargaining positions are weak. Registered Nurses can do better, especially if they are unionized, so it would an overgeneralization to say that they are all underpaid. It should also be noted that dental hygienist pay is raised to an average of $58,000 per year because dentists earn so much and can compete for the limited availability of qualified technicians with bachelor's degrees (Chen 2019). One could expect their pay and for other licensed technicians to diminish if vocational and technical school expansions become a national priority but no other reforms occurred, so they have no incentive to increase training opportunities for others.

There are not enough residencies for all of the people seeking them who graduate from US medical schools. Roughly 10 percent go without each year and cannot practice medicine until they do (Tan 2019). Some have had to wait several years. This shortage also makes it harder for persons who graduated overseas from finding positions in the USA and perhaps finding positions in countries like Finland instead, where they are welcomed. The American Medical Association is one of the biggest spenders on lobbying in Washington and should be viewed as a physician's union. Similar to some other unions, they seek to keep pay up by keeping the numbers of qualified people down.

Protectionism also keeps prices high

Unlike the lower-tier workers, the upper-tier workers have not been exposed to the global labor market to anywhere near the same extent. One cannot go to Europe to comparison shop if Medicare or Medicaid is paying the bills. Nor can pharmaceuticals be purchased from abroad, even if it were to save both the patient and employer money. Even so, there is still some medical tourism as the price difference can be so large that it is worthwhile without government or insurance contributions. Arguments justifying such protectionist legislation are not persuasive. Re-importing by oneself from Canada products that may have originated in the USA is somehow a safety issue yet shifting most of the production by US manufacturers to China is not.

The price levels for the medical non system raises the cost of all public services through the cost of insurance for public employees and the cost of running public clinics for those without insurance. It is no doubt one of the reasons why police respond to incidents better covered by psychiatric or other social workers. And, of course, the lack of access to mental health care contributes to the escalation of problems to where families cannot cope with one of their members any longer. It has also contributed toward the public works investment duplication and waste that arises from the abandonment of smaller towns and the migration toward cities. The Chartis Center for Rural Health found that 34 rural hospitals closed in the two-year period between February 2018 and 2020 (The Chartis Group 2020). State and local public health departments have shrunk by more than 56,000 employees nationwide since the recession of 2008 (Milman 2020), something that must have played a role in the chaos of the USA's response to Covid-19 (Farberman and Kelley 2020).

It is much harder to find a job with good health insurance in the rural areas. Between the steady stream of closings and the high pay that physicians can earn in the metro areas where people have better insurance and higher incomes means a shortage of same in the small towns and rural areas. Reversing the outmigration from rural areas and the public investment and growth management issues that it entails for cities and suburbs will probably not occur without a major increase in access and affordability of healthcare.

High incomes, high profits, high untaxed benefits all impede reform

The many players who are doing well by the system do not support many reforms. Sure, there are calls to reduce the insurance paperwork by physicians as it is a pain and requires some staff to deal with it. But this very inefficiency is what enables prices to increase incessantly. The insurance company, drug suppliers, hospital executives and physician practices can all earn more when prices increase in a synergistic fashion. The situation has actually worsened in recent years, with private equity funds getting in on the action by providing emergency room physicians, ambulances, and other vital services for which the "customers" cannot comparison shop (Webb 2019). Bringing in "out of network" specialists are a great profit opportunity and the cause of many of the "surprise bills" (Scofield 2019). And then there is an increase in so-called "concierge" service where one pays a very high retainer for a physician to be on call. Only a little over 20,000 physicians out of about 950,000 belong to Physicians for a National Health Program. Reform will not be coming from the physicians themselves.

It has already been noted several times that select workers have benefits that are far better than others, even working in almost identical jobs. One of the provisions of the Affordable Care Act of 2010 (ACA) was the implementation of a so-called "Cadillac Tax" that recognized that it violated horizontal equity of the tax code that some people could get services untaxed while others had to pay out-of-pocket with after tax income for the same services. The idea was that it would incentivize future labor negotiations toward salary and work rules instead of treating healthcare as something subject to collective bargaining. It would move the country toward healthcare being supplied on equal terms to all workers doing similar jobs with similar skills and wage levels, even if it still was not a basic human right for all. This part of the ACA has still not been implemented and postponed until at least 2022 (Eastman 2019), another strong indication of how difficult it is to reform benefits for the upper tier.

Comparison of healthcare to the UK and to Finland

There is some truth that an aging population and toxins in the environment can put more burden on healthcare providers and these are often offered as excuses for the rising costs in the USA. But surely this is not the whole explanation as other rich countries have aging populations, a legacy of pollution leftover from brownfields and ongoing air pollution as well. But they have not even begun to catch up with the USA on costs. The National Health Service in the UK and *Kela* in Finland have both seen some parallel private for-profit clinics open, and indeed other countries in the EU as well. This can place pressure on public health services as they cannot turn away patients that the private organizations can. This was evident in the recent Covid-19 outbreak in Italy where the private hospitals declined to help as it would cut into their profits (Disamistade 2020). But having the public option also places some competitive pressure on the private companies as well. The cost of having cataract surgery is about $4,000 in the USA, only about $2,000 at a private clinic in Finland. And, if one is willing to wait since it is not life threatening, close to free in the *Kela* system.

One big difference relevant to public finance is in the very high costs in the USA and as a result the percentage of the economy dedicated to healthcare. This, in turn, takes more disposable income out of other parts of the economy and has to be one of the main reasons that a high percentage of the population of the USA doesn't have money to deal with emergencies. Furthermore, with a national health system the stress level for most people is much lower as concern about surprise bills and personal bankruptcy if one gets sick is not always in the back of one's mind. There is much more personal freedom for people to pick employment based on what one prefers or matches their skills better instead of the healthcare benefits (or not). It is easier to start a small business and employers face a much fairer competition in their cost structures. In the USA, to borrow one of the terms some of my favorite pundits use, the "bottom feeders" like WalMart that are highly profitable but still refuse to provide adequate coverage have a cost advantage over the grocery store chain that has a legacy of providing decent insurance, even in years of limited profitability or loss.

In the USA, there is a relentless pressure to shift more medical-related costs onto employees to compete that does not exist in other countries. Expect ever more pressure for conversion of unionized jobs into ones based on contingent workers if healthcare coverage costs continue to increase faster than other costs. Any competition for contracts under a Green New Deal is going to be made even more divisive on this issue if healthcare for all is not introduced at the same time. It will scale up the same debate to why some people doing the same types of work have widely different benefits and why government is willing to pay such benefits for some people but not others.

Police in the USA: Immune from budget cuts

The police are almost always a significant portion of the budget of larger cities. When they are not, it is probably because of a huge public housing obligation and/or transit subsidy. New York City spends over $5 billion on police but it still represents less than 8 percent of the budget. More typical for larger cities would be a range from 25 to 40 percent (McCarthy 2020). While figures of up to 50 percent are sometimes quoted, comparisons are not always straightforward. In some states, the county sheriff or the state police will overlap in responsibilities, transit and housing authorities might have their own police departments, and so on. The significant aspect is not the exact amount, but the fact that the budgets do not get cut to the same degree when the pressure is on (Toussaint 2020a). To some extent, this is understandable because the police are taking on roles that would be done by social workers in other countries with more comprehensive health-care systems. Examples include wellness checks and psychiatric episodes that family members cannot manage. But like some other municipal unions, they are also very politically active and willing to spend money to protect their budget allocations (Barkan 2020; Perkins 2020).

Police in some jurisdictions have also been placed into a role of issuing many tickets and fines due to an insufficient local tax base and insufficient support from the state legislature for basic services. The Ferguson protests in 2014 were not just about an unwarranted death, but anger about the stopping of lower income people repeatedly to issue fines. State of Missouri support was so minimal that the police department was expected to fund the courts, which should, of course, be totally independent.

Quality and modernity of police vehicles and supplies versus other departments

While public housing and school buildings might be in serious need of a facelift and jails overcrowded, many police departments have fleets of SUVs and other large late model cars. This is reflected in the city budget as large purchase and fuel bills. It also sets a bad example from an environmental standpoint to use SUVs (Syal 2021). From a traffic safety standpoint, it is counterproductive. Large vehicles beget large vehicles. People are scared to be in a collision with a vehicle that might climb over the top of them or ricochet them into oncoming traffic like a billiard ball due to the huge weight difference. They are also so tall that the driver cannot see if there are children in front when in a crowd. SUVs are receiving increased attention in their role in deteriorating safety (Wilson 2020).

Much has been made of the military equipment in which police arrive to public demonstrations, but this has most likely come from a federal program of handouts of military surplus. The fiscal impact will come instead from massive amounts of overtime. The demonstrations after the George Floyd murder, for example, ironically enriched police as a group as do events like Republican Party conventions. Such events can lead to cuts in other basic services. Police are often organized with their campaign donations and voting so politicians fear them. Nor do politicians want to be viewed as soft on crime. This makes it very difficult to get reforms or impose budget cuts. Recent events that have included calls to defund the police may yet change the balance of power (Csongradi 2020; Toussaint 2020b). Shifts in spending to other departments could be quite transformative to the quality and quantity of other public services available.

Public Housing in the USA: limited by European standards

Some countries have a legacy of a substantial amount of housing that is public owned. Sometimes housing is controlled by membership in a union, like *Obos* in Norway. This may seem democratic, but it does not appear that way to outsiders like me who attempted to find a place to live but were not born in Norway. It is another form of upper tier differentiation that makes lives much harder or more difficult for otherwise similarly situated persons. But if there aren't such restrictions, some degree of public ownership generally provides some latitude to influence regional rent levels through subsidy increases or decreases and without the cooperation of private landlords.

Not so the USA. To address the increasing inability to afford market-rate rents, the USA has shifted largely to federal government funded vouchers instead, known as the Section 8 program of the Housing and Community Development Act of 1974. The ideas behind the voucher are that it allows the family to pick their own location, it disperses poverty thereby improving services available to the poor, and it is more affordable to city governments. In practice, there is widespread discrimination by landlords and roughly three-fourths of the people who could technically quality for a voucher don't receive them as it is not an entitlement (Kneebone and Holmes 2015).

Public housing: mostly at the bigger cities

There have been some prominent high-rise building complexes in the bigger cities such as Cabrini Green that gained a bad reputation for isolating people, for racial segregation and street crime. Many have been demolished. Conversion away from high rises to smaller and more dispersed units has been the name of the game. Furthermore, the total number of units available, even in metro areas that are growing in population has been steadily decreasing since 1997. (The reason for selecting this year as a reference will be evident soon.) Some cities have eliminated virtually all of their public housing, others have reduced it by over half while New York City is in the minority only reducing the stock by 3 percent. One reason is to escape the capital costs of maintenance and repair. The stimulus package in 2009 put $4 billion into public housing, but this was clearly insufficient. The most recent national survey I could find is from 2011 where the backlog was estimated at $26 billion (Kimura 2011). Looking at more current data for the largest operator of public housing puts the backlog of "major repairs" at $32 Billion for NYC alone (NYCHA 2019).

As with so many other types of publicly owned assets, states are mostly stingy and the Federal Public Housing Capital Fund is not growing in keeping with the need in either numbers of units or maintenance, so cities are apparently expected to shoulder much of the burden. One reason for the neglect of what remains has to be that this is a service strictly for the lower tier with no level of government setting a high priority. There are private organizations with suggestions that could be considered as part of any investments under a Green New Deal (NLIHC 2020; Mercy Housing 2020).

Legislation cancelling the Faircloth Amendment

One reason for the failure to meet the growing needs of a growing population was the Faircloth Amendment that passed Congress in 1998. It made it such that federal funds could no longer be used for an expansion of new units, only for replacement of existing units. This could very well be repealed in the near future (Andrews 2020). The population of the USA grows by about three million each year, much of it concentrating in or near a few major cities, making citizens and some elected officials ever more vocal on the need for below market rate housing. Furthermore, spending on affordable public housing could dramatically increase if the GND or something like it comes to pass, with figures of over $100B in new investment and efficiency improvements to existing housing stock being suggested. This level of spending would also have large implications for spending on transportation and other infrastructure to support densification and population increases.

Childcare

This public service can be placed in several organizing and funding categories, depending upon the situation. For many residents of the USA, the only childcare performed by non-parents is by the siblings and extended family and is unpaid. Few locations have preschool affordable to the lower tier. When schools are closed as the Covid-19 pandemic has highlighted, there is often no childcare for school age children either, as parents must work (Jaffe 2021). And many children depended upon schools for their lunch so a solution had to be found for that as well.

Under a GND, childcare facilities themselves can be a target for modernization, repairs, and new construction where they do not exist. Including paid childcare would bring more money into lower income communities. New income directed at parents could help them to take advantage of these childcare facilities, cover more meals when they are away and offset rents that might increase after a neighborhood receives these types of investment.

Availability or lack thereof of affordable childcare outside the home will have a large influence on the size of the workforce available during any GND. Childcare should therefore be integrated into investment and workforce training plans. It is discussed more in the next chapter.

Can a city handle all of this plus public works?

The answer to this question is usually: barely. There are a lot of responsibilities to handle. Most cities do not run large surpluses. They may end up in competition with other cities in the same region for a lucrative business that generates tax revenues but does not create too large of a burden. Or, conversely, they may seek to keep out the people who are generators of large costs. So, they want to attract the car dealerships and keep out the types of housing where there are likely to be school age children who will attend public not private or parochial schools. There can be some success at this by the clever use of zoning laws. In the old days, property covenants and private actors like real estate firms took care of the ugly task of filtering out who was going to be unwelcome. At the same time, people a city might want to retain in their tax base would be given competing incentives to move out from the city into unincorporated areas and new towns. This was certainly the case when the new Interstates made a beeline to the suburbs and low interest Federal Housing Administration (FHA) loans were available for new construction but not for rehabilitation of existing structures.

The outflow of the work sites for the upper tier had largely stopped and even reversed itself in a few cities that are attractive to the creative class or Robert Reich's symbolic analysts, as evidenced by the lagging popularity of suburban corporate campuses. These residents do not necessarily put big demands on the public schools or public clinics, but they do to the transportation infrastructure. When a city is already struggling to fill the potholes, how is to cope with the extra traffic and extra demand for transit when infill occurs? The perverse incentive then remains for municipal government to try to prevent specific people from residing who will be a burden.

There has been a rapid shift to working at home by much of the upper tier because of Covid-19, but it remains to be seen what happens after the epidemic is over. Perhaps exurban sites will become popular and exacerbate sprawl, or perhaps they will lower the highway and transit capacity needed for accommodating rush hour commuters, or a bit of both. Transportation is one public service where costs might go down.

In general, the investment situation is becoming more intractable. Many older cities and older suburbs need major replacements of hundreds of miles of local roads, water delivery systems, wastewater treatment plants, bus stations and depots, rolling stock, school buildings, recreation centers, and so on, that are well beyond the capability of the annual cash flow. Bonding is one way to raise money, but this is a number that might already have been dialed many times, perhaps for some items the public did not even want like stadiums or convention centers. The situation is compounded if major new projects are wanted or needed by the residents. Maybe they would like better flood control or better transit or childcare centers or other improvements that will make their city more livable or less expensive to conduct daily life. This will require major cash transfusions for a few years which could further increase an already high local burden.

An extreme example of what happens when a large project is internally funded would be the City of Arlington, Texas where property tax goes to a professional baseball stadium but not to a fixed-route transit system, despite a significant population of about 400,000. Property taxes assigned to all, but dedicated to for-profit companies is something that will no doubt be attempted again under the guise of the Green New Deal.

The argument that infrastructure is a local responsibility has prevailed, at least by default, and we have seen the results: stagnation in service levels and repairs on an *ad hoc* basis instead of using proper, more scientific asset management. In some locations, huge monthly bill increases are going to be necessary if the GND does not occur because short term capital might only be raised by billing current consumers for urgent repairs and for urgent safety issues, like eliminating toxins from the drinking water supply. Perfluoroalkyls or PFAs alone are estimated to affect 110 million people in the USA (Gardner 2020).

This description of towns being on their own for provision of basic public services and safety measures fits third world countries. The very definition of an advanced industrialized economy includes the ability to do long-term financing to keep assets in good repair, to make further improvements the public democratically can reach consensus upon, and to spread the public costs over generations of users and beneficiaries. It is not as expensive as it sounds, as not every city has major projects at the same time. All citizens should be able to depend on their city's turn coming for help from the state and federal governments when they need it. The reason that Erin Brockovich has continued with the same fights over toxins in water resources for 30 years is precisely the lack of organized plans of proper scope at higher levels of government to deal with investment plans, needed statutory changes, and enforcement. And there are similar experts in other public works silos repeating their same fights as well.

Increasing the state-level gasoline tax and transferring some or all of the additional revenue to local government would help a great deal, as the care and feeding of the auto would no longer be in competition with other basic services for the limited tax base like maintaining a safe water supply free of PFAs. There also simply has to be much more help from higher levels of government. Many projects that would be of immediate benefit take too long when the funding is a combination of local plus perhaps some funding from oversubscribed federal funding programs with a long wait list. It is no accident that Miami has poorly funded public schools and woefully inadequate transit. Great plans from the MPO but no means to fund them (Miami-Dade MPO 2016). Florida has no state income tax. Or that the Seattle area has been so slow with its transit build out or that it has such has high resident tuition at its public universities, even favoring non-residents who can be charged even more. When I started at University of Washington in the fall of 1973 it was $188 per quarter. Washington has no state income tax either.

Finally, it is a little bit late to be talking about local responsibility when the federal government gave all that "free money" to help create the low density and overly car dependent, inefficient urban form that metro regions must deal with every day. People in Seattle were helping to build freeways in Miami, and vice versa, through the 80 percent of the Highway Trust Fund that went to roads. Because the national gas and diesel tax has not increased since 1993 it no longer just drivers who are helping build each other's freeways. All taxpayers have been increasingly enlisted every year by the federal government through general appropriations.

It is not just civil, mechanical, electrical engineering and other traditional work associated with major public works, or smartphone apps that might more finely regulate utility usage, or technological gadgets, that are needed for a GND. Given the historical investment patterns and widespread government dysfunctionality, the GND will require major financial re-engineering, too. It is certainly do-able if there is the political will.

References

Action Committee for Transit. 2020. The Town of Chevy Chase and the Purple Line. Available at: http://actfortransit.org/purple_ChevyChase.html (Accessed December 1, 2020).

Allegretto, Sylvia and Lawrence Mishel. 2019. The Teacher Weekly Wage Penalty Hit 21.4 Percent in 2018, a Record Hightrends in the Teacher Wage and Compensation Penalties Through 2018. *Economic Policy Institute*, April 24. Available at: https://www.epi.org/publication/the-teacher-weekly-wage-penalty-hit-21-4-percent-in-2018-a-record-high-trends-in-the-teacher-wage-and-compensation-penalties-through-2018/

American Association of University Professors (AAUP). 2010. Administrative Costs Rise as State Support Dwindles: AAUP-CBC's Response to the Goldwater Institute's Report. August 27. Available at: 2010-AAUP-CBCs response to Goldwater Report.pdf.

American-Statesman Editorial Board. 2020. Endorsement: Prop A's Project Connect is a Steep But Overdue Investment. *Austin American-Statesman*. October 8. Available at: https://www.statesman.com/opinion/20201007/endorsement-prop-arsquos-project-connect-is-steep-but-overdue-investment

Andersen, Michael. 2020. Portland Just Passed the Best Low-Density Zoning Reform in US History. *Sightline Institute*, August 11. Available at: https://www.sightline.org/2020/08/11/on-wednesday-portland-will-pass-the-best-low-density-zoning-reform-in-us-history/

Andrews, Jeff. 2020. Affordable Housing Is In Crisis. Is Public Housing the Solution? *Curbed*, January 13. Available at: https://www.curbed.com/2020/1/13/21026108/public-housing-faircloth-amendment-election-2020

Appelbaum, Binyamin. 2019. Much Ado About a Little More Housing. *New York Times*, August 1. Available at: https://www.nytimes.com/2019/08/01/opinion/montgomery-county-housing.html

Barkan, Ross. 2020. How Did Police Unions get so powerful? *The Nation*, July 2. Available at: https://www.thenation.com/article/society/police-unions-nypd-history/

Bowen, Douglas John. 2013. Chevy Chase, Md., Still Fighting Purple Line. *Railway Age*, September 16. Available at: https://www.railwayage.com/passenger/light-rail/chevy-chase-md-still-fighting-purple-line/

Campbell, Colin. 2020. Five Years Later, Many across Baltimore Bitterly Lament Gov. Hogan's Decision to Kill the Red Line Light Rail. *Greater Baltimore Committee* (reprinted from The Baltimore Sun), September 16. Available at: https://gbc.org/baltimore-sun-five-years-later-many-across-baltimore-bitterly-lament-gov-hogans-decision-to-kill-the-red-line-light-rail/

CBS Baltimore. 2020. Hogan Remains Second-Most Popular Governor Despite Slight Approval Rating Dip. *WJZ13*, January 17. Available at: https://baltimore.cbslocal.com/2020/01/17/maryland-governor-larry-hogan-approval-rating-morning-consult/ (Accessed December 1, 2020).

Chen, Grace. 2019. Value of an Associates vs. Bachelors Degree. *Community College Review*, December 27. Available at: https://www.communitycollegereview.com/blog/value-of-an-associates-vs-bachelors-degree

Consensus Study Report. 2020. Strengthening Sustainability Programs and Curricula at the Undergraduate and Graduate Levels (2020). Chapter 4. Prepublication. *NAS Press*. Available at: https://www.nap.edu/25821/

Csongradi, Martin. 2020. Could Defunding Baltimore's Police Department Help Transit? *Greater Greater Washington*, June 17. Available at: https://ggwash.org/view/78098/how-could-defunding-the-bpd-could-help-transit

CV Match. 2020. Your Next Step in Excellence. *AcademicTransfer.com*. Available at: https://www.academictransfer.com/en/cvmatch/#matched (Accessed September and October 2020).

Davis, Carl. 2020. How Long Has It Been Since Your State Raised Its Gas Tax? *Institute on Taxation and Economic Policy*. February 26. Available at: https://itep.sfo2.digitaloceanspaces.com/022520-Gas-Tax-Policy-Brief.pdf; https://itep.org/how-long-has-it-been-since-your-state-raised-its-gas-tax/

Disamistade, Vale. 2020. No, Italy Is Not the Case Against Medicare for All. *The Nation*, April 14. Available at: https://www.thenation.com/article/world/universal-health-care-italy-coronavirus/

Eastman, Scott. 2019. The "Cadillac" Tax and the Income Tax Exclusion for Employer-Sponsored Insurance: Fiscal Fact 661. *The Tax Foundation*, June. Available at: https://files.taxfoundation.org/20190619103723/The-%E2%80%9CCadillac%E2%80%9D-Tax-and-the-Income-Tax-Exclusion-for-Employer-Sponsored-Insurance-FF-661.pdf

Editorial Board. 2021. Should Amtrak bring New Passenger Rail Service to Cleveland and Ohio? *The Plain Dealer*, February 13. Available at: https://www.cleveland.com/opinion/2021/02/should-amtrak-bring-new-passenger-rail-service-to-cleveland-and-ohio.html

Egan, John. 2020. Austin's $10 Billion Transit Package with 3 New Light-Rail Lines Drives Forward. *Austin Culture Map*, June 15. Available at: https://austin.culturemap.com/news/city-life/06-15-20-three-new-light-rail-lines-drive-10-billion-transit-plan-for-austin/

Farberman, Rhea and Brianna Kelley. 2020. The Impact of Chronic Underfunding on America's Public Health System: Trends, Risks, and Recommendations, 2020. *Trust for America's Health*. Available at: https://www.tfah.org/report-details/publichealthfunding2020/

Fleischer, Victor. 2015. OpEd: Stop Universities From Hoarding Money. August 19. https://www.nytimes.com/2015/08/19/opinion/stop-universities-from-hoarding-money.html

Goger, Annelies. 2020. Turning COVID-19's Mass Layoffs into Opportunities for Quality Jobs. *Brookings Institution*, July 23. Available at: https://www.brookings.edu/research/turning-covid-19s-mass-layoffs-into-opportunities-for-quality-jobs/

Government Accountability Office (GAO). 2020. Report to Congressional Addressees: K-12 EDUCATION School Districts Frequently Identified Multiple Building Systems Needing Updates or Replacement. Report GAO-20–494 Public School Facilities. June. Available at: https://www.gao.gov/assets/gao-20-494.pdf

Grabar, Henry. 2021. City Councils Are Villains of the Housing Crisis. Slate. April 29. Available at: https://slate.com/business/2021/04/city-councils-are-fueling-the-housing-crisis-thanks-to-ideas-like-member-deference-and-aldermanic-privilege.html

Herriges, Daniel. 2018. But Rich People Live Here, So We Can't Be Going Broke! *StrongTowns,* September 5. Available at: https://www.strongtowns.org/journal/2018/9/5/but-rich-people-live-here-so-we-cant-be-going-broke

HigherEd Jobs. 2020a. Assistant Professor in Mechanical Engineering (2 Positions). Available at: https://www.higheredjobs.com/faculty/details.cfm?JobCode=177201636&Title=Assistant%20Professor%20in%20Mechanical%20Engineering%20%282%20Positions%29 bioengineering (Accessed July20, 2020).

HigherEd Jobs. 2020b. Post Doctoral Researcher, Mechanical Engineering. Available at: https://www.higheredjobs.com/search/details.cfm?JobCode=177166282&Title=Post%20Doctoral%20Researcher%2C%20Mechanical%20Engineering human-robot swarm interaction (Accessed July 20, 2020).

HigherEd Jobs. 2020c. Postdoctoral Scholar - Mechanical Engineering. Available at: https://www.higheredjobs.com/faculty/details.cfm?JobCode=177271670&Title=Postdoctoral%20Scholar%20%2D%20Mechanical%20Engineering Neuroscience (Accessed July 20, 2020).

Jaffe, Sarah. 2021. Who Cares? *The Baffler. No. 57,* May. 2021. Available at: https://thebaffler.com/salvos/who-cares-jaffe?utm_source=Baffler+Readers&utm_campaign=08a853ef88-weekly_06022021&utm_medium=email&utm_term=0_3541d01f8a-08a853ef88-46816556

Jankowski, Philip. 2020a. Group Launches Campaign to Promote Project Connect, But Well-Funded Opposition Looms. *Austin American-Statesman*, July 25. Available at: https://www.msn.com/en-us/news/politics/group-launches-campaign-to-promote-project-connect-but-well-funded-opposition-looms/ar-BB179L0L

Jankowski, Philip. 2020b. Austin Proposition a Election: $7.1B Rail Measure Passes. *Austin American-Statesmen*, April 11. Available at: https://www.statesman.com/news/20201103/Austin-proposition-election-$7.1B-rail-measure-passes

Kelton, Stephanie. 2020. *The Deficit Myth: Modern Monetary Theory and the Birth of the People's Economy*. Public Affairs.

Kimura, Donna. 2011. Public Housing Faces $26 Billion in Capital Repairs. *Affordable Housing Finance*, January 1. Available at: https://www.housingfinance.com/news/public-housing-faces-26-billion-in-capital-repairs_o

King, Samuel. 2020. Austin And Cap Metro Board Vote To Create Entity To Guide Massive Project Connect Transit Plan. *KUT 90.5 Radio*, August 7. Available at: https://www.kut.org/post/austin-and-cap-metro-board-vote-create-entity-guide-massive-project-connect-transit-plan

Kneebone, Elizabeth and Natalie Holmes. 2015. Promise and Pitfalls of Housing Choice Vouchers Vary Across the Nation. *The Brookings Institution*, August 14. Available at: https://www.brookings.edu/blog/the-avenue/2015/08/14/promise-and-pitfalls-of-housing-choice-vouchers-vary-across-the-nation/

Legal Defense Fund. 2015. Baltimore Residents and Civic Groups File Title VI Complaint with United States Department of Transportation over Maryland's Discriminatory Decision to Strip Baltimore of Transportation Funding. December 18. Available at: https://www.naacpldf.org/press-release/baltimore-residents-and-civic-groups-file-title-vi-complaint-with-united-states-department-of-transportation-over-marylands-discriminatory-decision-to-strip-baltimore-of-transportation-fundin/

Levy, Alon. 2017. How You Can Tell Larry Hogan's Decision to Kill the Red Line Was Racially Discriminatory. *Streetsblog USA*, April 21. Available at: https://usa.streetsblog.org/2017/04/21/how-you-can-tell-larry-hogans-decision-to-kill-the-red-line-was-racial-discrimination/

Linton, Joe. 2020. Court Sides With Metro on Beverly Hills Subway Lawsuit, Again. *StreetsBlog USA*, May 18. Available at: https://la.streetsblog.org/2020/05/18/court-sides-with-metro-on-beverly-hills-subway-lawsuit-again/

Longreads. 2017. The Great Online School Scam. Excerpt from Cutting School: Privatization, Segregation, and the End of Public Education. *The New Press,* September 2017. Available at: https://longreads.com/2018/02/20/the-great-online-school-scam/

Maciag, Michael. 2019. States That Spend the Most (and the Least) on Education. *Governing Magazine*, June 4. Available at: https://www.governing.com/topics/education/gov-state-education-spending-revenue-data.html

Marohn, Charles. 2011. The Growth Ponzi Scheme, Part 1. *StrongTowns*, June 17. Available at: https://www.strongtowns.org/journal/2011/6/13/the-growth-ponzi-scheme-part-1.html

Maus, Jonathon. 2020. Election Recap: Metro Measure Loses, Wheeler Wins, and Nolan Grabs Metro Council Seat. *Bike Portland*, November 4. Available at: https://bikeportland.org/2020/11/04/election-night-recap-metro-measure-loses-wheeler-wins-and-nolan-grabs-metro-council-seat-322343

McCarthy, Niall. 2020. How Much Do U.S. Cities Spend On Policing? *Statista*, June 12. Available at: https://www.statista.com/chart/10593/how-much-do-us-cities-spend-on-policing/

Mercy Housing. 2020. Public Policy Priorities. Available at: https://www.mercyhousing.org/about/education-advocacy/ (Accessed December 2, 2020).

Miami-Dade MPO. 2016. Strategic Miami Area Rapid Transit (SMART) Plan. Available at: http://www.miamidadetpo.org/library/boards/TPO-Governing-Board/Resolutions/2016-26-mpo-board.pdf

Milman, Oliver. 2020. 2019 Was Worst Year for US Rural Hospital Closures in a Decade, Report Finds. *The Guardian*, February 19. Available at: *https://www.theguardian.com/us-news/2020/feb/19/us-rural-hospital-closures-report*

Mosler, Warren. 2010. The 7 Deadly Innocent Frauds of Economic Policy. August 13th. Valance. 117 pages.

National Low Income Housing Coalition (NLIHC). 2019.Changing Direction: What is the Future of Public Housing? October 17. Available at: https://nlihc.org/resource/advocacy-future-public-housing

New Faculty Majority. 2021. Facts about Adjuncts. Available at: https://www.newfacultymajority.info/facts-about-adjuncts/ (Accessed February 15, 2021).

New York City Housing Authority (NYCHA). 2019. NYCHA 2019 Fact Sheet. March. Available at: https://www1.nyc.gov/assets/nycha/downloads/pdf/NYCHA-Fact-Sheet_2019_08-01.pdf

Oldman, Iain. 2020. Project Connect Vote Propelled by Austin's Inner-City Voters. *Community Impact Newsletter*, November 4. Available at: https://communityimpact.com/austin/northwest-austin/transportation/2020/11/04/project-connect-vote-propelled-by-austins-inner-city-voters/

Partelow, Lisette, Jessica Yin, and Scott Sargrad. 2020. Why K-12 Education Needs More Federal Stimulus Funding. Center for American Progress. July 21. Available at: https://www.americanprogress.org/issues/education-k-12/reports/2020/07/21/487865/k-12-education-needs-federal-stimulus-funding/

Perkins, Tom. 2020. Revealed: Police Unions Spend Millions to Influence Policy in Biggest US Cities. *The Guardian*, June 23. Available at: https://www.theguardian.com/us-news/2020/jun/23/police-unions-spending-policy-reform-chicago-new-york-la

Pew Trusts. 2019. Two Decades of Change in Federal and State Higher Education Funding: Recent trends across levels of government. *Issue Brief*, October 15. Available at: https://www.pewtrusts.org/

en/research-and-analysis/issue-briefs/2019/10/two-decades-of-change-in-federal-and-state-higher-education-funding

Riley, Don. 2001. *Taken for a Ride: Trains, Taxpayers and the Treasury.* Centre for Land Policy Studies.

Rowlands, D.W. 2018. What Land Takings Will Be Required for Hogan's Beltway and I-270 Widening. *Greater Greater Washington*, August 30. Available at: https://ggwash.org/view/68847/what-land-takings-will-be-required-for-hogans-beltway-and-i-270-widening

Ryan-Collins, Josh, Toby Lloyd and Laurie Macfarlane. 2017. *Rethinking the Economics of Land and Housing* (p. 288). Zed Books.

Scofield, Jerri-Lynn. 2019. Private Equity and Surprise Medical Billing. *Naked Capitalism*, September 6. Available at: https://www.nakedcapitalism.com/2019/09/private-equity-and-surprise-medical-billing.html

Smith, Kevin. 2020. Crossrail on Course for Summer 2021 Opening. *International Railway Journal*, January 10. Available at: https://www.railjournal.com/passenger/metros/crossrail-course-summer-2021-opening/?utm_source=&utm_medium=email&utm_campaign=12591

Solomon, Joshua. 2020. U.S. Supreme Court Won't Hear Indian River County's Appeal of Brightline Lawsuit. *TCPalm (Treasure Coast Newspapers)*, October 5. Available at: https://eu.tcpalm.com/story/news/local/shaping-our-future/all-aboard-florida/2020/10/05/u-s-supreme-court-wont-hear-appeal-indian-river-countys-brightline-appeal/3624678001/

Sorentrue, Jennifer. 2018. Brightline Opposition Group to hold meeting tonight in Stuart. *The Palm Beach Post*, January 29. Available at: https://www.palmbeachpost.com/news/brightline-opposition-group-hold-meeting-tonight-stuart/cNpdMNR9o3zAhay7aXOW3M/

Spiker, Katie. 2019. Despite Focus from the Administration, Budget Falls Short on Much Needed Investment in Workforce and Education Programs. *National Skills Coalition*, March 12. Available at: https://www.nationalskillscoalition.org/blog/higher-education/despite-focus-from-the-administration-budget-falls-short-on-much-needed-investment-in-workforce-and-education-programs/

Syal, Rajeev. 2021. SUVs and Extra Traffic Cancelling Out Electric Car Gains in Britain. *The Guardian*, February 26. Available at: https://www.theguardian.com/environment/2021/feb/26/suvs-and-extra-traffic-cancelling-out-electric-car-gains-in-britain?utm_term=330b0c7c6e15f16ac-8228ca7d5acd5f8&utm_campaign=GuardianTodayUK&utm_source=esp&utm_medium=-Email&CMP=GTUK_email

T4America and Taxpayers for Common Sense. 2019. Repair Priorities. p 11. Available at: http://t4america.org/wp-content/uploads/2019/05/Repair-Priorities-2019.pdf

Tan, Shen Wu. 2019. Residency Problem Partly Leads to Physician Shortage. *The Washington Times*, December 10. Available at: https://www.washingtontimes.com/news/2019/dec/10/hospital-residency-shortage-medical-students-fueli/

Tank, Alisa. 2020. Physician Salary Report 2020: Salaries Rising Prior to COVID-19 Impacts. *Weatherby Healthcare*, June 17. Available at: https://weatherbyhealthcare.com/blog/annual-physician-salary-report

The Chartis Group. 2020. The Rural Health Safety Net Under Pressure: Rural Hospital Vulnerability. February. Available at: https://www.ivantageindex.com/wp-content/uploads/2020/02/CCRH_Vulnerability-Research_FiNAL-02.14.20.pdf

The Share Team. 2020. 10-Year Spending Trends in U.S. Education. The Resilient Educator. September 17. https://resilienteducator.com/news/10-year-spending-trends-in-u-s-education/

Timothy Gardner. 2020. U.S. Drinking Water Widely Contaminated with 'Forever Chemicals': Environment Watchdog. *Reuters*, January 22. Available at: https://www.reuters.com/article/us-usa-water-foreverchemicals/u-s-drinking-water-widely-contaminated-with-forever-chemicals-report-idUSKBN1ZL0F8

Toussaint, Kristin. 2020a. As Cities Make Deep Cuts Because of COVID-19, Police Departments are Keeping Their Funding. *Fast Company*, June 1. Available at: https://www.fastcompany.com/90511840/as-cities-make-deep-cuts-because-of-covid-19-police-departments-are-keeping-their-funding

Toussaint, Kristin. 2020b. ACLU's Executive Director says Defunding Police Budgets Will Be His 'North Star' Going Forward. *Fast Company*, June 4. Available at: https://www.fastcompany.com/90512811/alcus-executive-director-says-defunding-police-budgets-will-be-his-north-star-going-forward

Trickey, Erick. 2019. How Minneapolis Freed Itself From the Stranglehold of Single-Family Homes. *Politico Magazine,* July 11. Available at: https://www.politico.com/magazine/story/2019/07/11/housing-crisis-single-family-homes-policy-227265

US Bureau of Labor Statistics (BLS). 2020. Occupational Outlook Handbook. Home Health Aides and Personal Care Aides. *Office of Occupational Statistics and Employment Projections.* Available at: https://www.bls.gov/ooh/healthcare/home-health-aides-and-personal-care-aides.htm

Vigrass, J. William. 2014. Why the PATCO Hi-Speed Line Has Not Been Extended: Rapid Transit Planning in Southern New Jersey: March 5.

Vock, Daniel C. 2011. Kasich Shows No Desire for Cincinnati Streetcar. *Stateline*, April 1. Available at: http://www.stateline.org/live/details/story?contentId=563879

Webb, Olivia. 2019. Private Equity Chases Ambulances. The American Prospect. October 3. Available at: https://prospect.org/health/private-equity-chases-ambulances-emergency-medical-transport/

Wilson, Kea. 2020. American SUVs are Too Dangerous for UK Roads, UK Safety Experts Say. *Streetsblog USA,* July 22. Available at: https://usa.streetsblog.org/2020/07/22/american-suvs-are-too-dangerous-for-uk-roads-uk-safety-experts-say/ (Accessed November 24, 2020).

Woodworth, James L, Margaret E. Raymond, et al. 2015.Online Charter School Study. *Center for Research on Education outcomes (Credo).* Available at: https://credo.stanford.edu/sites/g/files/sbiybj6481/f/online_charter_study_final.pdf

8

SUGGESTIONS

> "What if its a big hoax and we create a better world for nothing?"
>
> *A character in a Joel Pett cartoon*

Almost none of the suggestions and insights offered in this chapter are original. Revisiting them from the perspective of systems analysis, however, can help explain why they have not caught on or have not been overly effective. Thus, the importance of systems analysis is discussed first.

The thesis of this book is that the main reason that the upper tier of the economic strata have not addressed the problems of infrastructure and public services is because either they or their constituency within the same strata are not personally affected and therefore not concerned. Often, they benefit from the status quo, receiving taxation and funding advantages. A more precise understanding of both who has the decision-making power and who are the beneficiaries must be taken into account in project design if implementations are to be spread more widely and more equitably. The importance of such financially related reforms is discussed next.

Given the very slow pace of repair and investment in public works in the USA relative to peers and its very large population means that that it must be exceptionally efficient going forward if it is to catch up and contribute more to worldwide environmental crisis mitigation. A few proposals for projects in the short-, medium-, and long-term conclude this chapter.

What is systems analysis?

Much of what is advocated for dealing with the various environmental crises is best referred to as "end-of-pipe" environmentalism. A literal example would be replacing the service pipes with lead in them that deliver from mainlines to houses and getting the cryptosporidium out of the water supply, as opposed to tracing the entire hydrological cycle to also see if one can also reduce the need for so much water delivery infrastructure and water consumption in the first place. Another less literal example would be to simply do a one-on-one substitution of gasoline-powered private cars and diesel-electric hybrid powered transit buses with hybrid or full electric cars that cost less to drive without any changes to street use or lifestyles that might encourage people to drive their private autos less (Lewis 2020; Hanley 2020). While there is an awareness that problems are interrelated by top academic scientists, even their suggestions tend

DOI: 10.4324/9781003245704-8

to be in the low hanging fruit of electrification of ground vehicles and more consideration of environmental justice as a sampling of interviews shows (Thompson 2020).

Systems analysis is the discipline where a system boundary is defined and studies are specifically designed and conducted to find any synergies between actions or policies usually perceived as independent interacting within this boundary and with items crossing into and outside the system boundary from outside. It often requires mathematical models. It is a bit like "whack a mole" the arcade game where one slams down one mole with a hammer, but another one pops up in an unexpected location. Interactions can be quite complex and result in unforeseen consequences. Some metrics are typically developed to identify interactions, such as percentage traffic increase due to densification of housing stock, or a so-called rebound effect due to the lower out-of-pocket costs to the consumer from driving a more energy efficient vehicle, and so on.

All proposals initially targeted for consideration or action by one governmental department related to the environment should as a matter of course first have a literature search to try to find any already performed systems analyses on this topic. The idea is to find potential unforeseen conflicts, potential partnering departments, and even perhaps totally different approaches. If they do not exist, or as is quite likely, the studies that do exist are out of date due to increasing specialization of academia and grants, such studies should be done before any commitments are made. There used to be an Office of Technology Assessment whose role was along these lines but not as comprehensive as this author advocates. It was disbanded by the US Congress in 1995. There have been calls for resurrecting it (Tudor and Warner 2019), but this time the system boundary should be widened to search for other affected parties and for unintended consequences.

If not totally unforeseen, consequences can certainly be undesirable and need to be identified early. An example would be the Corporate Average Fuel Efficiency (CAFÉ) standards, one of the cornerstones of federal environmental policy for decades. The effect has been offset by efficiency increases through technology advances that was used for higher horsepower for cars and by the gaping loophole that SUV-promoting lobbyists drove through: the first SUVs in 1990 were classified as trucks and hence exempt from safety features and CAFÉ standards. Furthermore, without a major increase in fuel prices through tax increases, the lower cost of filling one's tank during world price collapses meant that people drove more, the rebound effect again. This occurred while other policies were also being implemented intended to influence people to drive less. Another example was upgrading arterial roads to wide boulevards in efforts to speed up traffic to lower costs of commerce and to improve access to jobs. But it also decreased safety of surface streets which then, in turn, incentivized building grade separated motorways to mitigate it. These higher speeds then encouraged driving over longer distances and converted some pedestrians to motorists. There was a chain of events that might have been anticipated as a strong possibility.

Fare-free transit is another example of a situation where the big picture needs to be taken into account. It might seem like a good idea to promote transit use and to help lower income people and is already getting renewed attention from elected officials in cities in many countries, including megacities like Moscow and Los Angeles County. On closer inspection fare-free policy would cause adverse effects that need to be weighed as well. Replacing 20–40 percent of operating revenue might not be so easy. It could ultimately backfire if the system stops expanding out of fear of not being able to guarantee operating support to maintain a reliable operation because funding is often in jeopardy. One advocate is a US Representative from Massachusetts (Walker 2020). Despite the size of the Boston metro area, the regional trains run at substandard 90-minute headway during the midday and several times over recent years there have been feelers to cut service. This, despite the fact that new apartment buildings have arisen along the regional train lines based upon their presence. Furthermore, fare-free means that heavily used systems can get overloaded by people taking short trips on the busiest segments, people who could easily walk or bicycle thereby degrading services and increasing costs. In the end, as was shown in the widely cited case of Tallinn, Estonia, fare-free may not even increase ridership much (The Public Course 2013; City of Tallinn 2020; James 2020). In specific instances it could make sense, like rural and small systems that do not face the additional costs of peak hour surges and which only recover about 10 percent of costs from the farebox.

This type of policy question should periodically be revisited locally as revenue sources and policies change. Other possibilities could and should be investigated as well, like "fare capping" where fare payment media recognize the person has paid a maximum charge for one day, thereby helping lower income persons more directly, by measures that lower costs of operating and by measures that encourage people who can afford it to use transit more.

Governmental department divisions traditionally militated against systems analysis to maintain bureaucratic turf. There is increasing recognition of this problem as pressure for more sustainable development intensifies. But changing organizations and missions is easier said than done. Many players have an interest in the status quo of the urban development permitting and financing process. Firms selling vehicles, parts and fuel also have an interest in maintaining demand. At the risk of over generalizing, academic divisions have also solidified as their incentive structure increasingly rewards specialization to achieve promotions and attract funding, so their role under a push for sustainable development is likely to be limited to niche policy questions within silos and to technology development, barring some major policy changes toward public universities with respect to using them for systems-level policy analysis (Bruun and Givoni 2015).

An intense effort to reduce greenhouse gas emissions quickly will have to be highly interdisciplinary. In many regions, plans to conserve or even restore arable lands and forests on the perimeter of metro areas will also be necessary and highly interdisciplinary as well. Efforts will encompass scientific research, engineering alternatives analysis, investments strategy, workforce skills planning, rural/urban relations, purchasing from global versus more local supply chains, you name it.

Studies need to be selected and performed in a sequence such that short-term proposals are studied first and most rapidly. Plans are going to have to evolve rapidly as inputs are received from the various quarters. No department can be allowed to get too far ahead or drop too far behind or else consequences that will be regretted are likely. The voters should be selecting people who are up to the difficult task of leadership and these leaders, in turn, need to be selecting leaders of government agencies who can manage departments that are re-organizing themselves, perhaps rapidly expanding their budgets, or merging with others. Some of these efforts will be further complicated by multi-county and even multi-state jurisdictions. Ideological alignment and good intentions by elected officials are necessary but not sufficient.

Lower levels of government will always have difficulty to raise money alone

As has already been explained, it simply is not realistic for any changes involving large investments to be done unilaterally at lower levels. They need injections of substantial sums from time to time in specific locations to accomplish improvements that will be seen over the medium- or long-term. Lower levels of government can help bring short- and medium-term changes through statutory or zoning changes, some of which may require votes, depending upon the situation. Even policies that do not involve spending local money on physical investments to reduce CO_2 can be slowed or even reversed with the results of local elections. An example of good intentions that might need to be enabled by voting is a declaration by the *C40 Cities* to divest their assets and pension funds from fossil fuels (C40 Cities 2020). Some of these cities are going to have a lot more success than others given the commitments by their higher levels of government to date. The USA is not Norway or Spain but has to quickly start to act more like them.

Votes can encourage silo thinking

As has already been shown, polling and surveys clearly reveal that the public supports changes toward sustainability, at least in principle. But if it is true that the upper tier dominates the elected positions and senior leadership and technocratic positions in public agencies, there will be conflicts between their agencies' stated missions and their own shorter-term interests and perspectives. Voting on an array of separate and unrelated proposals, where it is even allowed, is just not likely to bring faster progress than in locales where voters are not asked or permitted to approve. Even more important from the standpoint of sustainability, the individual project-focused voting process is far too slow to address climate change, especially if it is several years before a vote can be repeated. The hapless mayors in Fulton County (Atlanta region) are now afraid to ask for the desperately needed BRT since adding more projects might jeopardize their increasingly inadequate existing funding, leaving them worse off than ever (Brasch 2021).

Initiatives and Propositions may seem to be a democratic way of prompting sluggish politicians but are problematic. The experiences from places like Washington and California demonstrate that Initiatives can even end up contradicting one another if priorities clash with one another or if agencies get tied up waiting for court rulings. Lobbying too vociferously and voting on one issue in one silo needs to be avoided, by having done due diligence in systems analysis. This will reduce the temptation to accept offers of resolutions that cause other problems to be aggravated.

Some successful initiatives have proven disastrous like Proposition 13 in California in 1978 that froze residential property taxes. It has played a large role in the chronic underfunding of public schools and the use of zoning by municipal governments designed to attract sales tax contributors like car dealerships and to repel families with school age children. Forty years later California has a truly massive housing shortage numbering in the hundreds of thousands of units. Ideal locations for apartment buildings over rapid transit stations remain as single family housing. The Seattle area is decades behind in its transit plan and has evolved into a smaller-scale copy of LA in large part because its rail projects were put to several public votes while highways were not. The approved funding level means the pace of construction is so slow that it is totally inadequate to meet the needs of a fast-growing region. It is also unfair to voters who have been paying since their youth but not be able to ride the trains until they have reached retirement.

Policy packages

Policies will be most effective when they are in packages that have been studied for their synergies and conflicts (Dijk et al. 2018). The whole is not necessarily the sum of the parts. It is common to hear statistics like transport is 30 percent of CO_2 emissions, buildings 25 percent, industrial machinery 25 percent, and so on, by category. But this is only true in an end-of-pipe situation where one is looking for small immediate gains, or in the economic parlance, changes at the margin. Switching ICE engines for electric motors will otherwise not change travel habits much except for a rebound effect because fuel costs are lower. Putting more insulation on some single-family houses is a second short-term change where the total of the two effects can be added together. But it is not the same thing as putting in nearby stores and sidewalks and building apartments that share more walls and have a smaller footprint for the same number of inhabitants. The latter package is a medium- to long-term change. The motorized travel reduction and the combined heat loss reduction cannot be estimated simply by adding two separate effects. Instead, one needs to compute the reduction in percentage of driving trips and the reduction in average trip length and the reduction in heat loss from fewer larger buildings using mathematical models that capture synergies. Guidebooks can be an effective way to disseminate this type of valuable information sponsored by professional societies and government agencies within particular traditional silos.

Equally important is to keep an eye out for tax regulations that undermine all of the other investment plans. For example, the Governor of New York capped property tax increases at 2 percent annually, which was an arbitrary restriction on struggling cities like Buffalo where one of the only investment means open to them was to increase the tax on the wealthy owners of newer properties who underpaid relative to older properties. See links in the website of the aforementioned *Strongtowns* for examples of inequitable property taxation relative to the services they receive. If institutions and the voting public could inform themselves about the anticipated combined results and votes could be held on such policy packages, it might be a very good way to overcome minority rule and irresponsible pandering to them, but this is rarely done.

Comparison to the UK: Central Government does not need to hold another vote for years

It would seem that the stronger central government makes jurisdictional issues simpler. It can apply a similar program over a larger area with less time spent negotiating and harmonizing with local practices. But this can cut both ways. It can also impede progress anywhere. The privatization of public works and utilities across the UK has been unpopular but has nevertheless persisted for decades. Many city and regional planning authorities gave up on receiving major assistance, such as Leeds with their requests for help with urban rail projects. In 2017, the Central Government initiated a policy of devolution of responsibility. While this was may have been partly done to finally respond to the public will for their metro regions to have more planning authority similar to that which Greater London retained, no doubt it saves the party base tax expenditures on the provinces as well. The previously mentioned example of Manchester recovering control of transit planning could be the beginning of a reversal of decades of emasculation but only if large scale investment assistance from the Central Government is available from time to time.

The lack of investment in public facilities that create anchors for employment, in alternatives to Heathrow, in modern, affordable public transportation and intercity trains in the northern parts of England has played a significant role in being unable to compete as places to conduct business and live well. This, in turn, has resulted in the need for duplicative new heavy infrastructure in the south while existing corresponding infrastructure up north has surplus capacity. The unaffordable combined housing plus transport cost for the people displaced from the north reflects this duplication and the pressure on land prices. The monetary and disruption cost of any Green New Deal in the Southwest and Southeast areas also will be much higher because of lack of reserve capacity in the existing public works that helps alleviate the hardships from shutdowns during construction. There is currently no major policy package that favors the north over the south sufficient to stem the flow let alone reverse it.

It is not just about promoting policies but about discouraging them as well. Choice of elementary schools is an example of something the Central Government should have dissuaded, at least in the Southeast with already very heavy congestion. Parents were driving their young children to schools for substantial distances at the height of rush hour, passing each other in opposite directions. Taking steps to equalize the quality of elementary schools instead would have been far better for the environment. A very good example of systems thinking.

In the UK, the impact from the previously mentioned fare-free proposal from a member of the Parliament similar to that proposed by a member of the US Congress would be severe due to the almost total lack of government operating support outside of Greater London. It is probably a good thing that the UK's Central Government does not want to try to impose this solution on already struggling local governments as a response to public dissatisfaction, at least so far. It is not beyond the realm of possibility. Like the Americans with Disabilities Act of 1990, a higher level of government can impose a mandate on lower levels of government, on public agencies, and its own government-owned corporations with no additional financial assistance for compliance yet still take political credit, like a recent settlement with Amtrak (Office of Public Affairs 2020).

Remove horizontal equity violations that benefit the upper tier

Definition: incidence of costs and benefits

The academic economic literature that evaluates public works often spoke of the "incidence" of the benefits of a project almost as an afterthought. This always seemed strange to me and I am sure to others, as the engineering methodology involves focusing upon identifying the needs of specific audiences as its starting point. Another downplayed aspect was the incidence of costs. "Economic Justice" is now the expression meant to capture the fact that this incidence of the costs is also a concern to someone, even if not necessarily of the institutions and people who conceived the plan. Future analyses of urgent problems are still going to have to be interested in one big number, like the total greenhouse gas or total water use reduction, but evaluations must start to look much more closely at the benefits and costs to the roughly bottom 80 percent and use this as a tiebreaker when several project alternatives are similar on the big numbers.

One extremely important approach for selecting projects is not directly about building of public works, *per se*, instead it tries to first make changes to improve horizontal equity, meaning more equal treatment and more equal incidence across the population with respect to the delivery and charging for public services and the taxing for any required subsidies. The user pays principle is the default, but when this is impractical, or some elements of society simply cannot afford to pay then other means are considered. The idea is that projects that do require building of public works can be achievable more quickly while greatly reducing the historical favoritism and resulting skewed distribution of public services toward the upper tier when more of them are equalized in treatment to the lower tier. Returning to Thomas Frank again, history suggests that populist movements might accomplish changes quickly if they can be initiated somehow, such as what the trauma of high unemployment created by the great depression did to so many workers or farmers anger against what the railroad monopolies did during the Populist era.

Property equalization (and possibly pension equalization too) would reduce resistance from the upper tier

A possible change that might have the largest impact of all on urban development equity in the short term is to remove depreciation that pertains to building rental and leasing businesses. Buildings are not like machinery that wears out and is an abuse of the concept. Today, even when land increases in value its owners can still depreciate it as a business investment. It explains why so much money goes into the Financial Insurance Real Estate (FIRE) sector. Unlike FIRE, manufacturing and retail are highly competitive, there is excess capacity in most sectors, and margins are low. By comparison, land remains finite. The situation has become so extreme that large buildings are used by the very wealthy as a way to store money and to avoid taxation. Selling, leasing, or renting of space as a landlord is a secondary concern. Prices go up and the places will stay vacant rather than come back down to attract tenants. Kevin Baker as a long-time resident paints a vivid picture of how increasingly high vacancy rates occurred even in supposedly prosperous and booming places like the Upper Westside of Manhattan (Baker 2018). Now both the depressed areas and the booming areas can have vacant storefronts.

Another housing example at the federal level is the mortgage interest deduction which makes larger houses more affordable for the wealthy, a policy promoting sprawl and more luxury units. At the state level, California's Proposition 13 has now evolved so that the benefits can be passed on to children (Albertson and Davidson 2018). This is egregiously unfair without any justification. It is creating an upper caste that can be counted on to resist efforts to purchase their houses under eminent domain. They have the equivalent of a huge capital gain since they pay much a lower property tax rate as long as they do not sell. This is a significant part of the reason why there is so little obstacle to densifying near transit in California.

Another one of the biggest horizontal equity violations in the USA is that some upper tier people are getting healthcare at no cost, except perhaps a token amount for prescription drugs. Others are doing similar work but must make co-pays, often on the order of 20 percent on six figure bills, plus significant percentages on drugs that have the highest prices in the world. All of this to be paid with after tax income. Even worse, if a member of the hapless lower tier does happen to have insurance, perhaps through a spouse, she/he may be denied treatment and pharmaceuticals as experimental by an insurance company which he/she may not have even chosen. As explained in the previous two chapters, the medical non-system will create several pathologies complicating work force hiring and controlling cost levels under a GND.

A current transport example of inequity is the extremely expensive success (purchase?) of Proposition 22 which among other things denies medical insurance to gig workers in the lower tier (Hussain and Bhuiyan 2020; Schor 2020). It will keep the cost of using Uber and Lyft down for the upper tier who might otherwise use transit and thereby not contribute to traffic congestion. Furthermore, this will be at the expense of the gig workers and of taxpayers who might be forced to pay their major medical and other social expenses instead of their non-employer "Transportation Network Company" that supposedly only supplies a software platform. Moreover, this replacement of taxis with TNCs might even be harmful on environmental grounds as research is showing that the reduced number of taxis is offset by increased purchases and cruising by TNC drivers in the USA (Liverpool 2021).

In the case of Proposition 22, its provisions cannot be reversed without a 7/8 supermajority. To this amateur lawyer, it seems it would be unconstitutional to effectively ban future legislatures or citizens from reversing it. That this kind of second-class citizenship could persist and even solidify is a strong statement on how the upper tier dominate legislation and jurisprudence even in Blue California. It has already started to embolden similar efforts in other Blue states (7 News Radio 2020) and might mean the only remedy for equity will involve Federal legislation. If Medicare for All or a new legal definition of employer succeeds, much but not all, of the debate about new gig business models will be obviated.

Furthermore, if pensions could also be made portable, it could certainly relax resistance to change. There simply has to be a lot of people who currently have an interest in postponing the day of reckoning for their particular business or industry that is no longer environmentally sustainable enough and obsolescent. Currently, industry can use the threat of closure and bankruptcy to get their employees to fall into line with their voting patterns and donations as well to help postpone this day.

Enforcing broadband contracts and access is long overdue

The telecommunications deregulation act in 1996 leaving the vast majority of investment and control in the private sector is clearly a failure with respect to public schooling and educational opportunity for lower income students. It is hard to argue that all students now have an opportunity to pull themselves up by their own bootstraps. In the old days, schools did not have money to buy textbooks or libraries, now students are given a responsibility to access the world from their homes in order to do their homework. Unlike most of its peer nations, the rural areas and even some more urban students are un-served by internet, either by lack of infrastructure, or by unaffordable charges, or both (Asher-Schapiro 2021). On the other hand, duplication of existing infrastructure can be expensive and wasteful (Rogoway 2020), so new public-private relationships must be negotiated, but not without first enforcing previous promises to expand access, another byproduct of oligopoly in the telecommunications sector (Rosen 2021). Fixing this will also help businesses in rural areas, yet another way to help address the need to slow the migration to urban areas.

Enforce other existing corporate environmental responsibilities as well

Many Superfund sites remain even 40 years after their identification. These are sites that meet criteria for being especially pernicious as opposed to mere brownfield sites. As global warming intensifies, there is a danger that they escape their confines faster than they might already be doing. There have been no additional polluter fees added to this program since 1995. With not enough money to deal with all of the existing sites, apparently the EPA can only issue idle threats to charge treble damages after they first get these clean-ups done themselves at their own expense and effort (Pollard 2021) with money the offenders know that the EPA does not have. Many oil and gas wells also remain unsealed even when the owners who profited from them are known. They have simply decided the bonds they paid are not large enough to worry about and/or the civil and criminal penalties they face are weak or non-existent (Sammon 2021).

Attention to the unfinished business of cleanup is not only important to prevent toxins from leeching into the ecosystem, they also tend to be concentrated around lower income communities and another example of the historic lack of concern for racial and economic justice. Furthermore, these restored sites can become loci for industrial redevelopment instead of greenfields that so many politicians have irresponsibly permitted and even promoted.

Remove healthcare costs from other public works costs

The focus here is on how to make short- to medium-term gains with respect to reduction of urgent environmental degradation. If healthcare costs could be transferred from public works or public service departments to a medical department instead of being a responsibility as a fringe benefit it could be transformative. In the worst case, all of funds for this medical benefit would be transferred at the time of takeover, but it would still decouple the cost of retaining and hiring new employees from what is a now significant percentage of operating budgets, a percentage that increases faster than inflation.

Shifting of medical costs to a separate department would also help to equalize the cost structure between school, transit, water, and other utility districts that can afford to pay decent benefits and those that cannot. This, in turn, would reduce the phenomena where people select sprawled locations for their residence, not because people prefer to live there but because of funding disparities in school districts. Medical expenses also greatly complicate pension funds, worker compensation charges and many other costs over which public agencies have little control and are outside of their core competencies.

It might even help some of the currently upper-tier members who discover the limitations of their free healthcare when they get injured, or fired, or their company gets merged into a different benefit plan, or their spouse has to decline a job in another city because of the "velvet handcuffs" of Nordic-style healthcare but in a US framework tied to their employer instead of their residency. Same for seniority and pensions, other sets of velvet handcuffs. Calling these possibilities to the attention of people who have not thought that they could be next might help to shift alliances and bring about change.

Then there is the political fallout for municipal elections that could make urban politics far more responsive to the lower tier. If bigger city police, transit, teacher, and other unions were no longer a privileged caste in a patronage relationship with elected officials they might stop voting and donating largely as a block during primaries. The competition would be very likely to improve and give new faces a chance. It might even help open the purses of some state governments that have a rural versus urban conflict. There is some merit to rural and smaller city representatives in the state legislatures when they argue that cities have much higher costs and that it is not fair to support better benefits than their constituents get. This reason or excuse would no longer be valid.

Tax lower densities higher: case study: Dallas

The user pays principle is generally not in use with public utilities serving residential areas. Average rates are used whether one lives in a McMansion or in an apartment building. This would be understandable for the quantity of electricity or water or natural gas that was used, but it is not equitable when it comes to the construction and maintenance of the infrastructure. The piping runs and cabling runs are much longer with low density development. By separating the physical infrastructure costs from the end-product purchase and delivery costs would have multiple benefits. As an example, the City of Dallas was studied in some detail with respect to how much adjustment could be made (Anderson 2018). It could generate more total revenues to help reduce maintenance backlogs without a vote. Of course, it would also save money for the lower tier in the short term and remove a subsidy to sprawl as a medium- to long-term benefit. Other cities could and should do similar studies and then propose adjustments. It is then a question of the political will to allow changes in the schedule of rates. It is another issue over which a mass movement is needed to support candidates favoring this reform.

Other public services like fire and police also cost more on a per capita basis in lower density areas because stations serve fewer people so driving distances and times are longer. It is also important to note that in the Dallas case, as in many other places, changing the property tax rate instead would require a change in a law which says all property must be taxed at the same rate. Annual increases are also capped at 8 percent regardless of actual need to clear the backlog of maintenance. Property tax changes might take much longer than a utility billing rate change, especially if politicians put it to a public vote enabling status quo defenders to mount a misinformation campaign that taxes will go up for regular workers, which they are likely to do if the idea builds momentum.

On the down side, depending on increasing the property tax means those responsible for maintaining public property find themselves hoping for annual increases in assessments as a means to clear the maintenance and environmental protection backlogs. This is a perverse incentive because it can aggravate housing affordability problems.

Furthermore, annual compounding of unpaid charges for eventual collection is not a solution. As the debt historian Michael Hudson is fond of saying: "Debts that cannot be paid will not be paid. The question is how it will not be paid." Other funding sources will need to be maintained as well.

Remove tax breaks for industry poaching

Good Jobs First puts the tax revenue losses from tax abatements to attract industry at over $19 billion in 2019 (Good Jobs First 2020). This is surely an undercount as it is difficult to independently collect a complete listing. In some places the amount can be very high and ongoing, such as the abatement for Boeing to retain their 787 Dreamliner plant in Washington State. Boeing had threatened to relocate to non-union South Carolina and indeed they did open a second factory anyway and will soon shut down the assembly line at the first. As seen in this and an earlier example, companies can and do renege on their commitments when there is no clawback provision.

Such competition at the expense of local and state taxpayers also has international consequences. Boeing's main competitor, Airbus Industries, felt pressured to shift more construction to Mobile, Alabama to sell military versions thereby also reducing the work and tax revenues at unionized plants in Europe and then in Canada through its acquisition of Bombardier. Some protectionist pressure for military purchases and Boeing's political clout as a sore loser played a role, but the fact also remains that both military and commercial airplane labor costs are lower in the deep south of the USA than in Europe or Canada. So Airbus probably liked this as it could use this to drive down wages. I would add that Hamburg, Toulouse, and Montreal all had decent transit systems whereas in 2018 Mobile County had a grand total of 29 fixed route transit buses for a population of 418,000 and only about 1600 ICU beds for the entire state. Thus, relocating to a city in Alabama is similar to relocating a megafactory to a rural area, something this area is ill equipped to handle.

Less dramatic examples are transit vehicle assembly plants and parts suppliers that get financial support from a state government, meanwhile this same state will not support transit in their own cities. How does this benefit the lower tier? Since it has proven hard to dissuade state and local elected officials to reduce this type of behavior and it is so widespread, there are ways to de-incentivize it through the Federal government's procurement law changes in the short term. It already has a list of requirements when they supply matching funds. Add one that requires that an estimate of the tax reduction value given to the bidder be added to the price during the evaluation phase to negate subsidies other vendors do not get. This estimate can be done by comparison to nearby companies and by peers building similar equipment. Had this been standard practice in the past, it is doubtful that the exodus of the automotive industry from the Midwest to the south would have occurred to anywhere near the same extent, at least for public sector product purchases. Large procurements from public agencies operating at the regional or state level already had enough market power to command attention. Trains are built in New York State for New York customers and electric buses are built in California for California customers for a reason.

It would be helpful for the Federal Government to also delete some of its provisions, in particular, its prohibition against specifying a percentage of local content because it makes it very much harder for a Green New Deal to distribute the benefits of employment and training to where it is most needed. It also raises costs when companies try to assign their own employees from far away on large scale projects rather than train locals. This is a requirement that favors large corporations and upper-tier unionized employees. It should also be noted that while public works and public services have been subjected to this requirement, the Pentagon has found ways to avoid it as evidenced by how contracts are distributed to many constituencies over a wide geographic region in order to make cancellation more politically difficult.

Comparison to Finland and the UK

The medical system is already a separate department with a separate budget rather than a burden for each department something which, as explained earlier, is not the case in the USA. This allows a given departmental operating budget to go much further especially for services where labor is a high percentage of the costs. Also, as explained earlier, the European Commission pressures all member countries to contract out public services. But it does not have the same implications as in the USA. Even when services are contracted rather than done inhouse, it largely removes the highly contentious issue of healthcare benefits from the negotiations and the motivation to cap the number of public sector workers and pay overtime instead, even when more employees are sorely needed, like school teachers and diesel mechanics for transit and garbage collection fleets. The competition can be based on judging the effectiveness and efficiency in a company's approach to dealing with urgent issues rather than a financial race to the bottom where they win instead through understaffing if superior benefits must be paid, or using staff that have inferior benefits and lack training if it is not required. After this dynamic of decline continues for a long time, it can degrade the skill level instead of increasing it.

Some proposals for the Green New Deal concept

Definitions: short term, medium term, and long term

It is useful to define three different time frames: short term is what occurs with effects seen almost immediately. Medium term changes require a few years because the effect from purchasing practices, consumer investment choices and/or statutory and policy changes do not show an impact immediately. The long term is after major investments are completed. All are important. Short term tends to lean toward what individuals can do without much participation by others, medium term requires some participation with government, while long term tends to be quite dependent upon government actions in accordance with a strategic vision, typically including large investments. How large the relative impacts can be needs to be the subject of study if suitable peers have not already been analyzed to get estimates. One cannot take the word of individual bloggers, scholars who reside mostly within their own comfort zone or silo, and not the equilibrium gap fillers, for these estimates.

Good starts in the short term can take place by individuals and local businesses making public purchasing and lifestyle decisions, but even such short-term measures will take some time to fully implement for maximum impact. It takes time for price signals to change in accordance with changes in demand due to lifestyles being altered and for building renovations and similar products of minor investments incentivized by consumer choice to reduce overall consumption. This will be true even with the best of intensions of elected officials and public agencies who do not try to obstruct them to defend existing interests.

Actions that require significant actions at governmental levels tend to be more involved to study and more difficult to implement. It is essential to try if government is to better reflect the will of millions of individuals who singly cannot bring about impacts whose measurements will sometimes be on grand scales. No longer just a question of people and small businesses making individual decisions, it is a question of how to move bureaucracies and to coordinate multiple players. It could be quite hard to persuade legislatures consisting of very comfortable members of the upper tier who do not personally feel the same hardships or whose businesses are not in the same decline as in lower tier dominated communities. There really is not enough time to building up the pressure needed. Some "free" money could work wonders as it did with the Interstate Highway Act.

Finding good mechanisms for more comprehensive improvements to public works spending

Global warming has put a sense of urgency into environmental actions. There is broad recognition that if it is to be taken seriously these actions must be on multiple fronts. A Green New Deal, or something similar, is thus both an opportunity and a necessity to finally bust the silos. Projects designed to disproportionately benefit the upper tier are not only going to continue to be inequitable but even tragic as the stakes are much higher this time. Efforts must be judged and distributed based more on scientific reasons and less on traditional considerations.

Even with investment plans and policy packages based on the most careful and comprehensive systems analyses, someone will also have to be keeping an eye out that investments do not work at cross purposes. It will almost certainly be the case that some projects would physically conflict with one another or have inadequate resources to do all elements simultaneously or in the most ideal sequence. In this case someone must decide what comes first. It is like the PERT charts that were used to identify the critical path of projects, that is where the bottlenecks might happen, but on a national level. There will also be staffing shortages for particular specialties, which mean that decisions also need to sequence the side investments in the workforce. The locations where work occurs and whether the workforce will be temporary are important considerations in any major plan. Think of the Grand Coulee or Hoover Dam in the 1930s or the production planning in the USA and Canada during the WW2 logistical emergency in the 1940s. Moreover, some project elements will involve the stemming of the emigration and even attracting people back to depopulated rural areas on a permanent basis. Thus, the GND represents a more holistic, interdisciplinary, and large-scale approach than has been the case for decades.

Daily life of individuals – a study from Leeds University

One place any Green New Deal or such can start is with the individual. There have been lots of suggestions on how to change one's lifestyle. Some sound good but are really of limited impact if not done properly, like recycling. Some groups have performed deeper analyses that come with quantitative estimates attached about the costs and benefits of a list of candidate actions. For example, from Leeds University in the UK comes a list with well researched suggestions about going vegan, adding solar panels, going car free with local transport, battery powered cars and taking fewer long-distance flights (Ivanova et al. 2020). These may need to be viewed as aspirations or directions one should be headed quickly rather than a list which can be done immediately. Vegan food can cost much more especially given existing agricultural subsidy policies and depending upon where one lives while solar panels and battery powered cars can require cash up front that people simply do not have in order to recover savings later. Going car free can be a real challenge indeed, especially in the USA and the UK.

One can add other ideas, such as choosing to support infill development by living in lofts over storefronts in districts where light industry has departed, or in new apartments where there used to be abandoned lots. In the above examples, these may not always be practical or even possible at all. Depending on where jobs are located, there are severe spatial mismatches between where work and housing are located (Ihlanfeldt 1994). Mountainous areas are better suited to ranging animals than farming vegetables. Car dependency is already lower in some areas for a variety of reasons. So, their specific situations needed to be studied by individuals.

The well off can help promote ready alternatives rather than give dogmatic advice and shame lower-tier people. One example is regions that have networks of disused railroad rights-of-way and other paths that can serve as bicycle and walking trails almost immediately or be readily incorporated. Metropolitan Washington, D.C. is expanding its network to more than 1,400 miles (2,300 kilometers) (Lazo 2020). Another example is to ask their City Council to stop opposing even modest support of transit even if they themselves do not need it. There are cases like suburbs of Detroit where transit service districts are not contiguous. Or suburbs of Atlanta where entire counties are without transit.

Trying to be a good citizen and follow advice reveals there are limits to what one can do as individual. Government has to be in the picture to enable and promote these things to some extent through changes in subsidy and tax policies, public investments, and changes in the *modus operandi* of entire sectors, such as agricultural practices and subsidies, and the locations and types of new housing starts that are permitted. Not all of these involve the same levels of government. Citizens will simply have to be more active, evolving their habits as government policies change, prices change, and alternatives become available. Then they must also close the feedback loop to generate a process of continuous improvement.

At the risk of going off on a tangent, similar opportunities exist and would be especially useful in developing countries if the USA and other rich countries ramp up efforts to help. They might yet recognize it is in their own interest to help aggressively boost CO_2 reduction efforts where events are moving too slowly, both for the sake of the climate and for employment. There could be a new generation of Peace Corp, Vista or City Year volunteers dedicated to transferring of best practices.

Judging how realistic proposals for restoring small towns are

Given the large number of suggestions available about where to live and with what lifestyle a concerned citizen must make an effort to see what is sensible and realistic. We really cannot all live in places like Snowmass, Colorado in solar powered single-family houses. This is just physically impossible with the current population. We would have to take down large numbers of alpine trees to farm and become vegans if we lived in a mountainous area and empty aquifers if too many of us lived in the same desert. And how would this solve the car dependency issue? There is no escaping that the majority of us will have to still live in cities of various sizes, they will just need to be more compact than in the past. But in the short term, this can be totally unrealistic and people must continue to reside where they are because it remains too expensive to move to one of the small number of thriving cities of the creative class until the supply of housing increases. Nor can they move to one of the other cities, larger or smaller, until there is some suitable employment.

Many would prefer to live in smaller cities and towns if it were economically viable. Even more so if they received some livability improvements. We know this because so many people left primarily because they could no longer make a living as farmers or factory workers. Compare most US towns in agricultural regions to what one can still see in southern European villages where getting children to day-care and to schools are less of a daily concern and headache. Many of the people working the fields just walk or ride their tractors instead of having to first drive cars or get a lift out to their fields. By contrast, in much of the rural US people live isolated in scattered farmhouses. Even houses within the nearest small town are often not in walking distance from one another. Take an internet tour down main streets with stores set back behind parking lots and vacant lawns adjacent to them and one can appreciate it would take a surprisingly long time to travel their length. Smaller towns can have their parking lots infilled to be more compact and to restore the downtowns with features like apartments over the tops of storefronts. Stores will then be in walking distance instead of behind an ocean of parking on the edge of a town without sidewalks.

Weatherization, appliance replacement and other familiar ideas

Much of the housing in the USA is either dilapidated or built in an era of very cheap energy or both. Insulation is something that has been talked about regularly and some incentives have been offered. Certainly, newer houses are built to a higher standard and information about energy efficiency of new appliances is available on the showroom floor models. Nevertheless, much remains to be done. Individuals can do a lot and legislation should be introduced for more instant rebates and various other short-term incentives to do so. In this way, more people of modest means will take action and take it sooner.

Promoting insulation can be further enhanced by governments investing in vocational education targeted at developing a suitable workforce. It should offer wages higher than current retail wages. Their services can perhaps be made available in a bundled price together with the supplies. Incentivization to commercial interests to build tighter factories and replace old equipment with newer electric motors and pumps is also needed but the policy tools are different since they can be less voluntary in nature, using regulations instead.

Both household and industrial improvement will probably not be assisted, and might be outright resisted, by the alliance of upper-tier building trades unions and elected officials and, once again, might require a mass movement demanding that a larger swath of the community participate in such work. The lack of such a movement was surely one of the reasons why this "no brainer" of weatherization is still not complete despite dating back to the energy crises of the 1970s. As discussed in an earlier chapter, this may already be occurring with mayors asking for regulatory changes for projects receiving federal funds. Another important reason for intermittent progress has been the dramatic swings of energy prices so that programs are not renewed by short term minded legislators.

Pick those projects first that reduce combined capital and operating costs from all infrastructure

Projects where concrete is being poured, asphalt is being laid and buildings are going up can vary a great deal in size and scope. Some efforts be quite minor in cost and yet pay a significant dividend in the short term. Charles Marohn of *Strongtowns* sensibly advocates for picking small investments that have the highest return in the short term (Marohn 2020). This can be done without additional revenue sources if one can successfully organize to block spending on further highway and subdivision expansion. He cites an example of putting a small amount of money into storage sheds that could enable local farmers to sell their wares close to downtown Muskegon, Michigan. His organization and others like the McHarg Center, Transit Center and T4America have an array of ideas (McHarg Center et al., 2020; Studer 2020). Another example is from Oakland, California where streets are being slowed down by planter barricades. Planting in them is being encouraged to teach skills and make daily life more pleasant (Hanzlik

2020). On a large scale, narrowing roads to install plant can also cool down a neighborhood leading to further savings in air conditioning.

Cities are not always passively awaiting their fate of continual shrinkage and have ideas to share with one another that do not need much help from higher levels of government. Not only are the oft recognized garage/alley apartments possible, cities with unaffordable storefronts can attract small sellers who only need limited or periodic selling space through zoning changes (Salvador 2020). New Orleans has had assistance from local universities to teach urban agriculture after it was partially abandoned after Hurricane Katrina (Wulfhorst 2020). This approach should be multiplied as it is clear that supply chains must shorten as global warming is taken more seriously, which creates opportunities for smaller cities and rural areas. My students and others elsewhere have identified similar opportunities near Pennsylvania towns, and, indeed, promoting selling space and local agriculture can cascade into longer term benefits. This can lead to further savings over time on an increasingly large scale as the number of cities following similar strategies multiplies.

Individual cities at modest analysis costs might discover that they could install district heating pipes from their central powerplants, install solar power units on buildings, rainwater harvesting systems, gardens on roofs, perforated parking lots to reduce flooding, and other such measures even with stingy and uncooperative state and surrounding local governments. They can start around major train and bus stations should they happen to have them because this also creates a focus for urban residential and commercial redevelopment. It might be that they can afford to issue bonds against the potential costs savings. There are some green energy businesses that are willing to self-finance, as long as they have enough long-term contracts based on sufficiently high rates. It could be that the city reduces its infrastructure costs, the residents see reduced rates, and the company makes a profit.

It does not have to be the city government itself, but any public agency with long-term contracting authority. This has already accelerated with transit agencies and schools covering their parking lots with solar collectors (Berg 2021). Getting such changes will not be equally easy in all locations, especially if there are regional power companies that jealously guard their monopoly powers. These types of alternative energy analyses should be revisited periodically especially after successful changes in regulatory and taxation policy at higher levels of government. Many energy technology companies are only too happy to visit and provide free help.

Pick projects that improve safety and public health

Making walking and bicycling safer often could be done with only minor investments. Some small access roads do not even need separate sidewalks, just better layouts to slow down cars and discourage parking in specific locations, strategic shortcuts through *cul de sacs*, and other inexpensive modifications. This can be later supplemented with better bus stops, bus lanes and queue bypasses, more street furniture, large billboard removal, and so on. There are quite a few advocates already for what has come to be known as the "complete streets" movement. One obvious direct benefit stems from reducing the need for cars to walk to stores, schools, and to work and all that this entails. But the chain of benefits is long. Community aesthetics improve (a benefit economists find hard to quantify) which in turn could lead to further walking and bicycling. If many people switch to non-motorized transport it will strengthen local commerce leading to diminished dependence on big boxes and less export of profits to billionaires like the Walton family living on Park Avenue and like Jeff Bezos living in Washington state that is without an income tax.

The public health community have become big advocates for transit because even short walks are good for health. Children have safer places to play with fewer cars on local trips and parents need to dedicate less time to chauffeuring. Safety will also improve as more people resist the temptation to drive home after drinking when there are affordable and practical alternatives. None of this could come a moment too soon. The USA has seen a reversal and decline in pedestrian safety over the last decade (McCarthy 2020; AAA Foundation for Traffic Safety 2021; Smart Growth America 2021) with children now dying at twice the rate of peer nations (Walker 2018). Florida leads the way in traffic mortality (Robertson 2021), perhaps not surprising with the very high percentage of advanced elderly who walk slowly across its numerous wide 50 mph (80 kph) arterial roads, its minimal non-motorized infrastructure investment and its minimal transit service. The prevalence of collisions with large SUVs has played a role (Wilson 2020a). One must also add the dramatic increase in "crew cab" trucks, crossovers, and oversized, overpowered luxury cars, both ICE and electric. The hood heights make it hard to see small people, and if hit, for the victim to bounce onto the hood instead of underneath. The Tesla "truck" with its sharp horizontal edge is a testament to the total abandonment of non-occupant safety regulation.

Hats off to the auto industry who deserve credit for their very successful marketing effort stimulated by a national policy of cheap gasoline and safety loopholes. Much has been written about the need for a larger fuel tax for a variety of reasons, but it still remains far too low. The forces against increases are formidable, especially at the federal level. Indeed, if there is any coherent policy it is to promote energy independence, which may be aggravating the environmental crises. Methane is the equivalent to far smaller quantities of CO_2 as far as contribution to GHG levels and has increased by about 12 percent over the last 20 years (Schiermeier 2020). A newer technique to release the harder to extract natural gas known as hydraulic fracturing, or fracking, releases methane through leaks to an uncertain extent, but any leakage clearly offsets and may even exceed the benefit of burning this increased 12 percent of natural gas over other fossil fuels. Deep sea drilling has already damaged the Gulf of Mexico and might soon damage the Arctic. To break this logjam of continued pandering to the extraction demands of the oil and gas industry is going to require a mass movement that overwhelms the US Senate membership imbalance favoring the oil states. Even reactionary state legislature typical of the oil producing states are gradually being forced to raise their fuel taxes for reasons other than the environment. The more they get raised, the more they will reduce demand.

The low tax mentality to which politicians pander seems to include the lower tier as well not the least because they are often amongst the most auto dependent.

During the Civil Rights movement people did not need racism explained to them. The harm of driving cheaply is not so readily obvious as a short-term interest conflicts with the long-term imperative. Even though the polls show that the majority of the public favors increases in gasoline taxes and protecting the environment would-be reformers must come bearing gifts, that is, a lot of other improvements in a policy package designed to make this more palatable to the people who are struggling to make ends meet. Any new expense, however well justified, should be compensated somehow and accompanied by a vision of a better tomorrow where daily costs might even come down. Indeed, some alternatives to driving must be a high priority and provided early without massive construction projects that take a long time to complete.

Electrification and technology boosterism can backfire

Many places have constituencies and advocacy groups whose sole focus seems to be pressuring public transit (and sometimes garbage collection agencies) to switch propulsion technologies. This approach should be resisted unless funding increases are extremely generous, service has already been sped up through preferential treatment, service is already very frequent, and there are few gaps in area coverage. Otherwise, it can backfire by putting more people back into their cars. In Washington State, King County Metro's recent estimate was that full electric buses cost at least 42 percent more annually to own and operate than diesel-electric hybrid buses (Ryan 2020). It is not only the more expensive buses, but new charging infrastructure along the routes and in the depots. Motor and charging technology can further limit the number of hours a bus can stay in service and the steepness of hills they can climb. With a fixed operating budget, in King County's hilly service area, this translates into major cuts in service. Similar cost increases are potentially catastrophic to minimal small city and rural operations where the removal of even a few buses means elimination of entire routes. The transit dependents are thus made to lead the fight against pollution with their jobs. The advocacy groups likely consist of members of the upper tier who are not dependent upon transit.

It also needs to be pointed out that propulsion technologies, fuels and prices are evolving. When the California Air Resources Board (CARB) mandated replacement of diesel buses with Compressed Natural Gas (CNG) buses three decades ago, it was a sound idea. Since then, CNG increasingly comes from fracking while now common diesel-electric hybrids use ultra-low sulfur diesel (ULSD) fuel, have substantially higher fuel efficiency than straight diesels, are quieter, and put less particulate matter in the air from their frequent braking than either CNG or straight diesel buses. California has had substantial success by toughening standards on straight diesel trucks, farm machinery, marine vessels, and so on, beyond national standards, so why continue to single out perennially underfunded transit systems for a diesel-electric hybrid ban and the transit shaming that goes with it? (Schwarzman et al. 2021). Better to concentrate the full electric buses and the CNG buses that emit less of the especially harmful microparticles than diesel-electric hybrids where there are the most pedestrians.

Similarly, school buses need a revisit. I was startled to find that all school buses in the USA were still not using ULSD, a genuine scandal considering that transit made the change before a 2010 deadline, a change which allows the installation of particulate traps at modest cost and high effectiveness (Austin, et al. 2019). Combining particulate traps plus modernizing the aforementioned huge backlog of dilapidated HVAC systems in school buildings should be done immediately if the goal is to protect student health. Demanding wholesale replacement of diesel engines or entire buses with money that schools do not have is probably counterproductive. Another example of systems thinking.

These types of decisions can be revisited periodically before every major purchase but based on the performance/cost packages available at the time, not with prejudice against specific propulsion technologies. For example, full electric buses are not without their drawbacks. Huge increases in batteries will also create their own industrial, supply chain and pollution challenges to replace some of those associated with fossil fuels (Picarsic 2020; UNCTAD 2020). Europe is creating laws about ethical sourcing and mandatory recycling and the USA will need to follow suit (Keynes 2020). A breakthrough in battery technology using something mundane like iron instead of precious metals is the holy grail, but it is irresponsible to plan on it (Searles 2020) or any other breakthrough, for that matter. For certain, there are going to be major recycling costs and concerns, further breakthroughs will only reduce these costs (Morse 2021). As another example, instead of aiming to replace cars one for one with electric powered ones of equal size, come up with a list of priorities for investment in infrastructure to incentivize rapid change in the existing mix that reduces the number of cars without damage to people who are already historically underserved.

Furthermore, US metro regions tend to have much longer trip distances than European ones of equal population, making weight reductions also important. In summary, take actions to reduce vehicle miles, reduce size and weight of replacement vehicles, reduce the need for auto trips and other short-term measures (Furth 2021). Take further actions to direct public and private investment to reduce average trip length over the medium and long term by densification and urban form restructuring for further gains. These two sides of vehicle technology and urban travel patterns are roughly equal in potential (Bruun 2013). If we luck out with technological breakthroughs, so much the better. None of other actions will have been wasted, the worst that can happen is that we made cities more efficient, liveable, and healthy at a higher monetary cost than otherwise.

Just because something is new and innovative does not mean it should automatically replace what is tried and true. Politicians in places with automotive related industries like Michigan and places with poor prospects to fix their severe transportation deficits, like South Florida, are trying to invite innovation experts to use their places as laboratories (Descant 2020a, 2020b). This is going to be working at the margins at best. This is either a cynical attempt to impress the public that something is happening or comes from an ideological belief that there are technological solutions to every problem.

Academic research on innovative approaches like Artificial Intelligence (AI) to help optimize existing services is no doubt mostly sincere but there is only so much one can do with sparse services (Flannery 2020). A good example would be Columbus, Ohio, where a $50 million "smart cities" grant was recently completed that tested various new technologies, including automation concepts like small community shuttles. Meanwhile, the existing transit system serving this metro area of nearly two million people is minimal. It has no rail lines and the last human-driven bus departs on almost all routes around nine in the evening. In the end, someone has to actually pay to install and operate additional services, and quite a few of them to boot, driver or no driver.

There are some technological boosterism bills being promoted in the US House of Representatives but also new climate plans promoting "smart growth" attempting to be a bit more holistic than just transportation but public utilities in general (Mulero 2020). These boosters have an easier time than advocates for funding of physical infrastructure investments as they need to pass only relatively simple bills unlikely to be opposed by lobbyists. It is free money and not threatening. It does not usually challenge commercial approaches; it boosts their Research and Development budgets.

On the other hand, Green New Deal advocates must consider that smart growth involves physical infrastructure involving multiple departments in multiple adjacent cities and any funding must be substantial, long term and reliable (Davis 2020) and policies must be coordinated. They also must be developed to prevent what is known as cannibalization of other sources that are temporarily more expensive. Newer energy sources and storage technologies will be coming on line at the same time as existing ones remain in service. Each one will have different times of day when they have peak output and optimal roles in balancing supply and demand. What one has seen in Germany and the USA is that natural gas systems have been left on when not needed due to their contractual requirements, which is not only wasteful but unfair to investors or taxpayers who might have to pay someone to wear out their equipment needlessly. Electricity for charging cars must be more expensive during peak demand hours and cheaper in low periods so that cars act like capacitors in the network, making it more efficient. And so on.

The C40 member cities in the USA start with a huge deficit compared to most of their sister cities, even against some cities in the developing world. Surrounding cities in the metro region that have not publicly made the same commitment will need to join the program as well in any serious attempts to negotiate a Green New Deal. There will be no technological bypass of actually spending money to create or increase the capacity of some public services.

Filling urban and suburban bus and rail gaps

People cannot use transit that does not exist, so the typical argument that people will not use transit cannot be assumed to be true without first trying. If there is an increase in frequency of existing service and in service hours, that is a first step. Putting in traffic signals that detect transit vehicles and queue bypasses for them will both lower their operating costs and increase ridership for the relatively modest sum of a few million dollars, that is a second step. It is equivalent to the cost of the annual operating cost of a handful of 40 foot (12 meter) long buses. These two steps can create a virtuous circle of further increases, the opposite of the downward spiral that occurred for decades.

Many places also need to fill huge gaps. If the area is of low density and the walking conditions are difficult, then demand-responsive smaller buses may be needed as well. Special attention will be required to reach the office and industrial parks in outlying areas to counter one of the consequences of unabated sprawl and over concentration of employees in the outskirts of a limited number of metro areas. The lower tier's work is continually being displaced to lower rent locales and the solution should not have to be buying and operating a car just to get to work. Smartphone apps can provide timed transfers to the larger fixed routes and one payment for the entire trip. Progress has been limited at bigger city transit agencies in large part because of the intransigence of labor unions under the existing patronage systems, not because the smartphone apps are immature. No responsible manager will create routes carrying less than, say, ten people per hour with drivers whose base labor rate is over $30 per hour and very expensive benefits. Not when there are so many other unmet needs at 100 persons per hour that can be served using large buses at only 20 percent higher total costs.

Populations are aging in place in auto dependent neighborhoods so this is another important demographic focus (Molinsky et al. 2020). The aforementioned improvements in demand-responsive smartphone apps also increase the possibilities for "mainstreaming" the disabled who used to require low productivity separate services and 24-hour advanced reservations.

There has been some justifiable criticism that the limited number of high-performance Light Rail Transit (LRT) and Bus Rapid Transit (BRT) systems and very limited rapid transit line extensions (like the Upper Eastside in Manhattan) have aimed excessively at easing the commute of the upper tier to central areas. This reflects who has political power. These can still be modified with new extensions and new connections to make them more helpful to the lower tier as well. The four-day workweek could benefit almost all workers as well as the environment.

Whether it is simply adding more service, adding extensions, or adding entirely new BRT or LRT corridors, cities need to be patient for a few years. People need time to discover these services and to alter their lifestyles. Eventually, the number of cars per household will decrease, training a new generation who will not be so auto dependent, and some income previously essential for commuting will become disposable. Not good for the gas stations and auto parts stores perhaps, but good for the book business.

Filling intercity bus, rail, and air gaps

The mainland USA is enormous. If as part of a Green New Deal we have decided that stopping the exodus from hundreds of smaller cities and towns to a limited number of ever-growing metro areas is an important goal then all transport modes available should be used in an integrated network. The current thinking that modes are competing with each other (McMurtry 2020) is not going to work. It only works between certain larger cities and along certain corridors with a string of smaller cities that lay between these two larger cities. If one sees where the new wave of intercity buses operate without operating subsidies they run in parallel to rail lines but at more affordable fares and in a few corridors between big cities without intercity rail. Amtrak has some *Thruway* services that connect a few cities off the main corridor with buses as do the large bus operators, but they are far from adequate in number. And many of the choices for where the aforementioned Essential Air Services operate are more a legacy of the earmarking process than anything else. Why does Johnstown, Pennsylvania that is only 70 miles (115 kilometers) from the Pittsburgh airport need service but not the other cities of similar size but farther away from a major airport? (McMurtry 2018).

The airline mode has traditionally been funded totally separately from the surface modes not only because of its distinctly different infrastructure needs, but because it is perceived as being important to the upper tier. Under a GND, more rigorous analysis and selection of routes and appropriate modes is needed to make better use of available funds (Schwieterman et al. 2017).

Using the same principle of hub-and-spoke already used by the airline industry and transit planners, known also in the jargon as a pulsing or timed-transfer system, is probably the best way forward. This method can connect many origins and destinations more times per day for an equal operating budget albeit with somewhat longer trip length and transfers as the tradeoff (Thompson and Matoff 2003). When other familiar modes like e-scooters, bike shares, car shares get connected and whatever else gets invented, perhaps hoverboards and e-unicycles, also become available at transfer locations, these places become "mobility hubs." Mobility as a Service (MaaS) smartphone apps are already mature enough that a convenient single ticket can be issued for an entire trip chain involving different companies (Gopal 2020).

There are other concepts being explored ostensibly using AI to simulate how a given region might be served using a clean slate including a mix of modes yet to be determined (Descant 2020c) but even with MaaS there will almost always need to be more spending on vehicles and operators to increase the volume of services, or what is the point? Transit planners are not so dumb, there is lots of experience how to operate the demand-responsive transit mode, there just are not enough zones where vehicles are actually available. Someone is going to have to pay for these other modes as well, except in the rare case that they can operate without subsidy.

AI is also being touted for an array of other public services besides transport where the same question might arise (Flessner 2020). Is it worthwhile technology if no money is available for staff to manage and maintain and hardware to operate these services, even if the AI research showed it would be helpful? One might only be supporting universities and consultants instead of the public at large the public might even end up having to pay for servers that consume energy for monitoring but without much improvement in output or delivery, something that itself should be a research project.

In the intercity setting, increasing the frequency of service along some of the bus and train mainlines is necessary because it then enables bus connections from cities near the corridor, per the aforementioned hub and spoke system. With moderate subsidy some smaller cities might even be close enough to receive direct connections to nearby larger hubs several times per day. Airplanes will still be the solution for some remote locations like mountains, sparse deserts, islands, and other places without hospitals where time savings can be very important. As confidence in the partnerships between companies from different industries increases and as demand builds, it will also be possible to negotiate joint prices between them. Think of a local transit ticket, the intercity train, and the taxi to the countryside cabin all for a combined price. And then a steep discount for several people traveling together. Then all of these services can better compete with car driving.

Then if and when this works, add even more small operators connecting to even smaller towns. Many of these smaller towns that presently cannot support a local taxi service might be able to do so if these companies had a base of scheduled trips to cities up the food chain. This is an example of painting a vision to people being asked to pay higher fuel taxes in the short term.

Large public works construction projects must have wider benefits and productivity improvements

The bigger the projects, the more the investment. Unless they have many parts that can be done in parallel, they take a lot of time to pour concrete. Sand of suitable quality for concrete is also becoming a scarce resource in some places. It is thus imperative that projects make up for this time where they provide no environmental benefit and perhaps for their high volume use of sand by having huge positive impacts later. They must be assessed for the specific distribution of benefits and costs upon particular communities and populations. For example, the California high speed rail project is moving slowly and will take a long time to really connect San Francisco Bay Area with the Los Angeles area competitively with airplanes, its original primary purpose. But in the meantime, it will make multiple stops in the Central Valley, something that the numerous airline flights do not do. These areas are historically more poverty stricken and need some stimulus and alternatives to agribusiness. They can also serve as alternative growth locations to slow down the population rush to the Bay Area and LA basin. So, this example project needs to be revisited whether these revised intermediate goals and delay of the full project are still worth the investment for huge over and underpasses in farmland.

There must also be productivity improvements as heavy construction has lagged behind other sectors which themselves have been only around 1 percent annually as a whole. From 2007 to 2019 productivity in the USA increased by a mere 0.7 percent for "industrial building construction" and actually decreased by 0.3 percent in "highway, street, and bridge construction" (Bureau of Labor Statistics 2020). This is something that would be of great interest to many cities and ideal for a national research program. It would go hand in hand with a plan to use large numbers of newly trained workers as city modifications intensify.

Relative size of US commitments

Peer countries are already experiencing major parts of their Green New Deals. The federal government of Germany has large infrastructure plans designed to shift people from their *autobahns* to long-distance trains (and buses as well) by allowing capacity investments and competition between operators to drive down fares. They have committed to €62 billion for the next five years while Deutsche Bahn (DB), their largest national intercity railway, committed to €24 billion (Briginshaw 2020). German states will also commit more for urban and suburban transit systems as well. Last year, Amtrak tried to cover a continent with $700 Million for the Northeast Corridor and $1.3 Billion for the remainder (Shepardson 2020). To compare with Germany, that would be $6.5 Billion for five years. And even this paltry level of funding has been perpetually in danger since its founding in 1971. One can go back to the George H. W. Bush Administration where his budget gave Amtrak a "kinder, gentler zero." Clinton and the second Bush Administration went along with efforts to force to it toward being self-supporting. At the conclusion of the second Bush Administration Congress then passed the Passenger Rail Investment and Improvement Act of 2008, also known as PRIIA, which requires states to support routes less than 750 miles (1,230 kilometers) long (Szabo 2011). This makes enthusiastic states fight with neighboring reactionary-led states to build corridors, as has been demonstrated by the aforementioned cases of Wisconsin, Iowa, and Ohio after the 2009 stimulus plans. In early November 2020 the Minnesota legislature declined to help fund a mere second train per day from St. Paul to Milwaukee and Chicago. After other contributions Minnesota's share was only $10 million and even included capacity increases for freight (Moore 2020). The governor then reintroduced a bonding proposal that would fund it (Progressive Railroading 2021). Two of the Midwestern lines that did get upgraded were never completed to the 110 mph standard. So the tough stance against even relatively small locally supported rail system development continues (Congressional Research Service 2019). The newest proposals and bills under the Biden Administration may finally reverse this, and contrary to a GND also turbocharge highway widening, but it is too early to say what actually happens.

In the urban and regional urban planning sphere, *Il-de-France*, otherwise known in English as the "Greater Paris Region" is building four more metro lines 15 through 18, extending line 14, and extending tram lines for a total of 200 kilometers (122 miles) with 68 new stations (Societe du Grand Paris 2019; Martin 2021). There is also a comprehensive sustainability program involving hydrogen buses, refueling stations and shared bicycles at all stations (Choose Paris Region 2020). Berlin is also planning a similarly huge transit expansion. Madrid already went through a prolonged period of continual construction for a very impressive rapid transit network. Even lower income Delhi has gone from no rapid transit at all in 1997 to a major system complete with a bus feeder network, thanks in part to generous help from Japan. By contrast, almost nothing in either new regional rail or rapid transit is scheduled for construction in the large metro regions of the USA, just a few miles here or a few miles there. To catch up, not only will funding have to increase dramatically, for the large cities rebuilding and extending their rapid transit and repairing or taming their freeways, construction costs and durations will have to come down dramatically. Anything involving tunnels will have to be done more efficiently than the 2nd Avenue subway if there is to be enough benefit to justify it, such as large volumes of new housing, a major decrease in car use for a major reduction in GHG, land preservation (sprawl reduction) and other environmental goals.

Can big corporations be broken up?

Antitrust prosecutions used to be based in large part on the theory that any firm that got too big posed a threat as it could get both excessive market and political power. This is why the oil conglomerates were broken up and railroad monopolies were regulated one hundred years ago. But the Milton Friedman school of thought expressed in his influential "Capitalism and Freedom" book from 1962 that one of the benefits from capitalism that economic and political power could be separated (Friedman 1962) has prevailed. In recent decades, the main test was short-term prices to the consumer, allowing mergers in many industries and predatory practices to go largely unchallenged. There is a minor consulting industry on the topic of whether customers will pay more or less as a result of mergers. It hires itself out to both the government and to industry, and sometimes both. Like something out of the satirical newspaper *The Onion*, it is an oligopoly characterized by extremely high hourly rates that might itself be in need of an anti-trust investigation (Eisinger and Elliott 2016).

This extreme concentration in several sectors related to public works has made it much harder to change the status quo. Finding ways to break them up or redirect them up is important for success: According to one study, the one hundred (100) largest fossil fuel producers and generated nearly 1 trillion tonnes of greenhouse gas emissions, 71 percent of global emissions. It is further stated in this same study that a *"huge acceleration of fossil fuel extraction has doubled their contribution since 1988. (Griffin 2017)"* They are now a powerful force for slowing down what needs to be speeded up instead. As are the "big box" stores that have relocated shopping to places requiring a car and cannot be served efficiently by transit or walking. In turn, this has led to the collapse of downtowns across the continent and all that entails for degradation of the environment and the choice of lifestyles available. As are the agribusiness players like beef packers, pork producers and vertically integrated chicken processors with their extremely polluting farms. The pollution is local and downstream and the profits are exported to distant owners.

It is generally believed that no action can be taken to break up these behemoths without new federal legislation which these same firms could succeed in preventing through campaign donations and lobbying. It is also commonly believed that corporations are legally required to maximize shareholder value and that therefore it is A-OK that they wreck communities until there is new legislation. This is not true (Stout 2012). Even if it were true, corporations would clearly be failing to maximize by any definition. Back in 1950s through the 1960s when antitrust laws were more aggressively enforced returns were always over 7 percent and then plummeted in the 1970s. They rose again during the dot.com bubble, but since it burst returns plummeted to only 3 percent today (CEPR 2019).

Managements have found creative ways to enrich themselves with extremely high salaries, quarterly bonuses, and accounting maneuvers like offshoring profits to avoid reporting profits in the USA thereby both avoiding taxation and sharing with external stock holders. Perhaps the most enabling change of all was SEC Rule 10b-18 implemented in November 1982. It allowed stock buybacks using profits rather they paying them out, which pumps up the value of the company stock. The management salary is tied to the value of the stock through bonus schemes.

It would be impossible to enforce maximizing shareholder value in any case, even if it were the law, as there are different classes of shareholders and different time horizons which one can consider. No law requires the planning horizon to be quarterly. In reality, corporations are granted limited liability when it is believed to be in the public interest since otherwise capital would not be risked due to risk of personal bankruptcy. Many charters can and should be challenged. Environmental and urban planning advocates could cajole or pressure politicians to challenge the alleged public benefits in order to revoke charters using existing legislation. Even if ultimately not successful, the exercise of requiring huge corporations to justify themselves would be enlightening and the data useful for planning.

Living with big corporations and their possible redirection

Because of the huge size of fossil fuel extractors and refiners, their numbers of employees and their global reach, any redirection must also be huge. They do have skills for constructing megaprojects successfully. One example to put them to work might be using public freeway rights-of-way as a cost-efficient method of installing solar panels on a large scale. Land acquisition is not needed and connections to the grid are easy. One study identified 127,000 acres (51,400 hectares) of suitable land (Descant, 2020d) near freeway exits. Furthermore, they span the North American continent so that the panels can be distributed across time zones to lessen east-west distribution to mostly the shorter north-south distribution distances. If the fossil fuel companies are not given the ongoing maintenance and distribution tasks as well, power utilities are also quite large though not as international and politically powerful. They too will need more redirection than they are already undergoing. Another intriguing example involving both industries would be the electrification of all of the east-west freight train mainlines that are now based on diesel-electric propulsion. The public would pay for the power distribution equipment and capital costs, the train operators for rail-related equipment, the power they use and their share of maintenance expenses. The money saved by them would translate into more competitive prices and thus more diversion from trucking to intermodal freight by shortening the so-called breakeven distance. The train corridors would also serve as readymade conduits for the very high voltage lines for long distance transmission to allow western power to reach the eastern seaboard during hot summer nights reducing the needs for fossil fuel (coal and natural gas) and nuclear power. Another example of systems thinking.

There are many other concepts to be analyzed. Because of water shortages, a high priority would be those projects having to do with aquifers, water supplies and distribution. Some would be more modest like repairing the leaks wasting trillions of gallons of water, while others can certainly turn out to be very expensive due to the long distances of piping runs. There can be further less expensive efforts like drip irrigation as has been helping farmers in climate-altered Pakistan use less fertilizer and 60 percent less water (Mukhtar 2020). There are also some major deconstructions (not in the literary sense but the literal sense) to be considered. As an example, the Snake River still has four dams in place that were slated for demolition already decades ago. Many elaborate fisheries could be closed and disassembled as they are limited in effectiveness since the native species get their DNA polluted or they stop spawning. Perhaps almonds and rice and other water-intensive growers could be assisted in finding new growing locales less dependent upon diminishing western water supplies. And so on. If a non-expert in one public works silo can list ideas, surely people who have spent decades within their silos can do so as well. Each city or region can then compile lists and classify the project as short, medium, or long term and set a list of goals and the objectives by which success would be measured. From there the deeper systems analysis can begin to identify synergies from joint projects as well as possible conflicts.

Comparison to Finland on Green New Deal plans

Finland has its hands partially tied with respect to investment plans because it is in the Eurozone. It has been expected to follow the Maastricht Treaty. It mandates an austerity policy of each member trying to stay below an annual deficit 3 percent of GDP. Nevertheless, it has clearly succeeded in doing public investments on a far higher level than the USA. It has a much higher level of taxation on fossil fuels so the competition against everything else for the funding of roads is much less. A more supportive populace with a legacy of support for political parties at lower levels of government that value continuing investment has prevented the near boycott of public investment in parks, transit, schools, etc., even under conservative governments, that has occurred in the USA at the Federal level and many state governments.

Expansion of the underground central heat piping network in the larger cities and the use of heat pumps to extract waste heat from factories, server farms, sewage plants, and building, is also in the cards. As prices rise, perhaps also extracting heat from the difference in sea temperature between the surface and the deep. Finland also is rare amongst western countries in that it actually recently completed a nuclear power plant. It will supply roughly 20 percent of the nation's electricity, a challenge for far northern countries with short days in the winter and limited wind. It was completed with the major delays and price increases one has come to expect for such projects. But it also comes with an underground long-term waste facility that will be watched by the USA and other nations as a possible role model for permanent safe storage.

The role for biofuels remains controversial in part because the full accounting and comparison to other fuels over the entire chain is difficult and needing specific resolution for particular sources and locations (EU Biofuels Chain 2020). Replacement of coal with wood pellets for urban electricity has been part of the sustainability plan, but this depends in large part on governments in the global south and the southeastern USA where states have weak governance and limited environmental concern. This is being increasingly recognized so its envisioned future role is reducing. If the GND is taken seriously on a more global scale, other places might soon reduce unsustainable logging and farming practices, bringing up prices in Europe. In that case, increasing local sourcing taking advantage of an abundance of clean water and forests in Finland might be able to respect the environment and provide a needed boost to rural and smaller city development. But whether it is a net positive for the environment remains controversial.

The path forward is not clear, as rural areas are still depopulating and the level of economic development spending must be increased in these areas if accommodating and stemming population migration is to be part of their equivalent of a GND. This is a common issue for most countries and requires urgent research projects, not just in the USA or Finland, but in almost every nation.

Related to use of biofuels is the preservation of topsoils, with some estimates saying that there is only about 60 years of use left without drastic changes (Arsenault 2014). Thus, there will be a big difference between using boreal forests with no adjacent farms as one sees in the far north and the semi tropical or tropical lands closer to the equator that feel the temptation for conversion to farming after a one-time stripping of trees, like has occurred in the Amazon basin, Indonesia and elsewhere.

Conclusions

Initially include even far-fetched concepts but keep in mind diminishing returns

It is much harder to add ideas later than to include them from the beginning. The Pentagon certainly does not hesitate to think about what might seem like science fiction. They even have DARPA, a major research funding agency. Furthermore, by inviting anyone to submit proposals a city even gets free advice from top experts whose companies usually charge a lot of money. Many recently publicized lists have quite distant ambitions like fossil-fuel free autos by 2050. Others can be quite a bit more challenging, such as switching 100 percent of automobiles in California by 2035 or perhaps switching water heating to all electric by some date only 10–15 years from now (Koseff and Gardiner 2020).

Being rigid about goals is a mistake. It is much better to get to something short of a 100 percent fully electric fleet like all public transit vehicles as stated in *The Biden Plan for a Clean Energy Revolution and Environmental Justice* (Stumpf 2020). There are always diminishing returns. It wastes money to work toward an ideal when there is the opportunity cost of not collecting the low hanging fruit elsewhere by moving on to other targets. More than one goal almost always needs to be considered. Returning to the car example, if pollution is the most important goal, get rid of the dirtiest cars first and don't worry as much about the cleaner ones. Even if full electric cars use less energy and pollute less once built, other problems remain like the resources and imbedded energy to build them, the expense of ownership and use, and the exclusion of people who cannot or will not drive (Wilson, 2020b). Most important of all is that their space inefficiency remains unaddressed. Systematic analyses using multi-criteria evaluation techniques that consider not just transportation, but the wider economy, environment and social impacts (Weisbrod and Stein 2021) need to become standard practice to prevent special interests and ideologues from making decisions that will be regretted later. No sense in repeating the mistakes of the past of not anticipating possible unintended consequences or making decisions where the process stays under the purview of one department.

There aren't firm limits on demand when investments change people's lives

Millions of persons have left the US workforce in the last two decade because of long commutes due to a combination of the mismatch of job and housing locations, stagnant wages, unreliable work schedules, perhaps coupled with lack of vocational retraining, lack of affordable childcare and lack of usable transit. The percentage of people of working ages 15–64 employed or seeking work peaked and held steady from 1996 to 2000 at over 67 percent and after the dot.com bubble burst began descending (Hipple 2016). By January 2021 it had declined to 61.4 percent (Trading Economics 2021). Taking into account the increase in population over the last 20 years, and with a current working age population of about 214 million (Rogers and Wilder 2020), this is roughly ten million fewer people in the workforce than an economy would have without this apparent increase in obstacles and disincentives.

We know from providing Americans with Disabilities Act transit services that when service options become more attractive, the word gets out, and more trip requests are made. If service has extended hours, reduced reservation time, or other such improvements, it opens more options for prospective passengers. One takes this into account by adding more service than one might have planned due to this induced demand. The same thing will happen with the general population when investments are made under the GND. If transit comes to more prospective job sites, the service is more frequent, if sidewalks and shelters are available, and so on, more jobs become attractive without the need for a car. And if pay increases then cars are also more affordable. All of these change the calculation of the cost of driving, the relative cost of driving versus transit, and the ease and time required for using transit, all of which might have made a job previously not worth taking.

It is important to stress that there is no "natural rate" of unemployment as the decision to work (for pay) depends on these transport-related factors plus non-transport factors like the previously discussed cost and availability of paid childcare. That the concept of a natural rate could continue to exist is more evidence that academia remains in silos. The recent analysis by the Congressional Budget Office whether an increase of the minimum wage would have an impact on the federal budget reflects this poor understanding of how many factors contribute to job seeking and acceptance (Auerback and Azmanova 2021). Investments should not be curtailed out of fear that too many people might be finding it viable to work (for pay) in the formal sector instead of staying home to do unpaid childcare or elder care. This would be a perverse result. Better to seek offsetting trip reductions for the hapless people who work several jobs or endure very long commutes. Both underemployment and overemployment can be reversed under a Green New Deal.

Base carbon counting and taxing on the end user not where products are made

If one really wants to move manufacturing back to the higher income countries and also create incentives to shorten supply chains, install taxes to be paid at the point of consumption. Otherwise, there is a perverse incentive to shift polluting industries to lower income countries and ones with weak regulatory power. Importing huge volumes of commodities that represent significant generation of CO_2 like ordinary Portland cement can also be a way to conceal carbon. If one compares the reduction in CO_2 in the USA in 2018 from the 1990 baseline it is really only about 11 percent GDP per capita not 19. Similarly for the UK, it is about 32 percent GDP per capita not 46 percent (Ritchie and Roser 2020). See Figures 8.1 and 8.2.

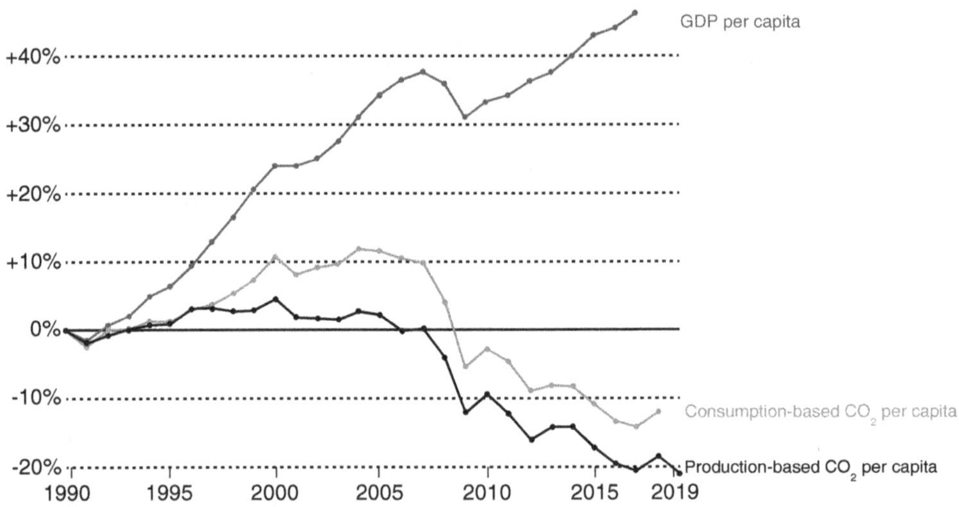

FIGURE 8.1 CO_2 emissions no longer linked to GDP growth after about 2005 in the USA, but reduction in emissions is overstated by almost double if place of production is used instead of place of consumption by end user.

Source: Ritchie and Roser 2020

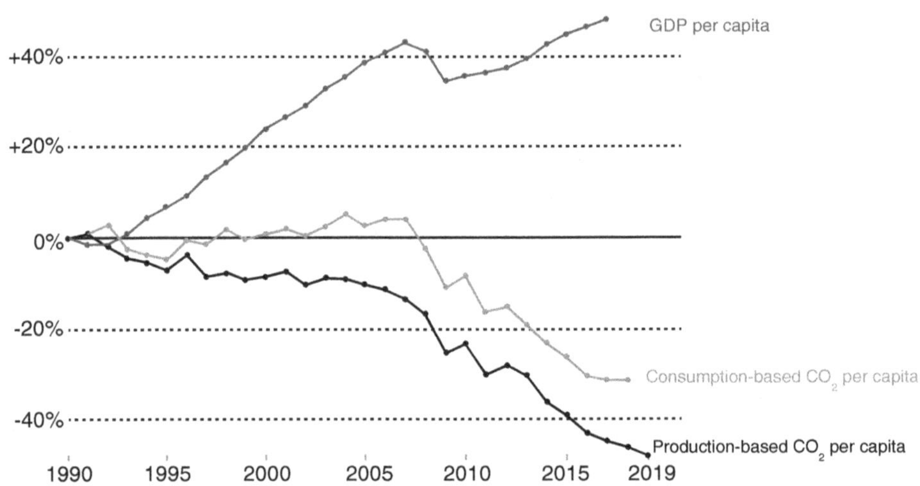

FIGURE 8.2 CO_2 emissions no longer linked to GDP growth after about 2005 in the UK, but reduction in emissions is overstated by significantly if place of production is used instead of place of consumption by end user. Reduction overall has been much larger in the UK than in the USA.

Source: Ritchie and Roser 2020

End-user prices must go up to incentivize reduction in consumption of CO_2 generating products, but there may also be some offsetting increases in manufacturing employment, reductions in transportation and other supply chain costs and environmental improvements visible in daily life, all of which makes this an easier political sell. This is a very important point. Developers of investment plans cannot listen to those who claim the USA is reducing its carbon footprint more than it really is because outsourcing does not solve the problem as far are the world climate is concerned. They must study the entire chain of imbedded energy from raw materials to final disposal before deciding. Not only is it morally unacceptable to expose people to the pollution from products which they are not rich enough to use and that they do not have the means to pay for cleaning-up after, either. The richer countries have demonstrated they can and will pass regulations to manage toxic chemicals and reduce emissions, even if not always so thoroughly. Certainly, they will do a better job than a country with low incomes and weak democratic institutions.

Do not let project size alone deter - consider modern monetary theory (MMT) instead

Thinking about a huge government budget and its unaffordability is a lifelong habit for most of us. The people voting for incessant increases in the Pentagon budget certainly have stopped worrying. Note that even with the huge deficits the USA has compiled year after year, there has been little net inflation on average. There is asset price inflation due to income inequality because the wealthy need places to store or invest their money and because Quantitative Easing has promoted it. There has also been inflation from price increases by those in the upper tier who have been shielded from both competitive markets and government regulation. But it has been compensated by intense competition for other businesses operating in the global "real economy driving down their prices and margins, and as a consequence, reduced or stagnant wages on the lower tier. There might even have been deflation except for the massive borrowing and debts such as credit cards, student loans, car loans, etc. that have postponed it.

As this book moves to final editing, some consumer product inflation seems to be developing. Certainly, lean global supply chains vulnerable to disruption and lack of retail competition due to decades of weak antitrust enforcement play a role at the moment. But the long term trend is unclear and investment in public works can break these trends. It can reduce the cost of living for the lower tier by making infrastructure more efficient resulting in lower monthly utility bills, lower transportation bills by reducing requirements for long commutes and car ownership, and lower operating costs to domestic businesses making them more competitive with foreign competitors. This in turn can create more employment in most locations albeit with reduced employment at locations involved in export products and in operating global supply chains.

The USA is now in a double standard where federal money is routinely allocated to military spending which is not an investment but at most an (over)insurance policy. But allocating money for public works that are genuine investments in the same way as public education is must be justified in Congress by "pay go" perhaps with increased taxes on the lower tier. It is worth familiarizing one's self with Modern Monetary Theory (MMT) and to let elected officials know your viewpoint. If you agree with it, tell them you are not buying their excuses for austerity. To simplify, it says that countries with sovereign currencies can simply make electronic entries into domestic bank accounts, the electronic equivalent of printing money, until capacities of certain sectors are reached and it is no longer equally cheap to add more, in which case inflation can start to occur. Meanwhile, state and local governments are seen as users of the currency instead of issuers and are often legally obligated to balance their budgets and must concern themselves more with how project bills will be paid.

As an example of the application of MMT, it is necessary to raise the gasoline and diesel tax at the local and state levels to remove the subsidy of the transport sector that has been so harmful to other public services by going so often to the front of the funding queue. But it is not necessary at the federal level in order to finance the GND. In fact, doing so while the states and local governments also raise their taxes will now work a hardship on the lower tier who still have no choice but to use motor vehicles but can now barely afford to make ends meet. (Raising federal taxes should have been done many years ago and vehicles would not be so large as they have become.)

In the case of the USA, the capacity crunch will most likely first be in the vocational skills as evidenced by the public project cost inflation so typical of what occurs in a city undergoing private sector building booms. The shortage extends into the public sector as well (Krupnick 2021). Thus, rapid training would have to be a part of any serious Green New Deal. President Biden's free community college proposal is a step in this direction. It would have to be aimed at strategic sectors and geographic locations as the sequence of investments unfolds. The cooperation or lack thereof by state and local governments and their political machines should be a more genuine concern than money as evidenced by delay and refusal of some state governments to distribute Covid-19 relief funds that would help the lower tier. Many elected officials will not want to put in their fair contribution based on ability to pay and will want to protect certain companies and classes of workers rather than distribute funds to the lower tier, even if the money came from the federal government.

Resistance from those in the upper tier invested into generous pensions, expensive houses and who have far above average medical plans can understandably be expected to resist rapid retraining of others as well. It might increase competition. Pensions that are made portable and medical care divorced from employment could lessen this type of resistance. Resistance can also be expected from corporate executives and from professionals in the cartel and oligopolistic sectors of the economy. But this resistance too must be lessened in order to bring public service operating costs down at the state and local levels.

There are going to be materials that have to be limited for environmental or toxicity reasons, or because of shortages, that can limit capacity for investment and project size. There have been wars in The Republic of the Congo over rare earths. A shortage of places to secure lithium for batteries is said by some to be the reason for the coup in Bolivia in 2019. China has the bulk of the needed rare earths identified so far which can bind them to the rest of the world the way that Middle Eastern oil did. Materials availability and ethical sourcing should be a more genuine concern than money and can be expected to be a new cause for geopolitical strife in a manner similar to oil over the last century (IEA 2021).

Reshaping of urban areas should be considered

Studying what the "optimal urban form" might be has been this author's ambition and if one recalls from the introduction, one of the motivations for the book. It is a very complex problem that, at least from my approach, requires mathematical operations research methods to capture the interactions of the commercial, residential, and recreational aspects of a city along with its supporting public services. But if successful it can be used as a "what if" analysis tool for city planners, for concerned citizens, and for students. With creative use one can explore questions like how much difference a change in power costs makes, how much difference building heights make, crowding standards make, whether the optimal profile of building heights to minimize greenhouse gas is the same one that has the lowest infrastructure cost burden, and much more. One can even dare to explore radical questions such as whether it makes sense to buy out some low-density sprawl to replace it with forests or wetlands. Or, how the city housing building height regulations and transit service levels should change if freeways were removed, something that many view as helpful to undo the legacy of racism (Dewey 2020; Fleischer 2020).

Indeed, many alternatives having to do with living space standards, building heights, (many cities currently have single family homes and tall apartment buildings and almost nothing in between in what has come to be called "the missing middle"), commercial versus residential space allotment, park sizes, parking space allotments, roof gardens, *ad in finitum*, could benefit from prior analysis to get closer to a smoothly functioning yet environmentally efficient district of a city on the first try. Rochester, New York is an example where the preliminary effort to replace a freeway is not nearly optimal (Popovich and Lu 2021). As problems become more urgent, what seems radical today might be mundane a few years from now. As a bonus, education in this type of analysis could be of great value for cities in poorer nations.

Finally, even if the traditional deficit hawks were correct that running huge deficits was endangering our grandchildren, which they are not, we would still need to spend money anyway or they will not have a prosperous future in any case. We must meet the challenge of climate change and water conservation to genuinely protect our grandchildren. Money will have to be spent in huge quantities to deal with the aftermath of storms and sea level rise. So why not try to make investments beforehand to try to avoid these crises and solve other liveability and societal problems at the same time? This can and should be done using a scientific approach that identifies conflicts and synergies, saves valuable time, and maybe even self-actualizes some people in the bargain.

References

7 News Radio. 2020. Battle Brewing Over Rights of Uber, Lyft Drivers in Mass. *WDBH*, November 16. Available at: https://whdh.com/news/battle-brewing-over-rights-of-uber-lyft-drivers-in-mass/

AAA Foundation for Traffic Safety. 2021. Research Brief Examining the Increase in Pedestrian Fatalities in the United States, 2009–2018. *American Automobile Association*, January. Available at: https://aaafoundation.org/wp-content/uploads/2021/01/20-1319-AAAFTS_Pedestrian-Fatalities-Brief_FINAL-122220.pdf

Albertson & Davidson, LLP. 2018. Can You Inherit Favorable Tax Treatment? November 15. Available at: https://www.aldavlaw.com/blog/can-you-inherit-favorable-tax-treatment-how-to-inherit-your-parents-house-and-their-low-tax-bill-too/ (Accessed November 24, 2020).

Anderson, Jon. 2018. Dallas Is Long On Maintenance Needs. Is There A Way To Generate More Intelligent Revenue? *FrontBurner*, September 12. Available at: https://www.dmagazine.com/frontburner/2018/09/dallas-is-long-on-maintenance-needs-is-there-a-way-to-generate-more-intelligent-revenue/

Arsenault, Chris. 2014. Only 60 Years of Farming Left If Soil Degradation Continues. *Scientific American*, December 5. Available at: https://www.scientificamerican.com/article/only-60-years-of-farming-left-if-soil-degradation-continues/

Asher-Schapiro, Avi. 2021. Our Education Lifeline': U.S. Battle Over Broadband Heats Up. *Thomson Reuters Foundation,* February 3. Available at: https://news.trust.org/item/20210203112838-qi2q7/

Auerback, Marshall and Albena Azmanova. 2021. What the Congressional Budget Office Doesn't Get. *The Nation*, February 17. Available at: https://www.thenation.com/article/economy/cbo-minimum-wage-unemployment/

Austin, Wes, Garth Heutel, and Daniel Kreisman. 2019. School bus emissions, student health and academic performance. *Economics of Education Review*. 70 (1): 109–126.

Baker, Kevin. 2018. Death of a Great American City: New York and the Urban Crisis of Affluence. *Harper's*, July (pp. 25–47).

Berg, *Nate. 2021.* The Clever Way Strapped Transit Agencies Are Saving Cash. *Fast Company*, February 25. Available at: https://www.fastcompany.com/90607913/the-clever-way-strapped-transit-agencies-are-saving-cash

Brasch, Ben. 2021. Fulton Mayors Tired of Fielding Ask for New BRT Tax to Help Traffic. , March 9. Available at: https://www.ajc.com/news/atlanta-news/fulton-mayors-tired-of-fielding-ask-for-new-brt-tax-to-help-traffic/RQNL6WUFAFGZXPWKBMWRRE7FVY/

Briginshaw, David. 2020. Germany Approves €86bn Rail Infrastructure Programme. *International Railway Journal*, January 15. Available at: https://www.railjournal.com/financial/germany-approves-e86bn-rail-infrastructure-programme/?utm_source=&utm_medium=email&utm_campaign=12591

Bruun, Eric. 2013. Chapter 5. Characterizing and Influencing Modal Relationships. *Better Public Transit Systems: Analyzing Investments and Performance*, 2nd Edition, pp. 124–144. Routledge: Abingdon, UK.

Bruun, Eric and Moshe Givoni. 2015. Sustainable Mobility: 6 Research Routes to Steer Transport Policy. *Nature* 523: 29. July 2. Available at: http://www.nature.com/news/sustainable-mobility-six-research-routes-to-steer-transport-policy-1.17860

C40 Cities. 2020. Divesting from Fossil Fuels, Investing in a Sustainable Future. *Press Release*. Available at: https://c40-production-images.s3.amazonaws.com/other_uploads/images/2600_DI_Declaration_Final_Draft_LAUNCH_LOGO.original.pdf?1600419997

Center for Economic Policy Research (CEPR). 2019. If Corporations Are Being Run to Maximize Returns to Shareholders, Why Are Returns So Low? November 7. Available at: https://www.cepr.net/if-corporations-are-being-run-to-maximize-returns-to-shareholders-why-are-returns-so-low/

Choose Paris Region. 2020. Interview with Lionel Grotto, CEO, Choose Paris Region. 2020. Paris Region Is Taking Sustainability To the Next Level: What You Need To Know. *Urban Mobility Company*, October 15. Available at: https://urbanmobilitycompany.com/content/daily/paris-region-is-taking-sustainability-to-the-next-level-what-you-need-to-know

City of Tallinn. 2020. Media Coverage on Free Public Transport. Available at: https://www.tallinn.ee/eng/freepublictransport/Media-Coverage-on-free-Public-Transport (Accessed November 24, 2020).

Congressional Research Service. 2019. Improving Intercity Passenger Rail Service in the United States. June 25. Available at: https://crsreports.congress.gov/product/pdf/R/R45783

Davis, Steve. 2020. New House Climate Plan Endorses Smart Growth America's Holistic Recommendations for Reducing Emissions. *Smart Growth America*, July 2. Available at: https://smartgrowthamerica.org/new-house-climate-plan-endorses-smart-growth-americas-holistic-recommendations-for-reducing-emissions/ Accessed November 24, 2020.

Descant, Skip. 2020a. South Florida Is Ripe for Transit Innovation, Experts Say. *Government Technology – Future Structure*, July 15. Available at: https://www.govtech.com/fs/transportation/South-Florida-Is-Ripe-for-Transit-Innovation-Experts-Say.html?utm_term=READ%20MORE&utm_campaign=Video%20Analytics%20Traffic%20Study%20Creates%20Baseline%20for%20Change&utm_content=email&utm_source=Act-On+Software&utm_medium=email

Descant, Skip. 2020b. Late-Night Transit in Miami Turns to Uber and Lyft. *Government Technology*, April 20. Available at: https://www.govtech.com/transportation/Late-Night-Transit-in-Miami-Turns-to-Uber-and-Lyft-.html

Descant, Skip. 2020c. Machine Learning Models Could Improve Transit in Chattanooga. *Government Technology*, December 1. Available at: https://www.govtech.com/computing/Machine-Learning-Models-Could-Improve-Transit-in-Chattanooga.html?utm_term=READ%20MORE&utm_campaign=Machine%20Learning%20Models%20Could%20Improve%20Transit%20in%20Chattanooga&utm_content=email&utm_source=Act-On+Software&utm_medium=email

Dewey, Caitlin 2020.Advocates Rally to Tear Down Highways That Bulldozed Black Neighborhoods. *Stateline*, July 28. Available at: https://www.pewtrusts.org/en/research-and-analysis/blogs/stateline/2020/07/28/advocates-rally-to-tear-down-highways-that-bulldozed-black-neighborhoods

Dijk, Marc, Moshe Givoni and Karen Diederiks. 2018. Piling up or Packaging Policies? An Ex-Post Analysis of Modal Shift in Four Cities. *Energies* 11(6): 1400. doi: 10.3390/en11061400

Eisinger, Jesse and Justin Elliott. 2016. These Professors Make More Than a Thousand Bucks an Hour Peddling Mega-Mergers *ProPublica*. November 16. Available at: https://www.propublica.org/article/these-professors-make-more-than-thousand-bucks-hour-peddling-mega-mergers

EU Biofuels Chain. 2020. The Not-So-Secret Solution to Decarbonising EU Transport. *EurActiv*, October 9. Availableat: https://www.euractiv.com/section/agriculture-food/opinion/the-not-so-secret-solution-to-decarbonising-eu-transport/

Flannery, Lee. 2020. Studying AI's Potential to Optimize Public Transit Systems. *Planetizen*, October 29. Available at: https://www.planetizen.com/news/2020/10/111035-studying-ais-potential-optimize-public-transit-systems

Fleischer, Matthew. 2020. Senior Opinion: Want to Tear Down Insidious Monuments to Racism and Segregation? Bulldoze L.A. Freeways. *Los Angeles Times*, June 24. Available at: https://www.latimes.com/opinion/story/2020-06-24/bulldoze-la-freeways-racism-monument

Flessner, Dave. 2020. Chattanooga, Tenn., Nets $110M in Smart City Research Projects. *Chattanooga Times/Free Press*, February 24, Available at: https://www.govtech.com/smart-cities/Chattanooga-Tenn-Nets-110M-in-Smart-City-Research-Projects.html

Friedman, Milton. 1962. *Chapter 1. Capitalism and Freedom.* University of Chicago Press

Furth, Peter G. 2021. Climate and Transportation Policy: Too Much Emphasis on EVs, not Enough on Smaller Vehicles, Fewer Vehicles, Fewer VMT. Blog. Northeastern University. Available at: http://www.northeastern.edu/peter.furth/climate-and-transportation-policy-too-much-emphasis-on-evs-not-enough-on-smaller-vehicles-fewer-vehicles-fewer-vmt/

Good Jobs First. 2020. State Tax Revenue Lost to Tax Abatement Programs 2019. Available at: https://taxbreaktracker.goodjobsfirst.org/prog.php?detail=state_list Accessed November 24, 2020.

Gopal, Venkatesh. 2020. Is Multimodal MaaS Just for Big Cities? *Urban Mobility Daily*, November 11. Available at: https://urbanmobilitycompany.com/content/daily/is-multimodal-maas-just-for-big-cities

Griffin, Paul. CDP (formerly Carbon Database Project). 2017. The Carbon Majors Database: Carbon Majors Report 2017. *CDP with Climate Accountability Institute*, July. Available at: https://b8f65cb373b1b7b15feb-c70d8ead6ced550b4d987d7c03fcdd1d.ssl.cf3.rackcdn.com/cms/reports/documents/000/002/327/original/Carbon-Majors-Report-2017.pdf?1499691240

Hanley, Steve. 2020. The Costs Of Owning A Conventional Car Are Far Higher Than People Think *CleanTechnica*. August 7. Available at: https://cleantechnica.com/2020/08/07/the-costs-of-owning-a-conventional-car-are-far- higher-than-people-think/

Hanzlik, Mae. 2020. Redesigning Slow Streets to reflect community & culture in East Oakland. *Smart Growth America*, November 9. Available at: https://smartgrowthamerica.org/redesigning-slow-streets-to-reflect-community-culture-in-east-oakland/?eType=EmailBlastContent&eId=31ce4992-d7e4-49ad-a525-e7b75eb72169

Hipple, Steven F. 2016. Labor force participation: what has happened since the peak? *Monthly Labor Review:* Bureau of (US) Labor Statistics. September. Available at: https://www.bls.gov/opub/mlr/2016/article/labor-force-participation-what-has-happened-since-the-peak.htm

Hussain, Suhauna and Johana Bhuiyan. 2020. What Happens After Uber, Lyft Win Big in California? *Los Angeles Times*, November 5. Available at: https://www.govtech.com/transportation/What-Happens-After-Uber-Lyft-Win-Big-in-California.html?utm_term=What%20Happens%20After%20Uber%2C%20Lyft%20Win%20Big%20in%20California&utm_campaign=Smart%20City%20Testbeds%20Are%20a%20Vital%20Part%20of%20Building%20Useful%20Tech&utm_content=email&utm_source=Act-On+Software&utm_medium=email

Ihlanfeldt, Keith. 1994. The Spatial Mismatch Between Jobs and Residential Locations Within Urban Areas. Proceedings of the Regional Growth and Community Development Conference, November 1993, Washington, DC, Cityscape 1(1). Chapter 11: 219–243. Available at: https://www.huduser.gov/periodicals/cityscpe/vol1num1/ch11.pdf

International Energy Agency (IEA). 2021. The Role of Critical Minerals in Clean Energy Transitions: World Energy Outlook Special Report. *IEA Publications France*, May. Available at: https://iea.blob.core.windows.net/assets/24d5dfbb-a77a-4647-abcc-667867207f74/TheRoleofCriticalMineralsinCleanEnergyTransitions.pdf

Ivanova, Diana et al. 2020. Quantifying the Potential for Climate Change Mitigation of Consumption Options. *Environmental Research Letters* 15: 093001 Available at: https://iopscience.iop.org/article/10.1088/1748-9326/ab8589/pdf

James, Owain. 2020. We May Not Be Ready for Fare-Free Transit, Though TDM Tactics Can Replicate Effects. *Mobility Lab*, October 29. https://mobilitylab.org/2020/10/29/we-may-not-be-ready-for-fare-free-transit-though-tdm-tactics-can-replicate-effects/

Keynes, Alex. 2020. New Battery Law Could Help Europe Lead the Green Battery Race *Transport and Environment*. November 12. Available at: https://www.transportenvironment.org/newsroom/blog/new-battery-law-could-help-europe-lead-green-battery-race?utm_source=Email+alerts+-+Transport+%26+Environment&utm_campaign=c3a357a3c6-EMAIL_CAMPAIGN_2020_11_12_01_52&utm_medium=email&utm_term=0_50e72c3d00-c3a357a3c6-120112474&mc_cid=c3a357a3c6&mc_eid=5f35fe3f86

Koseff, Alexei and Dustin Gardiner. 2020. California to Ban Gas-Powered Cars via Order by 2035. *San Francisco Chronicle*, September 24. Available at: https://www.govtech.com/fs/transportation/

California-to-Ban-Gas-Powered-Cars-Via-Order-by-2035.html?utm_term=California%20to%20Ban%20Gas-Powered%20Cars%20Via%20Order%20by%202035&utm_campaign=As%20Smart%20Cities%20Grow%2C%20Data%20Consolidation%20Efforts%20Should%20Too&utm_content=email&utm_source=Act-On+Software&utm_medium=email

Krupnick, Matt. 2021. Biden's Infrastructure Plan Would Create Plenty of Jobs, But Who Will Do Them? *The Hechinger Report*, June 3. Available at: https://hechingerreport.org/bidens-infrastructure-plan-would-create-plenty-of-jobs-but-who-will-do-them/

Lazo, Luz. 2020. Government Officials Adopt Plan to Expand Washington Region Trail Network to 1,400 Miles. *The Washington Post*, August 2. Available at: https://www.washingtonpost.com/local/trafficandcommuting/government-officials-adopt-plan-to-expand-washington-region-trail-network-to-1400-miles/2020/08/01/f651239c-d32e-11ea-9038-af089b63ac21_story.html

Lewis, Michelle. 2020. EVs Are Now Cheaper to Run than ICE Cars Per Year in the UK. *Elektrek*, July 22. Available at: https://electrek.co/2020/07/22/evs-cheaper-per-year-ice-cars-uk/

Liverpool, Layal. 2021. Uber and Lyft Operating in US Cities Linked to Rises in Car Ownership. *New Scientist*, January 6. Available at: https://www.newscientist.com/article/2264144-uber-and-lyft-operating-in-us-cities-linked-to-rises-in-car-ownership/#ixzz6m9Oy0EIL

Marohn, Charles. 2020. Building More Roads Won't Help Fix America's Economy. *CNN Business Perspectives*, October 2. Available at: https://edition.cnn.com/2020/10/02/perspectives/road-infrastructure-pandemic-recovery/index.html

Martin, Reece. 2021. Grand Paris Express Demystified. *CoMotion News*, January 21. Available at: https://comotionnews.com/2021/01/21/grand-paris-express-demystified/

McCarthy, Niall. 2020. U.S. Pedestrian Deaths Hit Highest Level in 30 Years. *Statista*, March 2. Available at: https://www.statista.com/chart/17194/pedestrian-fatalities-in-the-us-by-year/ Accessed November 24, 2020.

McHarg Center, Transit Center, T4America. 2020. A Green New Deal for City and Suburban Transportation. March. Available at: https://transitcenter.org/wp-content/uploads/2020/03/20.03_GND-Transit_use_v4.pdf

McMurtry, Ian. 2018. Flood City Folly: How U.S. Taxpayers Funded the "Airport for Nobody" *Airline Geeks*. March 2. Available at: https://airlinegeeks.com/2018/03/02/flood-city-folly-how-u-s-taxpayers-funded-the-airport-for-nobody/

McMurtry, Ian. 2020. Amtrak 2035: Does Amtrak Finally Have a Strong Plan Against Airlines? *Airline Geeks*, October 24. Available at: https://airlinegeeks.com/2020/10/24/amtrak-2035-does-amtrak-finally-have-a-strong-plan-against-airlines/

Molinsky, Jennifer, Whitney Airgood-Obrycki, Rodney Harrell and Shannon Guzman. 2020. Which Older Adults Have Access to America's Most Livable Neighborhoods? An Analysis of AARP's Livability Index. *Harvard Joint Center for Housing Studies and AARP Public Policy Institute*, October. Available at: https://www.aarp.org/content/dam/aarp/ppi/2020/10/which-older-adults-have-access-to-americas-most-livable-neighborhoods.doi.10.26419-2Fppi.00115.001.pdf

Moore, Janet. 2021. Minnesota Funding for Second Train to Chicago Thwarted. *Star Tribune*, November 4. Available at: https://www.startribune.com/minnesota-funding-for-second-train-to-chicago-thwarted/572974172/

Morse, Ian. 2021. A Dead Battery Dilemma. *Science* 372(6544): 780–783. Doi: 10.1126/science.372.6544.780

Mukhtar, Imran. 2020. With Water Scarce, Pakistan Helps Farmers Grow More With Less. *Thomson Reuters Foundation News*, September 30. Available at: https://news.trust.org/item/20200930020936-fq54d/

Mulero, Eugene. 2020. New House Bill Promotes Transportation Technologies. *Transport Topics*, October 30. Available at: https://www.ttnews.com/articles/new-house-bill-promotes-transportation-technologies (Accessed November 24, 2020).

Office of Public Affairs. 2020. Justice Department Settles with Amtrak to Resolve Disability Discrimination across Its Intercity Rail System. *Department of Justice*, December 2. Available at: https://www.justice.gov/opa/pr/justice-department-settles-amtrak-resolve-disability-discrimination-across-its-intercity-rail

Picarsic, Nathan. 2020. Risky Business: The Hidden Costs of EV Battery Raw Materials. *Automotive World*, November 23. Available at: https://www.automotiveworld.com/articles/risky-business-the-hidden-costs-of-ev-battery-raw-materials/?fbclid=IwAR0We06AiBnT1bR62vQpqEiQuUU19LtM-dID2OuIWO1aisNFvcvOPs0GQ57M

Pollard, Amelia. 2021. Can Biden's Infrastructure Plan Save the Superfund Program? *The American Prospect*, April 27. Available at: https://prospect.org/environment/can-biden-infrastructure-plan-save-the-superfund-program/

Popovich, Nadja, and Denise Lu. 2021. Can Removing Highways Fix America's Cities? *New York Times*. May 29. Available at: https://www.nytimes.com/interactive/2021/05/27/climate/us-cities-highway-removal.html

Progressive Railroading. 2021. Minnesota's Walz Includes Second Twin Cities-Milwaukee-Chicago Train in Bonding Proposal. February 21. Available at: https://www.progressiverailroading.com/amtrak/news/Minnesotas-Walz-includes-second-Twin-Cities-Milwaukee-Chicago-train-in-bonding-proposal--62794?oly_enc_id=7687H8293156H9R&utm_medium=email&utm_source=-prdailynews&utm_campaign=prnewsletter-2021

Ritchie, Hannah and Max Roser. 2020. CO_2 and Greenhouse Gas Emissions. *OurWorldinData.org*, August 2020. Available at: https://ourworldindata.org/co2-and-other-greenhouse-gas-emissions

Robertson, Linda. 2021. Walking Is Hazardous to Your Health in Florida, the Deadliest State for Pedestrians. *Miami Herald*, March 11. Available at: https://www.miamiherald.com/news/local/article249723078.html

Rogers, Luke and Kristie Wilder. 2020. Shift in Working-Age Population Relative to Older and Younger Americans. *US Bureau of the Census*, June 25. Available at: https://www.census.gov/library/stories/2020/06/working-age-population-not-keeping-pace-with-growth-in-older-americans.html aged 15 to 64 (213,610,414).

Rogoway, Mike. 2020. Muni Internet in Oregon County May Cost $1 Billion. *The Oregonian*, October 6. Available at: https://www.govtech.com/network/Study-Muni-Internet-in-Oregon-County-May-Cost-1-Billion.html?utm_term=Study%3A%20Muni%20Internet%20in%20Oregon%20County%20May%20Cost%20%241%20Billion&utm_campaign=Utah%20Expands%20Connected%20Vehicle%20Project%20to%20Include%20More%20Autos&utm_content=email&utm_source=Act-On+Software&utm_medium=email

Rosen, David. 2021. Confronting the Digital Divide: New York City vs. Verizon. *The Nation*, February 24. Available at: https://www.counterpunch.org/2021/02/24/confronting-the-digital-divide-new-york-city-vs-verizon/

Ryan, Dan. 2020. Metro's Fleet Will Be All-Electric, Also Much Smaller. *Seattle Transit Blog*, November 2. Available at: https://seattletransitblog.com/2020/11/02/metros-fleet-all-electric/

Salvador, Ashley. 2020. Best of 2020: Legalize Accessory Commercial Units. *Strongtowns*, December 8. Available at: https://www.strongtowns.org/journal/2020/12/8/best-of-2020-accessory-commercial-units

Sammon, Alexander. 2021. Biden's Promising, Problematic Plan to Plug Orphaned Oil and Gas Wells. *The American Prospect*, April 14. Available at: https://prospect.org/environment/bidens-promising-problematic-plan-plug-orphaned-oil-gas-wells/

Schiermeier, Quirin. 2020. Global Methane Levels Soar to Record High. *Nature*, July 14. Available at: https://www.nature.com/articles/d41586-020-02116-8

Schor, Juliet B. 2020. California Voters Decide Uber and Lyft Drivers Are 'Contractors' as Gig Workers Continue Search for a Livable Wage. *Government Technology*, November 5. Available at: https://www.govtech.com/workforce/California-Voters-Decide-Uber-and-Lyft-Drivers-Are-Contractors-as-Gig-Workers-Continue-Search-for-a-Livable-Wage.html?utm_term=California%20Voters%20Decide%20Uber%20and%20Lyft%20Drivers%20Are%20%27Contractors%27%20as%20Gig%20Workers%20Continue%20Search%20for%20a%20Livable%20Wage&utm_campaign=Smart%20City%20Testbeds%20Are%20a%20Vital%20Part%20of%20Building%20Useful%20Tech&utm_content=email&utm_source=Act-On+Software&utm_medium=email

Schwarzman, Megan, Samantha Schildroth, May Bhetraratana, Álvaro Alvarado, and John Balmes. 2021. Raising Standards to Lower Diesel Emissions. *Science* 371(6536): 1314–1316. doi: 10.1126/science.abf8159

Schwieterman, Joseph P., C. Scott Smith, and Riley O'Neil. 2017. Transportation Gaps: The Most Heavily Traveled Intercity Routes Without Express Coach or Rail Passenger Service in the United States. November 17. Available at: https://las.depaul.edu/centers-and-institutes/chaddick-institute-for-metropolitan-development/research-and-publications/Documents/Transportation%20Gaps%202017.pdf

Searles, Katie. 2020. EV batteries Composed from Deep-Sea Rock Reduces Carbon Footprint. *City Transport and Traffic Innovation*, September 22. Available at: https://www.cittimagazine.co.uk/news/electric-vehicles-charging/ev-batteries-composed-from-deep-sea-rock-reduces-carbon-footprint.html?utm_source=CiTTi+MOVE+exhibitors&utm_campaign=ae09951f50-EMAIL_CAMPAIGN_2017_12_06_COPY_01&utm_medium=email&utm_term=0_fc7e670c7d-ae09951f50-130155177

Shepardson, David. 2020. Trump Proposes Cutting Amtrak Funding, Boosting Infrastructure Spending. *Reuters*, February 10. Available at: https://www.reuters.com/article/us-usa-trump-budget-transportation-idUSKBN20429Q

Skip Descant 2020d Reimagining Interstate Rights of Way Could Bring Energy Boon. *Government Technology – Future Structures*, October 9. Available at: https://www.govtech.com/fs/infrastructure/Reimagining-Interstate-Rights-of-Way-Could-Bring-Energy-Boon.html?utm_term=READ%20MORE&utm_campaign=Reimagining%20Interstate%20Rights%20of%20Way%20Could%20Bring%20an%20Energy%20Boon&utm_content=email&utm_source=Act-On+Software&utm_medium=email

Smart Growth America. 2021. Dangerous By Design 2021. Available at: https://smartgrowthamerica.org/dangerous-by-design/?eType=EmailBlastContent&eId=e52be738-d0e7-4a23-b713-1b5d6dd8413e

Societe du Grand Paris. 2019. Le Grand Paris Express en résumé. November 21. Available at: https://www.societedugrandparis.fr/gpe/le-grand-paris-express-en-resume#les-couts-financements (Accessed November 24, 2020).

Stout, Lynn. 2012. The Shareholder Value Myth. How Putting Shareholders First Harms Investors, Corporations, and the Public. Chapter Two: How Shareholder Primacy Gets Corporate Law Wrong. Penguin Random House.

Studer, Quint. 2020. Best Practices and Bright Ideas for Renewing American Communities. *Strongtowns*, October 30. https://www.strongtowns.org/journal/2020/10/29/best-practices-and-bright-ideas?utm_content=buffer3c305&utm_medium=social&utm_source=facebook.com&utm_campaign=buffer&fbclid=IwAR0qox9PtQCzgLaD49dVxm17E1k290s5wntDu2YIFO688Eq1cCjo1yB-3Gwg (Accessed 24 November, 2020).

Stumpf, Rob. 2020. President-Elect Biden Wants Zero-Emission Public Transit for Cities With 100,000+ People. *The Drive*, November 9. Available at: https://www.thedrive.com/news/37500/president-elect-biden-wants-zero-emission-public-transit-for-cities-with-100000-people

Szabo, Joseph C. 2011. Statement before U.S. Department of Transportation before the Subcommittee on Railroads, Pipelines and Hazardous Materials Committee on Transportation and Infrastructure. *U.S. House of Representatives*, March 11. https://www.transportation.gov/testimony/implementation-passenger-rail-investment-and-improvement-act-2008

The Public Course. 2013. Free Public Transport Barely Increased Number of Passengers in Tallinn. August 19. Available at: http://www.baltic-course.com/eng/transport/?doc=79254

Thompson, Andrea. 2020. Here's How Scientists Want Biden to Take on Climate Change. *Scientific American*, November 12. Available at: https://www.scientificamerican.com/article/heres-how-scientists-want-biden-to-take-on-climate-change/

Thompson, Gregory and Thomas Matoff. 2003. Keeping Up with the Joneses: Planning for Transit in Decentralizing Regions. *Journal of the American Planning Association* 69(3): 296–312.

Trading Economics. 2021. United States Labor Force Participation Rate 1948-2021 Data | 2022-2023 Forecast. Available at: https://tradingeconomics.com/united-states/labor-force-participation-rate Accessed March 17, 2021.

Tudor, Grant and Justin Warner. 2019. Congress Should Revive the Office of Technology Assessment. Here's How To Do It. *Brookings Institution*, December 18. Available at: https://www.brookings.edu/blog/fixgov/2019/12/18/congress-should-revive-the-office-of-technology-assessment-heres-how-to-do-it/

UNCTAD. 2020. Special Report No. 13: Commodities at a Glance. Special Issue on Strategic Battery Raw Materials. *United Nations*. Available at: https://unctad.org/system/files/official-document/ditccom2019d5_en.pdf

US Bureau of Labor Statistics. 2020. Focus on Productivity: Construction Industries. US Department of Labor. https://www.bls.gov/lpc/construction.htm

Walker, Alissa. 2018. U.S. Kids Die from Traffic Fatalities at Twice the Rate of Other Wealthy Nations. *Curbed*, January 10. Available at: https://archive.curbed.com/2018/1/10/16871152/traffic-deaths-children-vision-zero (Accessed November 24, 2020).

Walker, Alissa. 2020. Why Bus-Loving Rep. Ayanna Pressley Wants Transit to Be Free. *Curbed*, July 2. Available at: https://www.curbed.com/2020/7/2/21308773/ayanna-pressley-free-transit-equity

Weisbrod, Glen and Naomi Stein. 2021. Public Transport Evaluation. Manuscript version, Appearing as Chapter 11 in The Routledge Handbook of Public Transport (2021). Corinne Mulley, John Nelson and Stephen Ison, Editors. 630 Pages. Available at: https://www.routledge.com/The-Routledge-Handbook-of-Public-Transport/Mulley-Nelson-Ison/p/book/9780367418724

Wilson, Kea. 2020a. American SUVs are Too Dangerous for UK Roads, UK Safety Experts Say. *Streetsblog USA*, July 22. https://usa.streetsblog.org/2020/07/22/american-suvs-are-too-dangerous-for-uk-roads-uk-safety-experts-say/

Wilson, Kea. 2020b. Study: We Can't Fix Transportation-Related Climate Emissions with EVs Alone. *Streetsblog USA*, October 2.Available at: https://usa.streetsblog.org/2020/10/02/study-we-cant-fix-transportation-related-climate-emissions-with-evs-alone/

Wulfhorst, Ellen. 2020. Gardening in Katrina's Wake: Growing Food Helps Rebuild New Orleans. *Thomson Reuters Foundation*, August 26. Available at: https://news.trust.org/item/20200826081455-gink8/

INDEX